WOMEN WHO SHOCKED THE NATION

WOMEN WHO SHOCKED THE NATION

Diane Canwell

breedon **books**
PUBLISHING

First published in Great Britain in 2002 by
The Breedon Books Publishing Company Limited
Breedon House, 3 The Parker Centre,
Derby, DE21 4SZ.

DEDICATION

For my Dad

ISBN 1 85983 287 3

Printed and bound by Butler & Tanner, Frome, Somerset, England.

Cover printing by Lawrence-Allen Colour Printers, Weston-super-Mare, Somerset.

CONTENTS

Acknowledgements … … … … … … … … … … … … … … … … …6

Introduction … … … … … … … … … … … … … … … … …7

Till Death Us Do Part … … … … … … … … … … … … … … … …8

Saucy and Scandalous … … … … … … … … … … … … … … …28

Regal Relations … … … … … … … … … … … … … … … …44

Pistols and Petticoats … … … … … … … … … … … … … … …73

Passing Strangers? … … … … … … … … … … … … … … …81

Love Kills … … … … … … … … … … … … … … … …104

A Bitter Pill … … … … … … … … … … … … … … … …130

Heinous Horrors … … … … … … … … … … … … … … …163

Felonious Females … … … … … … … … … … … … … … …176

Cradle Rockers … … … … … … … … … … … … … … …189

Bibliography … … … … … … … … … … … … … … …214

Index … … … … … … … … … … … … … … … …215

ACKNOWLEDGEMENTS

I would like to thank Steve and Ray at the Metropolitan Police Museum for their assistance in finding factual information and some excellent illustrations, and the Public Record Office for the superb facilities they provide for researchers.

A few illustrations were supplied by The Press Association and Getty Images.

Thanks also to Uncle Chris for his continued interest and Vera and John Sutherland and my two sons, Alun and Stuart, for their encouragement. My main thanks must go to my partner, Jon, for his love, support, encouragement and tolerant patience.

INTRODUCTION

THIS BOOK looks at the lives of nearly 180 women through the ages. Some murdered; some robbed; some simply scandalised society because of their behaviour. All of them, in their own way, shocked the nation.

Many months ago I was carrying out some picture research at the Metropolitan Police Museum when I encountered my first truly wicked and shocking woman. She was Styllou Christofi, and although many other women mentioned in the book surpass her for their acts of violence and the scope of their crimes, she still remains one of the most chilling women that I have ever encountered. Her case was somewhat overshadowed by her contemporary, Ruth Ellis, whose crime, incidentally, occurred in very much the same area of London.

I have tried to be even-handed with the women that are included in this book and make no value judgements about their comparative wickedness or notoriety. However, if, from the tone of the book, my personal opinion does manage to creep in, I apologise.

What has been particularly interesting is the fact that many of the women who did genuinely shock the nation carried out acts, not necessarily murder, which would no longer have any real impact on our society. They would certainly not attract many column inches in newspapers nowadays. What is particularly significant about some of the women is that there appears to have been no real delineation between crimes carried out by women and crimes carried out by men. There are women thieves, forgers, confidence tricksters and, on the other hand, there are women who have sought fame and fortune, not necessarily in that order, in the armed forces and on foreign soil. In times when women were considered to be precious and delicate, we find a vast number of them abandoning their assigned roles in life to become what we would now call hardened and habitual criminals. Others took enormous risks and often paid the ultimate price for their decisions.

A book like this can only hope to scratch the surface of the activities of women and it has been particularly difficult to include some women who have never done any other person an ounce of physical harm. I have had to place these alongside some women that I really would have preferred not to write about. I did feel, on the other hand, that this book would not be complete without the likes of Rose West, Myra Hindley and Amelia Dyer. I have not chosen to give these women any greater coverage than the others, as their crimes, although shocking, are no more or less significant than those of other women.

My hope is that you will find this book a 'jolly good read'.

Diane Canwell

CHAPTER ONE

TILL DEATH US DO PART

Although many women resorted to the use of poison to deal with aggressive, violent, or simply unwanted husbands, this option was not open to all. It is interesting to note just how many women who plotted the downfall of their husbands resorted to involving other people in their plans. Sometimes these conspiracies got so out of hand that many people found themselves facing a judge and jury.

LITTLE DID **Alice Arden** realise, when she involved several other people in the murder of her aging husband, that the courts and executioners would be overworked for weeks in their pursuit of justice.

Alice Arden had married Thomas Arden in 1544. Alice was the stepdaughter of Sir Edward North. Since her teens she had been having an affair with Richard Mosby, one of her stepfather's servants. Rather reluctantly she had married Thomas and moved to Faversham, but seems to have continued her affair with Mosby. It is supposed that Alice assumed that her elderly husband would not survive for very long, but she was to be sadly mistaken. The longer he lived, the more she loathed him and on a number of occasions she tried to poison him, although she only managed to make him feel sick.

Alice contacted a man called Green, whom she knew had once had a property dispute with her husband. Green worked for Sir Anthony Agers, and on a trip to London, accompanied by his colleague Bradshaw, they encountered a murderous individual called Black Will. He had quite a reputation for robbery and killings in France while he was a soldier. Green propositioned Black Will and offered him £10 to kill Thomas Arden. Green then wrote a letter to Alice telling her what he had planned.

Black Will, of course, had no idea what Thomas Arden looked like so, accompanied by Green, they went to St Paul's and saw Thomas Arden walking through the churchyard. Black Will wanted to kill him there and then, but Green said that it was too public a place, and that now Black Will had seen Arden he could make his plans to carry out the killing at a better time. Green was obviously a little wary of Black Will, but they had established that Thomas Arden was living in his London house, so they contacted, through Alice, Arden's servant Michael. Michael agreed to leave a door open for them so that Black Will could enter the house and kill his master.

In the event another servant closed the door and Black Will could not get in, so the conspirators agreed a new plan to kill Arden on his way back from Rochester to London on Rainham Down. Michael was fidgety about this idea as he feared that Black Will would kill him as well. Black Will lay in wait for Arden but somehow missed him.

Black Will, meanwhile, had taken on an accomplice called George Shakebag. The pair met Alice Arden and decided on a new way to kill her husband. Again they missed him at Faversham despite an elaborately laid plan. They then involved Mosby directly, along with his sister.

While Arden was away they hid Black Will in a cupboard in the parlour of their Faversham house. Mosby and Michael also lay in wait. When Arden walked into the parlour they sat down to play cards and at a pre-arranged signal Black Will emerged from the closet and started strangling Arden with a towel. Mosby hit Arden with a pressing iron and they thought they had killed him. They dragged him into another room, but he was still groaning, so Black Will stabbed him and after that Alice stabbed him seven or eight times in the chest. They then cleaned up the murder scene and threw the towel and knife into a tub near a well close by. Eventually they took Arden's body and dumped it in a field near the churchyard, not far from Arden's own back garden.

It did not take long for somebody to stumble on the corpse, particularly since Alice had told her neighbours that her husband had not returned from business. Such was the farce surrounding the conspiracy and murder that the killers had failed to notice that they had left their footprints in snow, leading to and from the house.

The mayor and several others went straight to the Arden's house and, after initially denying it, Alice confessed. All that remained was for the authorities to round up the conspirators. Alice Arden, her daughter, Michael and their maid were thrown in prison; Mosby was arrested at his employer's home, where they found some incriminating evidence. He too confessed his involvement.

When the arrested conspirators were put on trial they were all happy to incriminate one another and those still at large. Michael was executed in Faversham, joined by Alice's unfortunate maid, who was burned at the stake. Mosby and his sister were hanged at Smithfield. Green was still at large but he was eventually captured and hanged. Black Will was also eventually captured and hanged, and Shakebag died resisting arrest in Southwark. Even Adam Fowle, the local innkeeper, was arrested and imprisoned. His only crime had been to serve Alice and Mosby food and drink at one of their meetings, and thankfully he was later released.

Alice Arden was burned at the stake at Canterbury on 14 March 1551. An enormous cheering crowd enjoyed the spectacle.

* * * * *

Another murder conspiracy that went hopelessly wrong involved **Catherine Hayes**. She had been born in 1690 as Catherine Hall and at the age of 15 she had become a prostitute for a group of army officers. When she was around 23 she secured work in the

*Catherine Hayes,
prostitute and
conspirator.*

household of the Hayes family, who were farmers. It did not take Catherine very long to lure John Hayes, the eldest son, into her bed, and they secretly married in 1713.

Catherine had kept in contact with some of the army officers, and had arranged for them to press-gang John into the army on his wedding night. While John was being dragged away the rest of the officers spent the night in bed with Catherine. Somehow the situation was sorted out and the couple moved into a cottage on the Hayes's farm. Catherine still kept to her old ways, however, and often lured unsuspecting males into her bed as soon as her husband's back was turned.

Eventually they moved to London in 1719 and John set up a business as a pawnbroker, moneylender and coal merchant. His business flourished and they had several servants, a handsome home and a carriage. It seems that whatever her husband gave her, Catherine wanted more. His simple method of dealing with this was to cut her allowance every time she asked for something else.

Matters came to a head in 1725 when Thomas Billings took up lodgings at the Hayes's home. He was a tailor, but there were two other sides to Billings that John was not aware of. Firstly, Billings was Catherine's illegitimate son, and secondly, they had begun an incestuous relationship.

Catherine also managed to secure the sexual favours of Thomas Wood. The Warwickshire man was a close friend of her husband and had moved into the house. Billings, Wood and Catherine now hatched a plot to do away with John Hayes.

On 1 March 1725 Billings and Wood, in order to get some Dutch courage, drank six pints of wine each at a local inn with John Hayes and then returned home. Sat in the

parlour they bet Hayes that he could not drink another six pints. He did and then promptly collapsed on the floor. After lying unconscious for a short period, Hayes got up and tottered off towards the bedroom. Billings hit him over the head with a hatchet and his screams awoke Mrs Springate, who was also a lodger in the house. Catherine went to head off the woman while Wood and Billings finished off Hayes.

Having completed their task they then had to decide what to do with the body. In order to prevent the body from being identified, Catherine had the two men hack off her husband's head, wrap it in rags and put it in a bucket. They threw it into the water at Horseferry Wharf. Unfortunately the tide was out and the head landed in the mud. They then went back to the house to cut up the body and pack it in a trunk, which they then abandoned in a pond on Marylebone Fields.

The following morning a man called Robinson, who was the watchman at Horseferry Wharf, saw a bucket on the riverbank. When he went to investigate he saw John Hayes's

Attempting to strangle Hayes as she was burnt alive.

head lying in the mud below him. He handed the remains over to the authorities. They used a rather unusual method to identify the head.

The blood and mud was cleaned off the head and the hair was combed. It was then placed on a spike with a notice attached to it. The notice asked anyone who recognised the face to contact the authorities. Identification came in the form of a man named Bennett, who was certain that it was John Hayes's head. The authorities went round to the Hayes's home and arrested Catherine and Billings, whom they had found in bed together. They also arrested the poor Mrs Springate. It also did not take the authorities long to pull the trunk from the pond.

Wood, meanwhile, had fled the scene, but rather stupidly returned to London and was promptly arrested. It was he that first confessed and the unfortunate Mrs Springate was released from prison.

The trial ended on 9 May 1726, but by then Wood was already dead, having died of a fever while in prison. Billings was hanged and placed in a gibbet near the pond on Marylebone Fields. The fate of Catherine Hayes was far more unpleasant.

She was strangled and burned at the stake. A rope was put round her neck and the executioner began to strangle her, but someone had lit the fire too soon and flames burned the executioner's hand before Catherine was unconscious. A delighted crowd watched Catherine Hayes being burned alive.

* * * * *

Ann Beddingfield was married to John, an industrious farmer and well-respected resident of Sternfield in Suffolk, and they had two children. Because the farm was so busy John took on a young 19-year-old man called Richard Ringe as his assistant. Ann immediately fell in love with Richard and began to hate John.

Once Richard realised how Ann felt about him, he found it impossible to avoid temptation and the two became lovers. Ann felt such contempt for her husband that she told Richard she wanted to do away with him. Richard refused to be party to the murder until Ann had promised him that he would share the fortune she was to inherit.

It would seem that despite the gravity of the deed the couple were planning, Ann found it impossible to remain discreet. Her maidservant was to testify later that Ann had said to her one morning 'Help me put on my ear-rings; but I shall not wear them much longer, for I shall have new black ones. It will not be long before somebody in the house dies, and I believe it will be your master.'

Richard, meanwhile, went and bought some poison. He told one of his colleagues in the household that he would like her to mix it with the rum and milk that she served her master each morning. The girl refused but said nothing to anybody about the conversation she had had with Richard. A further attempt to poison John Beddingfield failed. Apparently the man was feeling unwell and Richard was instructed to serve him some cold water, to which he added arsenic. John was not so unwell, however, that he did not notice a white sediment in the bottom of the basin and refused to drink the water. It would appear, however, that John did not suspect the white sediment to be arsenic for nothing further was said about the incident.

Having failed in their attempts to poison John, Ann and Richard came up with another plan, which this time did not fail. Ann, having refused to spend the night in her husband's bed, was asleep in the room next door with her maidservant. Richard crept through their bedroom and into the one occupied by John. He tied a cord around John's neck and strangled him. Ann and the maidservant were awakened by the scuffle that took place and when Richard entered the bedroom he said to Ann 'I have done for him' to which Ann replied 'Then I am easy'.

The coroner's inquest in March 1763 gave a verdict of 'death by natural causes' with the explanation for this being that John had somehow strangled himself with his own bedding. None of the servants were called to give evidence at the inquest.

Ann and Richard were now free of John. But, it would seem, Ann now lost all interest in Richard and began to despise him in the same way that she had turned against John. The maidservant who had shared her bed, however, had ideas of her own.

As soon as she had received her wages for the quarter from Ann, the maidservant went to the authorities and told all that she knew. Ann and John were arrested and brought to trial at the Lent Assizes. During the trial medical experts admitted that they had seen some marks of violence on John's body and after a very short time the pair were sentenced to death. They travelled to their execution at Rushmore, near Ipswich, on the same sledge, Ann declaring until the very end that she was innocent. Richard had made a full confession but when Ann was tied to the stake she confessed her guilt and declared that she deserved to die.

* * * * *

Elizabeth Barber, also known as Elizabeth Daly, had been born in Deptford in 1752 and had a series of convictions against her. Apparently she had once stabbed a man called Thomas Seerles and had been imprisoned in Maidstone for a year for this offence. She was married to a man called Barber at one time and had children with him. He, according to accounts, was an honest waterman who was well-respected in the local area. However, the two appear to have separated when her imprisonment left her husband devastated.

By 1804 Elizabeth was living with a man called John Dennis Daly in Greenwich. Apparently he was a poor college man and the couple lived in lodgings in the same house as a lady called Ann Ward. Their neighbour was later to testify that she had heard scuffling from the Dalys' room on 14 October 1804, the night of Elizabeth's partner's murder. She had heard the scuffling noises and then about half an hour later she had heard Elizabeth shouting 'Murder! Bloody murder! My husband has stabbed himself, and is dead enough. Will nobody come to my assistance?'

Ann Ward, together with another neighbour, rushed to the Dalys' room and saw the man sitting in a chair with his head lolled to one side. His shirt had been opened and a knife wound on his chest had been washed and cleaned. The women were very distressed and called for the authorities. Elizabeth, meanwhile, sat smoking her pipe and claiming that Daly had stabbed himself.

Her claims were ignored, however, and she was found guilty at the trial. The judge pronounced the death sentence, to which Elizabeth responded that she wanted her body to be saved for her children rather than being sent for dissection as was the norm. She was hanged on 25 March 1805 and before leaving the prison for her final journey she made a full confession.

* * * * *

The Summer Assizes for the county of Norfolk in July 1807 saw the trial of **Martha Alden** for the murder of her husband, Samuel. Samuel was a quiet and industrious husbandman and the couple lived with their son in a small cottage near Attleborough.

Several witnesses gave evidence at Martha's trial, many of whom were friends and neighbours of the couple. Edmund Draper told the court that he, Martha and Samuel had been drinking together at the White Horse pub on Saturday 18 July. Martha had left the two men and taken their son home with her, but Edmund and Samuel had continued drinking for some time after her departure. The two men had walked home together, with Edmund leaving Samuel at his cottage. Apparently Samuel was a little worse for drink but Edmund delivered him safely to the Aldens' cottage and saw no one else in the vicinity.

In the early hours of the following morning, another neighbour, Charles Hill, had got up early and was making his way to Shelf Anger Hall to see his daughter. As Hill approached the Aldens' cottage at about 3am he had noticed that the door was ajar and then he saw Martha standing outside her home. When he had asked her what on earth she was doing at that time of the morning, Martha had claimed that she had been to fetch water from the pit in the garden.

The next day, Monday 20 July, Martha had paid a visit to another neighbour, Sarah Leeder. She had told Sarah that she needed to borrow a spade because a sow had managed to get into her garden and damaged some of the potato crop. Sarah had lent Martha a spade which had been engraved with the initials J.H. At about 11pm the next night Sarah had left her house and gone onto the local common in search of some missing ducks. She had found the ducks in a small pit or pond, beside which was a larger one known as Wright's Plantation. Sarah noticed something floating in the larger pond and had prodded it with a stick, but because the light was so bad she had been unable to identify what it was and had returned home for the night. She returned to the pond the next morning and on closer examination she could identify the two hands of a man and a shirt stained with blood. Sarah called a local boy to alert the neighbourhood that there was the body of a man in the pond and went home. She had returned again, after composing herself at home for 10 minutes, to discover that the body had been taken out of the pond. She could then identify the body as being that of Samuel Alden, despite the fact that the man's body had been chopped, with the head virtually severed. Sarah made her way immediately to the Aldens' cottage and saw her spade standing beside a grave-like hole that had been dug by the side of the garden. There was blood inside the hole. Martha Alden's cottage was searched later that day and a blood-stained bill-hook was found in a cupboard.

An old friend of Martha, Mary Orvice, told the court that on Sunday 19 July Martha had called at her house and asked her to return to the Aldens' cottage with her. She confessed to Mary that she had killed Samuel and showed her the body lying on the bed; Mary had also seen the bill-hook lying beside the body. The two women had then put Samuel's body into a corn sack and taken it from the house to the edge of the garden, where Martha had covered it with earth. The following night they had moved Samuel's body from the cottage garden to the pond and the next morning the two had cleaned the cottage.

It didn't take the jury long to find Martha Alden guilty of the murder of Samuel and on 31 July 1807 she was executed on Castle Hill. It was reported that 'an immense concourse of spectators' were present but that Martha behaved with decency during the whole execution.

* * * * *

Despite the fact that Arthur Reginald Baker was already married, he and **Emma 'Kitty' Byron** lived together as man and wife. By all accounts Kitty was a pretty 23-year-old, who was very happy and very much in love with her common-law husband. She was a milliner's assistant and Reg, as he was known, was a stockbroker. They lived together in lodgings in Duke Street, in the West End of London. They had been living together for several months when things turned sour.

Apparently Reg liked his drink and often became violent with Kitty when he was under the influence. Kitty, besotted with her man, did not tell anyone about these violent episodes and remained loyal to Reg. On 7 November 1902, when their landlady, Mrs Laird, went to investigate disturbing noises in Kitty and Reg's flat, Kitty was predictably defensive and sheltered the drunken Reg from Mrs Laird's eyes, claiming that they had simply been playing games. However, when the noise continued until 1.15am, Mrs Laird returned to the flat, only to find Kitty on the landing, dressed only in her nightdress, crouched in an attempt to avoid Reg's blows. The following morning Mrs Laird told the couple that she had no choice but to ask them to vacate the flat.

The calm before the storm seemed to last through the weekend, with Kitty giving the appearance that all was well. Until, that is, Mrs Laird's maid relayed a conversation to Kitty that she had overhead between the landlady and Reg. Apparently he had told the landlady that Kitty was not his wife and he had blamed all the arguments on her. He claimed that Kitty was classless and that he would ensure she had gone by the next day. Kitty responded to this news with the statement 'I'll kill him before the day is out'.

On 10 November, the day of the Lord Mayor's Show, Kitty went into Oxford Street and bought a strong-bladed knife. Fighting her way through the crowds with the knife concealed in her muff, she made her way to the Lombard Street post office, where she sent a telegram to Reg at the Stock Exchange. The message she sent read 'Dear Reg, Want you immediate importantly. Kitty.' When Reg arrived at the post office an argument began, with him refusing to pay for the message and Kitty giving him the money needed to pay the bill. The argument continued out onto the street outside the post office and suddenly Kitty brought out the knife from her muff and stabbed Reg twice, once through the back and once through the chest. As Reg fell to the ground, dying instantly, Kitty fell over his body, crying and sobbing 'Let me kiss my Reggie. Let me kiss my husband.'

Kitty Byron did not give evidence at her trial, nor did the defence counsel bring forward any witnesses; the prosecution brought forward 20 witnesses. She pleaded not guilty in December 1902, with her defence counsel claiming that she had bought the knife in order to commit suicide and not to kill Reg. The defence counsel pleaded manslaughter but the judge summed up in favour of a murder conviction, stating 'If I had consulted my own feelings I should probably have stopped this case at the outset.' It took the jury just 10 minutes to return their verdict of guilty of murder, but they strongly recommended mercy. Kitty was sentenced to death.

After the Home Secretary received a 15,000 signature petition he granted a reprieve and the death sentence was commuted to one of life imprisonment. In 1907 the life imprisonment sentence was reduced to one of 10 years, of which Kitty served six; she was released in 1908.

* * * * *

The childless Percy and **Edith Jessie Thompson** had been married for six years when Freddy Bywaters came into their lives in the summer of 1921. Percy, a shipping clerk, was apparently a very 'feet on the ground' type of person, while Edith, a manageress at a milliners, was dramatic and romantic in nature. The 19-year-old Freddy was flamboyant and attractive.

Freddy was eight years younger than Edith, but when they met on a holiday in the Isle of Wight they were immediately attracted to each other. It wasn't long before they began a secret affair, to which husband Percy was totally oblivious for some time. He, it seems, also liked young Freddy and invited him to stay with them at their home in Ilford until the SS *Morea*, the ship on which he served as a clerk, sailed again.

Things seemed to tick along quite well until an argument developed in early August, resulting in Percy hitting Edith. Freddy witnessed this violence and sprang to Edith's defence, telling Percy that he should divorce his wife. This argument resulted in Freddy

Frederick Bywaters, Percy Thompson and Mrs Thompson in the garden at Ilford.

leaving the Thompson's home and staying instead with his mother until September, when his ship sailed.

It was after Freddy had left in September that Edith began writing him incriminating letters. Apparently her pet name for him was 'Darlint' and through her letters she encouraged his jealousy of Percy and discussed the possibility of either poisoning her husband or putting ground glass into his food. She had, it seems, been putting poison in Percy's tea and wrote to Freddy that her husband had complained of the tea tasting bitter. She also complained that the ground glass was not having any effect on Percy by writing 'I used the light bulb three times, but the third time he found a piece, so I've given up until you come home.' It became a regular habit for Edith to cut out articles from the newspapers regarding death by poisoning and to send them to Freddy. When enclosing such paper clippings on one occasion, she was obviously concerned that her intentions would cause a strain on the newly formed relationship: 'This thing that I am going to do for both of us – will it ever – at all, make any difference between us, darlint? Do you understand what I mean? Will you ever think any the less of me?'

Edith continued writing to Freddy, a total of 60 letters, until he returned to England in the September of 1922 and the couple resumed their secret meetings. On the evening of one of these secret afternoon meetings Edith and Percy had been to a theatre in London with some friends. They travelled back to their home in Ilford by train and while they were walking from the station to their house Freddy leapt out of the shadows and stabbed Percy with a knife. Edith was heard to scream 'Oh don't! Oh don't!' and Freddy ran off, leaving Edith to seek help from a passing couple, shouting 'Oh, my God, will you help me, my husband is bleeding'. By the time help was summoned in the form of a doctor, Percy had died.

Edith Thompson, whose husband was murdered by her lover.

It didn't take long for the authorities to suspect Freddy Bywaters as being the secret attacker, or to find his pile of letters from the dead man's wife. The pair insisted from the outset that there had been no murder plot between them and Freddy told the authorities that he had not meant to murder Percy. He told the police 'I loved her and I could not go on seeing her leading that life. I did not intend to kill him. I only meant to injure him. I gave him an opportunity of standing up to me as a man but he wouldn't.'

Despite Edith's defence counsel's claim that her letters to Freddy were inadmissible evidence, they were brought forward as evidence against her. She claimed that she had only written of poisoning as a way of keeping his interest in her alive and Freddy claimed that he never believed she had any intention of carrying out the acts she had written to him about. The post-mortem carried out on Percy Thompson showed no trace of any toxic substance or glass in his body.

In his summing up, the judge, Mr Justice Shearman, made clear his own view of the guilt of the couple. He told the jury that he considered they had committed a vulgar and common crime. The jury, it seems, was in agreement with the judge and returned a guilty verdict. Both Edith and Freddy protested their innocence in loud voices when the verdict was passed.

There was an appeal on the grounds of the judge's biased summing up; there was also a petition signed by thousands of people, but no appeal was granted and the two were hanged. Freddy Bywaters, despite accepting that he had to pay for a crime he had committed, wrote 'For her to be hanged as a criminal is too awful. She didn't commit the murder, I did. She never planned it. She never knew about it. She is innocent, absolutely innocent. I can't believe they will hang her.'

* * * * *

There was never cause for an appeal in the case of **Marguerite Fahmy** in 1923, but there was great debate about her motives for killing her husband. Marguerite was a 23-year-old Parisian born into a working-class family. She had given birth to an illegitimate daughter when she was only 15 and had then turned to prostitution. After spending some time in a high-class brothel, she had learned how to dress well and attract wealthy men.

By 1923 she was a wealthy woman who had married the Egyptian Prince Ali Kamel Fahmy Bey. They had met 10 years before in Cairo and the millionaire Ali had been instantly intrigued by Marguerite and her beauty. Ali, by all accounts, was determined to have Marguerite for his own and began showering her with expensive gifts and writing her many romantic letters, full of promise. Eventually Marguerite succumbed to Ali's charms and promises and accepted his marriage proposal. There were some conditions, however, attached to a marriage to the wealthy man. His new wife was obliged to adopt the Islamic faith and, she later found out, she did not have the right to divorce him.

Their problems, it seems, began on their honeymoon on the Nile on Ali's luxury yacht. Marguerite later claimed that her husband's sexual preferences and demands caused her severe problems and that his threatening behaviour towards her made her fear for her life. She had sent a letter to her Parisian lawyer, to be opened only in the event of her death, in which she wrote that she formally accused Ali of causing her sudden death or disappearance. When Ali's yacht docked in Luxor he had Marguerite locked in her cabin and gave instructions to the crew that she was not to be released.

Not long after this Ali began working at the Egyptian Embassy in Paris and the couple were often seen by hotel guests and theatre-goers in the French capital having screaming rows in public. On one of the many occasions when violence was a part of the dispute, Ali punched Marguerite and dislocated her jaw.

Things came to a head in July 1923 while the couple were holidaying in London. They were staying in a luxury suite at the Savoy Hotel and had, apparently, been witnessed having arguments. One of the reasons for their disharmony on this occasion was a recent visit Marguerite had been forced to make to a doctor. She had been suffering from severe discomfort resulting from what she had termed 'the unnatural lovemaking practices' of her husband and had been given some treatment. When the treatment failed to alleviate the discomfort, the doctor said that an operation was required. The couple had argued about where the operation should take place, with Marguerite wishing to return to Paris but Ali insisting it should be carried out in London. The argument continued at the theatre and over dinner that night. Marguerite refused to dance with Ali and threatened to smash a bottle over his head. A band was playing in the Savoy Grill while they ate dinner and the leader later testified that he had asked Marguerite if she had any request. She had replied that music was not in her mind at that time because her husband had just threatened to kill her. The couple then retired for the night to their suite.

At about 2.30am one of the hotel's staff, John Beattie, was walking past the Fahmys' suite. The door had burst open, he told the court, and Ali had run into the corridor, complaining loudly about an injury Marguerite had given him on his face. Marguerite had also entered the corridor, but had said something in French that Beattie had not understood. The couple returned to their suite and Beattie had begun to walk away when he heard three gunshots. Beattie ran back and saw Ali lying in the corridor with an obvious head wound which was bleeding profusely and he saw Marguerite throw down a pistol.

At her trial, which opened in September 1923, Marguerite was defended by Sir Edward Marshall Hall and Sir Henry Curtis-Bennett. She appeared in the witness box and told the jury of her fear of Ali and of her miserable marriage to him and of his perverted sexual practices. When cross-examined by Percival Clarke, she was asked why she had not left him. Marguerite had replied that she had not wished her friends to know of her miserable marriage and that Ali would have found her and brought her back to him whatever she had attempted to do.

In his summing up Sir Edward told the jury that he considered Ali to be a 'treacherous Egyptian beast' and that Marguerite had made only one mistake and that was to marry an Oriental. He closed his summing up by appealing to the jury to 'open the gates where this Western woman can go out, not into the dark night of the desert but back into the light of God's great Western sun.'

Marguerite Fahmy was found not guilty of murder and not guilty of manslaughter after the jury had deliberated for only one hour. The details of Marguerite's past character had not been heard in court, but had been ruled as inadmissible evidence by the judge.

* * * * *

Another couple whose constant rows caused disquiet among their neighbours were Michael Scott Stephen and **Elvira Barney**. She was the daughter of the wealthy Sir John and Lady Mullins and, by all accounts, was arrogant and spoiled from an early age. Her marriage at the age of 23 to the American, John Sterling Barney, had only lasted a year and she had resumed her lifestyle in London's swinging high society after their separation.

Elvira, now 27, had several affairs before she met Michael, aged 24, with whom she set up home in 21 Williams Mews, Knightsbridge. Apparently the couple drank a lot and

regularly held riotous and noisy parties. They also had numerous loud and violent arguments. During one of these quarrels a neighbour, Mrs Hall, later testified that she had seen Elvira fire a shot at Michael. Apparently this had occurred after Michael had arrived in the mews in the early hours of the morning and had been shouting up to the couple's window. Elvira had told Michael to go away but he had returned and she, from the window, had fired a shot and shouted 'Laugh, baby; laugh for the last time.' Mrs Hall, under cross-examination, confirmed that the following morning the couple had left the mews together in an amicable manner.

On the night of 31 May 1932 Elvira and Michael went to a party at the Café de Paris where they both became the worse for drink. Elvira later testified that they had arrived home at around 2.30am and had made love. Soon after their lovemaking they had started to quarrel and this was confirmed by evidence given by their neighbours, who had heard shouting. They had also heard Elvira cry 'I will shoot you'. Elvira claimed that the argument was an ongoing one from earlier in the day and she said that Michael had threatened to leave her. She had begged him not to leave and he had grabbed the gun from behind a cushion on an armchair. She claimed she had struggled with him to take the revolver from him and that the gun had gone off accidentally. Elvira claimed that she was unaware of how badly hurt Michael had been because he had been the one to tell her to get a doctor and she maintained that he had told her it was not her fault.

Elvira did, however, telephone her doctor and summoned him by shouting 'For God's sake come at once. There's been a terrible accident'. By the time the doctor arrived Michael had died and the doctor summoned the police. When told that she would have to accompany the police constable to the station, Elvira slapped the officer across the face and shouted 'I'll teach you to put me in a cell, you foul swine!' Having made her statement at the police station Elvira was released, but arrested again three days later.

Elvira was defended at her Old Bailey trial on 3 June 1932 by Sir Patrick Hastings. The forensic evidence against her was strong and suggested that the gun had been fired from a distance. A gun-maker was called to give evidence and he confirmed that the gun used was one of the safest ever made and it was unlikely it could have been fired accidentally.

Despite the fact that the jury found Elvira not guilty of murder and not guilty of manslaughter, there were several unanswered questions. There was a bullet hole in the wall of the bedroom the couple shared; there was no smoke or any scorch marks on Michael's clothes or hands or around the fatal bullet wound.

The huge crowds outside the Old Bailey cheered Elvira as she left a free woman at the end of her trial and shortly afterwards she sold her story to a Sunday newspaper:

> I write in tears… People think of me as an exotic woman who was on trial for her life. They forget that my greater tragedy is with me yet. The man I loved more than anything else in the world is dead and now that I have come back to the freedom which I once shared with him, I am reminded in a thousand different ways of all that he meant to me.

Four years later Elvira was found dead in a hotel bedroom in Paris.

* * * * *

The summer of 1935 saw the nation riveted by the Rattenbury murder case – a tragic and intriguing crime of passion. It would leave a distinguished Canadian architect dead, a teenager languishing in prison and the woman in the case driven to take her own life.

Alma Victoria Rattenbury married Francis in 1925; he was 30 years older than her. Although Francis had been born in Leeds, he had moved to British Colombia in his twenties and had carved out an extremely successful career as an architect, gold prospector and property speculator. Both Francis and Alma had been married before but by 1935, with Francis in retirement at the age of 67, they were living at Villa Madeira in Bournemouth. They had two sons, Christopher and John, and seemed to have a reasonably comfortable lifestyle.

Sometime before they had taken on a teenager, George Stoner, as a chauffeur. He had claimed to be 22, but was in fact 18. It was not long before he was sharing Alma's bed and was deeply in love with the older woman. Alma was shocked when she found out how old he really was and tried to end their affair, but they quarrelled and George told her that he could not live without her. They continued their relationship. Alma later claimed that she had not had sex with her husband for nearly six years, and that her husband wanted her to live her own life.

Alma Rattenbury.

Francis was a rather solitary man who drank too much whisky, lapsed into depressive moods, was often morose, talked of committing suicide and was deaf; this enraged Alma.

Although their lifestyle was comfortable, Alma took drugs and was often not really in full control of her actions. Certainly her behaviour around the time of the murder, on Sunday 24 March 1935, is difficult to explain if she was not under the influence of some substance.

When the police were called at 2am on the Monday morning they found Francis Rattenbury severely battered, but alive, sitting in his chair. He never regained consciousness and died in hospital four days later. On that night Alma, probably drunk in addition to having taken drugs, danced around the room with a gramophone playing at full blast, babbling incoherently, but at times saying 'I know who did it. I did it with a mallet. Ratz had lived too long.' Later she said 'I would like to give you £10. No, I wouldn't bribe you.' Later she said 'I did it. He lived too long. I'll tell you where the mallet is in the morning. I shall make a better job of it next time. I made a proper muddle of it. I thought I was strong enough.' Eventually a doctor arrived and gave her some morphine to make her sleep.

The police returned on the Monday morning and arrested her for attempted murder. She then made a statement:

> About 9pm on Sunday, 24th March 1935, I was playing cards with my husband when he dared me to kill him as he wanted to die. I picked up the mallet. He then said 'You have not got guts enough to do it.' I then hit him with the mallet. I hid the mallet outside the house. I would have shot him if I had a gun.

The 31-year-old woman was arrested and over the next few days many secrets of the Rattenbury household found their way into the newspapers. George Stoner claimed that he had been called by Alma at about 10.30pm that night. She had told him that her husband had been shot and that there was blood running from his head as he sat slumped in an armchair. She had told Stoner that she did not know how this had happened.

The newspapers were full of the relationship between Alma and George Stoner. In the spring of 1935 Alma had conned her husband out of £250, claiming that she had to go to London for an operation. She had spent five glorious days in hotels with Stoner and they had even exchanged rings. They had returned to Bournemouth on Saturday 23 March and found Francis in a very depressed state. He had agreed, finally, to visit a friend in Bridport the following day.

George, too, found himself arrested and was asked about his relationship with Alma and what he knew about the frenzied attack on Francis. He claimed that he had seen Alma kiss Francis good night as he peered at the couple through the French windows.

As Alma disappeared up the stairs, he had crept into the room and smashed Francis continually over the head with a mallet. He then calmly went upstairs to tell Alma.

The police were in a quandary; both Alma and George had independently confessed to attacking Francis but their stories were contradictory and they had both claimed responsibility. They were both charged with the murder and their trial began on Monday 27 May 1935. There were hundreds of people hoping to gain access to the court but it was already largely filled with newspaper reporters.

The court heard Stoner plead not guilty and then Alma Rattenbury claimed she was not guilty. In court Alma changed her story and claimed that George had not wanted her to go with Francis to Bridport and that he had attempted to hurt Francis in order to stop the trip. When she saw her husband sat with blood pouring down his face she became hysterical and drank so much whisky that by the time the police arrived she was so drunk that she did not know what she was saying. Despite Alma's change in evidence, George would not implicate Alma. Both defence counsels admitted that their clients were almost certainly under the influence of cocaine at the time, although it seems clear that George had never taken cocaine as he failed to recognise what it looked like in court.

Faced with the contradictory evidence, a packed court heard the jury return a verdict of guilty for George Stoner but not guilty for Alma Rattenbury. The crowd both inside the court and those assembled outside booed when they heard the verdict. Stoner was sentenced to hang and despite her acquittal Alma was distraught and hysterical.

Three days after the trial ended, Alma boarded a train for Christchurch. She walked down to the river bank and calmly wrote a note on the back of an envelope, which read: 'One must be bold to do a thing like this. It is beautiful here and I am alone. Thank God for peace at last.'

With that she stabbed herself six times. Three times the blade pierced her heart.

Her death released Stoner from his vow of silence regarding Alma's involvement in the murder. He wrote a letter to his solicitor claiming that he had crept into Alma's room that night and found her in a terrible state. They heard a groan from downstairs and they both ran down to see Francis slumped in a chair with terrible head wounds. Stoner saw a mallet lying on the floor, the one that he had borrowed to drive tent pegs into the ground for the children. He had kicked it underneath the sofa.

Despite this new evidence the Home Secretary turned down his appeal, but reprieved him from the death sentence. In the event, he served just seven years and distinguished himself as a soldier during World World Two. He later married and passed out of the public eye.

It seems clear that Alma's acts that night must have been carried out while she was under the influence of drugs and alcohol. The press tracked down people that she had known in Canada who attested to her violent behaviour when she was under the influence. As for her suicide, she could not face the death of her innocent lover when she knew that she was guilty but saved from the hangman's noose.

* * * * *

A trial that heard claims that a gun had gone off as a result of a struggle was that of 43-year-old **Freda Rumbold** in 1956. She was married to Albert and the couple lived in

Bristol. According to Albert's mother's later testimony, 'Freda was a very odd person, particularly at the time of the full moon.'

Albert, according to Freda, had strange sexual habits and this often resulted in her choosing not to share his bed, preferring to sleep on the landing of the house or in her daughter's bed. He owned a 12-bore shot gun and friends of Freda's testified that she had asked them to obtain cartridges for her for it. Freda had also been known to obtain loans in her husband's name and to forge his signature on cheques.

At her trial the jury was told that on the night of 25 August 1956 Freda had shot her husband in the head as he had slept in his bed. She had drenched a towel in perfume and placed it under the bedroom door and hung a sign on the door handle that read 'Please do not enter'. Albert's family and friends became suspicious and were not satisfied with Freda's answers to their questions about Albert's whereabouts. They called the police and the officers who attended the house to investigate had found the body. Despite Freda's claims that the gun had gone off as a result of a struggle, forensic evidence regarding the angle of the entry of the bullet into Albert's head forced the jury to find her guilty. She was sentenced to life imprisonment.

* * * * *

Sheila Garvie was another woman who complained that her husband's sexual demands were abnormal, perverse and unwelcome to her. Sheila and Maxwell Robert Garvie had been married for nine years and they lived a comfortable life with their three children at West Cairnbeg farm, Kincardineshire, Scotland. They had been married in 1955 but by 1964 Max obviously thought that his sex life with Sheila had become stale and began looking elsewhere for excitement. He became very interested in pornography and nudism and his demands on Sheila increased.

Much to the shock of locals, Sheila found a way to satisfy her husband's sexual needs. In 1967 she had met the 22-year-old Brian Tevendale and his sister Trudy Birse. The foursome would spend most weekends together at the farm, with Sheila and Brian gradually becoming more than sexually involved with one another. Trudy was married to an Aberdeen policeman and she, apparently, found Max's sexual needs quite acceptable. Often the partners would change places during the course of the night, or one of the men would share his bed with both of the women. Despite the fact that Max found the whole situation very satisfactory, Sheila and Brian began to make plans to run away together. Unbeknown to them, however, Max was aware of their plans and arranged for Brian to be 'mugged' one night. They did manage to get away together in March 1968, but Max found out their whereabouts and managed to 'persuade' Sheila to return home.

On 14 May 1968 Max left the farm for the last time. He attended a meeting of the Scottish Nationalist Party at Stonehaven and was last seen at around 10pm that night. Despite pleas from Max's sister, Sheila refused to report Max missing and it was not until five days later that the police were informed. His car had been found parked across a runway at the Fordoun Flying Club, and despite intense searching of the surrounding area, he had not been found. Sheila, apparently, had confidentially told her mother, Mrs Watson, that Max had been killed, and she had hinted that Brian was involved. Mrs

Watson told the police about this conversation with her daughter and on 16 August Sheila and Brian were arrested, together with a young friend of the Tevendale family, Alan Peters.

On 17 August Max Garvie's body was eventually found in an underground tunnel at Lauriston Castle. He had been shot through the neck and it was thought that the battering to his head had been carried out with a gun barrel. Sheila Garvie, Brian Tevendale and Alan Peters were all charged with murder.

Their trial, in November 1968, caused shock and scandal in the surrounding area. It became public knowledge that the foursome had enjoyed their sexual exploits at West Cairnbeg farm. However, Sheila and Brian, who had been so inseparable in the past, now blamed one another for the murder of Max. Brian claimed that Sheila had shot Max during a struggle and that his only involvement had been to assist in the disposal of the body. Sheila, on the other hand, claimed that she had known nothing of the death because she had been asleep in bed when the killing had taken place. Alan Peters backed Sheila up in court, claiming that Brian Tevendale had shot Max Garvie in bed and that he and Brian alone had disposed of the body.

The jury came back with a verdict of not proven against Alan Peters. However, both Sheila Garvie and Brian Tevendale were found guilty of murder and sentenced to life imprisonment. This verdict seemed to satisfy the local population, who were so outraged and repulsed by the reports of the activities at the farm, that they thought that the couple deserved to be punished.

* * * * *

Fifty-two-year-old **Muriel McCullough** lived in Ailsworth, Cambridgeshire with her 48-year-old insurance executive husband, Bill. On 18 November 1981 Muriel telephoned the local police station and reported that their house had been burgled. When PC Gregory arrived at the house Muriel informed him that she had been away, staying with friends in Hale, in Cheshire, and that on her return she had found that the house had been broken into. She claimed that she was unaware of what had been taken as she had been too frightened to check the rest of the house.

When the police constable checked upstairs he discovered the corpse of Bill McCullough lying in his bed. The man had been shot in the head. PC Gregory was immediately suspicious of the circumstances and told Muriel that her husband was upstairs ill; but she refused to go up the stairs. When the policeman told her that her husband was not ill but dead, she was even more adamant that she would not go and see his body.

It transpired that Muriel was not present at the house when the murder took place but alarm bells started to ring when it was discovered that Bill McCullough had been insured to the tune of £110,000.

Muriel had been married once before and her first husband had died of a heart attack. When the police looked into the McCullough's financial situation it became clear that they were deeply in debt and, as a result, Bill had turned to drink and had regularly assaulted Muriel.

The breakthrough in the investigation came when a friend of Muriel's, Joe Scanlon, told the police that he had been threatened by two Liverpudlian men, Collingwood and Kay. He had met them before and had arranged for Muriel to meet them too. Collingwood and Kay were brought in for questioning and the former told them that Muriel had paid them £8,000 to kill her husband. Scanlon's story had been different. He had told the police that Muriel had simply employed them to beat her husband up. Collingwood went on to make a full confession, in which he admitted that Kay had driven him to the house and that Muriel had left one of the side doors open. He had gone upstairs and found Bill McCullough asleep in bed and he had shot him in the head.

The McCulloughs had only been married since 31 December 1980, and in less than two years Muriel McCullough, along with Collingwood and Kay, found herself facing a murder trial at Birmingham Crown Court. As a result of Collingwood's admissions, he chose to plead guilty and implicated the other two defendants. They were all found guilty and sentenced to life imprisonment.

* * * * *

Many of these women were obviously pushed to the limits of their endurance or were faced with the prospect of having to remain with a man they felt nothing but contempt for. A different kind of desperation and forcefulness is required to calmly plot the execution of a husband. Given the extreme circumstances it is not surprising that so many of these women chose very badly when it came to the actual killing and the choice of those who would be their accomplices.

CHAPTER TWO

SAUCY AND
SCANDALOUS

There are many women that stand out in history for their outrageous or scandalous behaviour. Many, of course, have provoked sexual scandals, such as Christine Keeler or Cynthia Payne. Others were simply immoral as far as the public and the authorities were concerned. Still more behaved in ways which society could not accept, choosing lifestyles with radically different morals.

NO SELF-RESPECTING chapter on scandalous behaviour could fail to include the story of **Lady Godiva**, even though her shocking act was for all the best intentions. She had a fascinating life and as a widow in 1028 she believed that she was dying and left all of her estate to Ely monastery.

She survived, however, to marry Leofric, the Earl of Mercia, about 10 years later. Leofric had earned his fortune in the mutton trade and they moved from Shrewsbury to Coventry, where it became Leofric's responsibility to collect taxes on behalf of the king. Exact dates are difficult, but some time during the reign of Edward the Confessor, the citizens of Coventry were suffering from crippling tax demands, exacerbated by a new tax which was to stretch their finances even further.

Godiva and Leofric established a Benedictine monastery, the remains of which lie under the war-damaged Coventry Cathedral. Despite numerous charitable acts by Leofric at the request of Godiva, he refused to listen to his wife's pleas to do something to alleviate the tax burden on the citizens. At length he told her that if she rode through the market during the day, naked, then he would find the money to pay the new taxes himself. The following day, accompanied by two clothed women servants, she did just that, and it is said that all of the inhabitants of Coventry, grateful for her action on their behalf, stayed indoors and shuttered their windows to save her embarrassment. According to legend, the only one who did look was a tailor called Tom who looked through a crack in the shutter of his window and was struck blind, and thus became the original 'Peeping Tom'.

Godiva outlived her husband and several monasteries enjoyed her patronage for many years. She left all of her riches to the church when she died.

* * * * *

Mary Carleton was born on 11 January 1642 and although her father was an Englishman, Mr Meders, in her dreams she was a German princess. Her first husband was a shoemaker called Stedman, but she ran off and married a surgeon from Dover. She was then tried for bigamy in Maidstone but was released on a technicality. Mary then moved to London where she married John Carleton, but the authorities again caught up with her and she found herself committed to Newgate and then tried at the Old Bailey. Again she was acquitted.

Between her last two marriages Mary had spent some time in Germany and had become close to an older man who showered her with jewels and money. She promised to marry him but ran off, taking many of the old man's possessions with her. She then returned to London, where she met and married Carleton.

She had returned to England in March 1663 and from then on was known as the 'German Princess', claiming to be Lord Henry van Wolway's daughter. Carleton met Mary at the Exchange Tavern where she was staying. He clearly thought that she was of noble blood and she did nothing to persuade him otherwise. Carleton was the brother-in-law of Mr King, who kept the inn, and it was King who first had his suspicions about Mary. King was the one who handed Carleton the following letter which had arrived anonymously at the inn:

> Sir, I am an entire stranger to your person, yet common justice and humanity oblige me to give you notice that the pretended Princess, who has passed herself upon your brother, Mr John Carleton, is a cheat and an imposter. If I tell you, Sir, that she had already married several men in our county of Kent, and afterwards made off with all the money she should get into her hands, I say no more than could be proved were she brought in the face of justice.
>
> That you may be certain I am not mistaken in the woman, please to observe that she has high breasts, a very graceful appearance, and speaks several languages fluently,
> Yours unknown
> T.B.

As quickly as Mary had come into John's life, she disappeared and took up with a 50-year-old man whom she also married and robbed. Again Mary was on her way, this time masquerading as a demure virgin. Her new landlady introduced her to her young nephew and the two soon became lovers.

This time Mary's method of escape was even more ingenious. She forged a letter which told a sad tale and she showed it to the young man. Apparently Mary's brother had died and this had left her the sole beneficiary of her father's estate. Suffice to say that Mary, through a series of deceptions and forged documents and tales of her history continued to rob, defraud and lie to lovers and potential lovers for many years.

Her downfall began when she was arrested for stealing a silver tankard in Covent

Garden. She was brought to trial and convicted at Newgate, and was sentenced to death. This sentence, however, was commuted to transportation and she was sent to Jamaica. Somehow she managed to return to England and, carrying on in her normal way, she met and married a wealthy man in Westminster. Having robbed him of £300 she then left and invited several new acquaintances of hers to attend a play with her. While at the theatre she stole a total of £600-worth of money and jewellery from her guests before disappearing into the night.

Finally, in December 1672, she was found out and imprisoned until her trial took place on 16 January 1673. Despite the fact that Mary pleaded that she was pregnant, examination by several women proved that she was not, and she was hanged on 22 January. Apparently she appeared more gay and brisk than ever before on the day of her execution, and when her irons were removed she pinned the picture of her husband, Carleton, on her sleeve, and carried it with her to Tyburn. Before her execution she told the people that she had been a very vain woman, and expected to be made a precedent for sin; that though the world had condemned her, she had much to say for herself; that she prayed God to forgive her, as she did her enemies. Mary was buried in St Martin's churchyard.

* * * * *

The scandal attached to Mary Carleton as a polygamist was shocking, but a case that came to light 70 years later, in 1746, rocked the establishment to its foundations and found it floundering to find a charge to lay at the offender's door. Over a number of years **Mary Hamilton** had dressed as a man and followed through her disguise by marrying polygamously no fewer than 14 different women.

Several women scandalised society by dressing as men.

Her case came to trial at the Quarter Sessions in Taunton, Somerset, and it seems that the court had never before encountered a case such as this one. To begin with they floundered to find a charge but since the marriages had all been carried out in a church, it was finally suggested that Mary Hamilton should be charged on a count of bigamy.

What is particularly amazing is that Hamilton's 14th wife, Mary Price, had been married to her for over three months before the case came to court. She appeared as a witness against Hamilton and told the court that she was lawfully married and that they had slept and lived together as man and wife and that at no time had it ever occurred to her that Hamilton was not a man. It is not clear whether or how the marriage was or was not consummated.

The court concluded that Hamilton should be imprisoned for six months and during that time be taken to Taunton, Glastonbury, Wells and Shepton Mallett to be whipped in public. The punishment was carried out in the particularly cold winter of 1746.

* * * * *

The Mary Hamilton case was not an isolated incident. **Ann Marrow** was convicted of a similar offence on 5 July 1777 before the Quarter Sessions in Westminster. Ann had been masquerading as a man for some time but from the charges it does not seem that there was a sexual element to her multiple marriages. Ann had married three different women in order to defraud them of their money and possessions. After having been found guilty she was sentenced to three months imprisonment and to be pilloried at Charing Cross on 22 July. It seems that her behaviour had provoked a great deal of interest and anger in the city. There was a massive audience when she was put in the pillory and she was pelted by the crowd to such an extent that she lost the sight of both of her eyes.

* * * * *

Lady Emma Hamilton had humble beginnings but her exceptional beauty and scandalous behaviour has left her a well-known part of British history. She was born in the Wirral in 1765 as Emily Lyon, the daughter of a blacksmith. She moved to London in her early teens and quickly swapped her occupation as a nursery maid for the far more exciting role of a painter's model.

George Romney painted several portraits of her but as Emily Hart she became the mistress of Sir Harry Featherstonhough and then Charles Greville. Greville was the nephew of Sir William Hamilton who was, at the time, the British Ambassador to Naples and a wealthy widower. Greville passed Emma, as she had become known, over to his uncle, and she was duly packed off to Naples early in 1786. To begin with Sir William was unsure that he wanted to become involved with a woman 40 years younger than himself, but they eventually formed a relationship that led to their marriage back in London towards the end of 1791. It seems their relationship was based more on mutual understanding than sexual passion, despite the fact that the two were very much in love with one another.

Around seven or eight years later, after having established herself as a friend of the Queen of Naples, Marie Caroline, Emma met and fell in love with Lord Horatio Nelson.

Unlike her relationship with her husband, this was a far more physical union, despite the fact that Nelson was also already married. When Emma gave birth to Nelson's daughter, Horatia, in 1801, it signalled the end of Nelson's marriage to Frances.

Emma's relationship with Nelson was brought to an abrupt end by his death at the Battle of Trafalgar on 21 October 1805. Despite having been left legacies by Nelson and later by her husband, Emma fell into debt and died a virtual pauper in Calais in 1815. By then she was 50 years old, and only the generosity of some of Nelson's close associates saved her from spending her last days in a debtor's prison.

Horatia Nelson considered her mother's life to have been so scandalous that despite accepting that she was Lord Nelson's illegitimate daughter, she refused to recognise Emma as her true mother.

Lady Emma Hamilton, mistress of Nelson.

* * * * *

Kitty O'Shea was born Katharine Wood in Essex in 1845, the last of her parents' 13 children. Her father was Sir John Page Wood and her mother Lady Emma, and Katharine was tutored at home by her father. In 1867 she married Captain William O'Shea but it seems that William was not good company for Katharine. He was often away from home and lived a life full of drinking and gambling outings that left them nearly bankrupt. By 1875 their marriage was virtually over.

In July 1880 Katharine met Charles Stewart Parnell. They immediately fell in love with one another and began a long and complicated relationship. On 16 February 1882 Katharine gave birth to Parnell's first child, Claude, but he died shortly after birth. Katharine was to give birth to two more girls between 1883 and 1884 and by 1886 she and Parnell were living together. Katharine received a very special Christmas present from her husband on that Christmas Eve, in the form of a divorce petition, citing Parnell as co-respondent.

The event which had triggered off this rather belated divorce request after 15 years of separation and nearly 10 years of her relationship with Parnell was the death of one of Katharine's aunts on 19 May. O'Shea wanted some of the aunt's inheritance but Katharine refused to negotiate. This triggered off a divorce case in court on 15 November 1890. Parnell was found guilty of ruining the O'Sheas' marriage. Following this scandal Parnell's party demanded that he resign, which triggered a party split and the end of Parnell's political career. At the time Katharine was referred to as 'that bitch, that English whore did for him. She put the first nail in his coffin'. Kitty was the name given to her by her Irish critics and was a term used to describe prostitutes.

Katharine and Parnell married on 25 June 1891 but by 6 October Parnell was dead, aged just 45. He died in Katharine's arms. Shortly after his death Katharine had a nervous breakdown and after her recovery she could never seem to settle. She lived in many houses in the south of England until her death in 1921. It has always been believed that if Parnell had never met Katharine, Home Rule for Ireland would have been achieved. She is, therefore, reviled by many Nationalists as bringing about the downfall of the 'Uncrowned King of Ireland'.

* * * * *

The mid-1890s, as far as Irish history is concerned, will always be associated with the libel action brought by Oscar Wilde against the Marquis of Queensbury. News of this scandal vied with the tragic story of **Bridget Cleary**. Bridget lived with her husband Michael in Clonmel in County Tipperary. She was 26 and her husband, it appears, was quite mad. He believed that his wife had been replaced by a faerie, which accounted for the fact that she appeared to him to be taller than he believed her to be.

In March 1894 Michael confronted Bridget, accusing her of being not his wife, but a faerie who had taken over her body. Over the next few weeks, with the assistance of family and neighbours, Bridget was systematically tortured in their attempts to confirm that she was not, in fact, Bridget Cleary. It culminated in Michael and several others pouring lamp oil over Bridget and burning her to death.

They were brought to trial and found guilty of manslaughter. Michael Cleary was given 20 years hard labour. It emerged in the trial that Bridget had fallen ill after catching a chill and on Saturday 9 March a doctor had confirmed that she was suffering from bronchitis. She had been given the last rites by a priest and the family had believed that she would surely die, but because she had recovered Michael had thought that magic was involved. Those that were anti-Irish and particularly those that opposed Home Rule used the Bridget Cleary case to demonstrate how savage and primitive the Irish peasants were, in their opinion, and claimed that they should never be given the opportunity to decide issues for themselves.

* * * * *

Marie Stopes was born in Edinburgh in 1880. Her mother, Charlotte Carmichael, had been the first woman to try to attend university in Scotland. Her experiences in education shaped both her life and that of her daughter Marie. Marie graduated from University College in 1901 and became a doctor of science in 1905. She supported the Women's Suffrage campaign and later joined the Women's Freedom League. After several failed relationships she married Reginald Gates in 1911, but as far as Marie was concerned, his old-fashioned and Victorian ideas about women forced her to seek a divorce just five years later.

Her first book, *Married Love,* was refused by a number of publishers during World War One. The book argued that men and women should have an equal relationship in marriage. It was finally published in March 1918 and was reprinted six times within the first year. It was, however, banned in America for being an obscene publication.

Marie's next book, *Wise Parenthood*, about birth control, brought her into direct

Marie Stopes's book Married Love *scandalised the nation.*

conflict with established views and her advice was often referred to as obscene or lewd. She drew enormous criticism from Roman Catholics and from the Church of England, but, with the assistance of her second husband, Humphrey Roe, she opened the first of her birth control clinics in Holloway, London, on 17 March 1921.

Marie met Margaret Sanger, an American nurse, who had fled to Britain in order to avoid charges relating to a birth control article she had written in her own newspaper back in 1915. Sanger now wrote a pamphlet in Britain and it was widely believed that both she and Marie Stopes should be charged with selling obscene publications.

Marie Stopes dedicated all of her life to the crusade for women's rights, and lobbied both the education authorities, to stop them from sacking married female teachers, and the Inland Revenue, to have women taxed separately from their husbands. She is now remembered for her pioneering attempts to allow women the right to prevent unwanted births. She died in 1958.

* * * * *

Emmeline Pankhurst was born in Manchester in 1858 and was already attending Women's Suffrage meetings with her mother in the early 1870s. Emmeline's comfortable middle-class background provided her with a conventional education. Both her mother and father had, for the time, radical political beliefs and feminist ideas. After returning from a finishing school in Paris where she was sent at the age of 15, Emmeline met Richard Pankhurst in 1878. She was 20 and he was 44, but her father was happy for them to marry. They had four children between 1880 and 1885 and all became staunch supporters of the Women's Suffrage movement.

Emmeline and her husband helped set up the Women's Franchise League and both joined the Indpendent Labour Party. Richard died from a perforated ulcer in 1898. Emmeline continued her political career, founding the Women's Social and Political Union in 1903 and in 1905, faced with the media's complete disinterest in women's rights, the new generation of Pankhursts found themselves at the heart of more direct action.

Emmeline Pankhurst and her daughter Christabel shocked the nation with their fierce campaign for women's right to vote.

On 13 October 1905 **Christabel Pankhurst** was arrested and charged with assaulting a police officer who was trying to evict them from a Liberal Party meeting. She was found guilty of assault and fined 5s. She refused to pay and was sent to prison. The event caused considerable uproar at the time as it was the first time that a British woman had ever used violence in support of Women's Suffrage.

Emmeline Pankhurst joined her daughters in London in 1907 and although she was

in her fifties, she spent the next seven years in and out of prison. She brought further attention to their cause by subjecting herself to 10 hunger strikes. All of the suffragettes were released on 10 August 1914, just six days after the outbreak of World War One. They agreed not to continue their militant activities and took advantage of a £2,000 government grant to organise a demonstration. It was attended by 30,000 people.

By October 1915 the Pankhursts were using the WSPU newspaper to accuse the government of being 'more German than the Germans'. In 1917 Christabel and Emmeline formed the Women's Party, calling for equal pay, equal rights in marriage and more opportunities for women.

Emmeline toured Canada after the war and then joined the Conservative Party. This led to an enormous public row between her and her daughter, Sylvia, who was still a socialist, which was added to by the fact that Sylvia had given birth to an illegitimate child. Until her death in 1928 Emmeline refused to see her grandson.

One of the Pankhurst supporters, **Emily Davison**, committed suicide by throwing herself underneath the hooves of the king's horse during the Epsom Derby in 1913. She had been imprisoned eight times and had been force-fed nearly 50 times. Her funeral attracted 2,000 people. Suffragette radicals would often chain themselves to railings outside the Houses of Parliament or Downing Street and were probably one of the first groups in Britain to use civil disobedience as a means to give publicity to their cause.

* * * * *

Unity Valkyrie Mitford died an unrepentant Nazi on 28 May 1948 in the West Highland Cottage Hospital in Oban. Her parents, Lord and Lady Redesdale, were eccentric pro-Germans who found themselves in much-reduced circumstances after World War One. Unity had been born on 8 August 1914 and from an early age inherited her parents' xenophobia, obsession with German mythology and pathological distrust of the unknown.

Unity was beginning to show a distinct interest in Fascism and her sister, Diana, four years older than her, had already married Oswald Mosley. Unity met Mosley on 14 June 1933, shortly after his return from an audience with Mussolini. Just five days later she tried to join the British Union of Facists at their headquarters in London. She then travelled to Oxford and told the Facists there that she knew Mosley and convinced the leader of the Oxford group, Vincent Keens, to allow her to join the party. From then on she habitually wore a swastika and became violently opposed to Jews.

She travelled to the Nuremburg Rally in August 1933, where she first met Hitler, and in the spring of the following year she convinced her parents to let her go to a finishing school in Munich, where she could learn German. Around this time she witnessed a Jewish man being beaten and was heard to say 'Jolly good. Serves them right. We should go and cheer.' During her time at the finishing school she always wore a black shirt and black leather gloves and attended Nazi ceremonies in the local area.

She was determined to meet Hitler again. For some time she stalked the German leader, turning up in his favourite restaurants and always pushing herself to the front of a crowd at formal occasions. Hitler began to notice her and although it is not believed that she ever became his mistress, she managed to join his entourage. Her parents went

*Aristocratic Nazi
Unity Mitford.*

to Germany over the winter of 1934–5 and found their daughter a changed woman. She became close friends with Goebbels and his wife, as well as Julius Streicher, the notorious murderer of German Jews. She denounced several people in Germany that criticised Hitler and the majority of the British that remained in Germany took elaborate steps to avoid her. She attended the 1936 Olympic Games but by now her close association with Hitler had been blocked by the arrival of Eva Braun. Any hope that she may have had regarding a closer relationship with Hitler had now passed. There were rumours that Hitler had asked her to marry him and this appeared in the British press, but the suggestion was violently denied by her father.

When she came back to England shortly before the Czechoslovakian crisis she joined a group of Facists in Hyde Park bent on disrupting a Labour Party rally. She caused a sensation by producing a swastika banner and making a Facist salute. Members of the crowd grabbed her and threatened to throw her in the Serpentine.

She moved back to Germany and was given a flat that had been confiscated from its Jewish owners in Berlin. She decorated it with Nazi memorabilia and she told a friend 'When I'm obliged to quit Germany I'll kill myself.' By now, of course, the world was sliding towards war. By August 1939 it became clear that Britain and Germany would soon be at war with one another. In the days before war was declared she listened desperately to news on the radio.

On 3 September, just as war was declared, Unity drove to the Ministry of the Interior and gave back all of her Nazi insignia, along with her farewell letter to Hitler. She then drove to the English Garden in Berlin and shot herself. The bullet lodged in her brain but failed to kill her, and Hitler visited her in a clinic on 8 November. She asked to return to England, and it was widely thought that she should be imprisoned as a traitor. Instead she was hidden by her family until after the war, when her mother took her to the island of Inchkenneth. She spent her last days dying from meningitis brought on by an abscess in her brain. It had been a specialist's opinion after she shot herself that the bullet should never be removed.

* * * * *

Just before the outbreak of World War Two, in May 1938, a Dundee hairdresser was imprisoned in Perth Prison after an MI5 investigation. **Jessie Jordan** was the widow of a former German soldier and had used her address as a post box for mail to and from German agents in Britain and the United States. She was arrested following the discovery of a German spy ring in the United States and at the time her case created a sensation. She was charged under the Official Secrets Act and spent four years in the Scottish prison.

* * * * *

Margaret White was known as Lady Haw Haw. She was the assistant secretary of the British National Socialist League and the wife of William Joyce, their leader. She and William left Britain in August 1939 and headed for Germany. From 10 November 1940 she broadcast pro-German propaganda from Berlin. Her husband had established himself as Lord Haw Haw, a much-hated and reviled German propagandist. The couple were arrested in Germany on 28 May 1945 and appeared at the Old Bailey on charges of treason. They both denied treason on the basis that they were German citizens, having become naturalised in 1940. This ruse did not save her husband, who was hanged in 1946. Margaret was deported and interned. Her imprisonment was short and she returned to Britain, where she died in 1972.

* * * * *

1945 also saw the beginning of **Melita Norwood**'s long career as a KGB agent. She passed many secrets to the Soviet Union until 1972 and is credited with being the spy that revealed the secrets of atomic warfare, allowing the Soviets to produce a nuclear weapon of their own only a year after the Americans dropped their bombs on Japan. She later claimed that her intention was simply 'I wanted Russia to be on an equal footing'. But it was idealism that had begun her involvement.

Melita Norwood, the elderly KGB agent.

She had joined the Communist Party in the 1930s and had begun spying for the Soviets just four years after Stalin had ceased to rule. She worked for them for 40 years and her motive was not greed, as she received very little financial support. She was awarded the Order of the Red Banner, the KGB's highest decoration, and her role did not come to light until Vasily Mitrokhin, a KGB archivist, defected in 1992. Among the names of spies that he provided to MI5 was that of Melita Norwood.

She had worked for the British Nonferrous Metals Research Association as a secretary and very secret and sensitive documents passed across her desk every day. She would take copies of these and pass them on to her KGB contact. She visited Moscow in 1979 but refused to take any financial reward for her services. Her story hit the headlines in the late 1990s following research by a journalist, David Rose. The public was stunned that MI5, despite knowing what she had done, had never interviewed her, let alone taken any legal action against her. By this time she was 87 years old, and it was not considered in the public interest to prosecute this retired woman that lived in South London.

* * * * *

There has rarely been a political scandal which involves all the elements of sex, prostitution, drugs and spying to rank alongside the Profumo Affair. John Dennis Profumo was made Minister for War in Harold Macmillan's cabinet in July 1960. Six years earlier Profumo had married the actress Valerie Hobson, but a chance meeting in

July 1961 was to lead to his fall from grace and the defeat of the Conservatives at the General Election in September 1964.

Profumo and his wife were attending a party at Cliveden near Maidstone in Kent. It was the home of Lord Astor, who had also agreed to allow his friend Dr Stephen Ward to rent one of the cottages on the estate for £1 a year. Among Ward's guests was the 19-year-old nightclub hostess, **Christine Keeler**.

Three years before, after an abortion, Christine Keeler had moved to London and begun working as a topless dancer. On the fateful evening of 8 July 1961, Keeler was swimming naked in Astor's swimming pool when he, accompanied by Profumo, encountered her. The swimming pool party was invited to another gathering at the pool the following evening. Among the guests was a Soviet naval attaché, Eugene Ivanov, who was in fact a spy. Soon after Profumo and Ivanov were both sharing Keeler's bed. Although the two never met, MI5 was already beginning to take an interest.

Stephen Ward (1912–63), an osteopath and talented artist, was visited by MI5 at his flat in Wimpole Mews and told in no uncertain terms to steer clear of Ivanov. They also paid a visit to Profumo as gossip had begun to circulate about his indiscreet relationship with Keeler. Profumo had only been seeing Keeler for a few weeks and he now broke off all contact with her.

Keeler continued to sleep with a variety of men and became close friends with **Mandy Rice Davies.** She frequently slept at Ward's flat. One of Keeler's ex-boyfriends was a West Indian drug dealer called Lucky Gordon whom she had left after he had threatened her with a knife and repeatedly raped her. Gordon was desperately searching for Keeler and for a short time they were reconciled but he returned to his violent ways and Keeler even threatened to kill him. Having jettisoned Gordon, she returned to Ward's flat and later struck up a relationship with Johnny Edgecombe, an associate of Gordon. There was a confrontation between Edgecombe and Gordon in which the latter tried to smash a chair over his rival's head and received a knife wound on his face for his trouble.

Despite MI5's warnings, Ward still saw Ivanov, who managed to convince Ward to try and arrange a meeting with British Members of Parliament, as he had been unofficially authorised to help diffuse the Cuban Missile Crisis. In the event he only saw William Shepherd, who simply passed on the content of the conversation to MI5.

Meanwhile, Edgecombe had turned up at Ward's home with a gun that had belonged to Keeler. The door was answered by Mandy Rice Davies and after she had refused to let him in Edgecombe shot at the door and then tried to hit Keeler, who was looking out of the window. Edgecombe was arrested but the incident began to bring the rumours and the gossip about Keeler and Profumo back into focus.

With Edgecombe's trial fast approaching, Keeler realised that she would have to admit to having owned the gun, of having been the cause of the dispute between the two West Indian men and that there was also the possibility that her relationships with Ivanov and Profumo would emerge under cross-examination. Ward, meanwhile, tried to disassociate himself and claimed that Keeler, much against his better judgement, had been using the flat to have sex with Gordon and Edgecombe and that she continually smoked drugs. The press were desperate to find the truth and all but named Profumo as one of Keeler's many lovers.

The dam broke just a few days before Edgecombe's trial. Keeler had fled to Spain and in Profumo's absence in the House of Commons the Labour MP George Wigg directly asked the Prime Minister for an explanation. He said:

> There is not an honourable Member in this House who in the last few days has not heard rumour upon rumour involving a member of the Government Front Bench. The Press has got as near as it can – it has shown itself willing to wound, but afraid to strike. I rightly use the privilege of the House of Commons to ask the Home Secretary to go to the Despatch Box – he knows the rumour to which I refer relates to Miss Christine Keeler and Miss Davies and a shooting by a West Indian – and on the behalf of the Government, categorically deny the truth of these rumours. On the other hand if there is anything in them, I urge the Prime Minister to set up a Select Committee, so that these things can be dissipated and the honour of the Minister concerned freed from the imputations and innuendoes that are being spread at the present time.

In his written statement to the House Profumo admitted meeting Ivanov and Keeler through their mutual friend Ward. He denied any impropriety and threatened to sue if anyone suggested otherwise.

Christine Keeler, the model involved in the infamous political scandal known as the Profumo Affair.

Ward, meanwhile, openly admitted to George Wigg and to MI5, as well as the Home Secretary, that Profumo had slept with Keeler. The police had also received information that Ward was nothing more than a pimp and had procured various women, including Keeler and Rice Davies, for well-connected gentlemen. Ward was later to be charged with living on immoral earnings.

By now Profumo realised that there was no way out and on a holiday to Venice he considered his position and told his wife of his affair with Keeler and the fact that he had lied to the House of Commons. He wrote a letter of resignation to Macmillan, who was delighted to receive it. Both letters were published in the newspapers.

Ward's trial was to be the undoing of everyone else. Keeler found herself in prison for nine months for perjury and as for Ward, he took an overdose of barbiturates on the eve of the end of his trial. He had told a friend 'Someone had to be sacrificed, and it was me. When the establishment want blood they get it.'

Profumo's career had been ruined, not because of his relationship with Keeler, nor because she was also sleeping with a Russian spy – he had lied to the House of Commons and this was unforgivable. Ivanov's cover had been completely blown and he found himself back in Russia.

Keeler never described herself as a prostitute and in court on 17 May 1963 she said 'I never considered myself a prostitute or a call girl. Stephen said you have to have the mentality of a prostitute, which I didn't have, and it was not quite so wrong just once or twice sleeping with a man and having some money from him; a man I knew and liked.'

* * * * *

April Ashley was born George Jamieson in 1935, one of 10 children. Apparently George was a sickly child and was largely ignored by his mother, Ada. At 15 George followed his father and many of his brothers to seek a career as a sailor but on his second trip to America he was put ashore in Los Angeles after attempting to commit suicide.

1953 found George back in Liverpool, where he had been born, being treated in hospital with psychiatric problems. After a brief stay in London, George then holidayed in 1956 in France, and was taken on by the Le Carousel nightclub in Paris, where his feminine looks earned him a job as a female impersonator. He held down the job for four years, meeting many well-known celebrities. After saving a considerable sum of money George travelled to Casablanca where he had a sex-change operation and was reborn as April Ashley.

April became one of the most sought-after models of the 1960s and eventually married Arthur Corbett, the son of the 2nd Lord of Rowallan in 1963. Her secret came to light at the end of the 1960s when it was finally revealed that she had once been a man. A hugely scandalous divorce case came to an end on 2 April 1970 when Justice Ormond declared that her marriage was null and void and therefore she was not entitled to any divorce settlement. April's modelling career fell apart when she suffered a heart attack in 1975 which prompted her to retire even further into the background. For some time she lived in Hay-on-Wye and then moved to France, Spain and finally to America. She visited her former husband, Lord Rowallan, in Spain and was at his bedside when he died on 24 June 1993.

* * * * *

February 1987 saw **Cynthia Payne** accused of running a brothel, and for 13 days, the public and the media were fascinated, outraged and shocked by a procession of 'working girls', transvestites and numerous friends of Cynthia.

This was not the first time that Cynthia had found herself before a court. In March 1965 she was fined at Marlborough Street Court for keeping a brothel, and again in October 1966. In court again in 1974 and the following year, she was finally sentenced to six months in 1980 for controlling prostitutes. After that she made a considerable living from her reputation as a professional madam and was known as 'Madame Cyn'.

The police, not very ably led by Inspector Colin White, had been desperate to catch Cynthia during one of her notorious parties, where gentlemen would purchase luncheon vouchers which they could then exchange for various sexual favours. Cleverly none of the women, other than Cynthia, handled money at these events. When the police finally raided 32 Ambleside Avenue they had already infiltrated the party with undercover policemen. As the court was to hear, this was not the first time that the

police had been present at one of Cynthia's parties.

The police and the prosecution completely bungled the case, wheeling in numerous witnesses who either flatly denied any wrongdoing, or simply contradicted evidence that the court had already heard. Whatever the truth and fiction, everyone rallied around Cynthia, although it still came as a great surprise when on the final day of the trial, at 11.32am on 11 February 1987, the jury retired and took five hours to consider their verdict.

The court was packed when the jury finally filed back in just before 5pm. On the seven counts of controlling prostitutes Cynthia was found not guilty. For the majority of the public and all of her supporters, who by now included all of the media reporters and photographers, the verdict was a triumph, and when asked what she was going to do now that the case had been concluded, Cynthia simply replied 'Have a party'.

Cynthia Payne, accused of running a brothel and controlling prostitutes.

* * * * *

Unlike the majority of women in other chapters of this book, the women of this chapter who behaved in a scandalous way did not break the law. Some actively chose a different lifestyle that would bring them into conflict with their peers. None of them intended to do any physical harm, but most managed to cause grief and outrage by their behaviour.

CHAPTER THREE

REGAL RELATIONS

Looking back over the last 25 years of the 20th century, the innumerable royal scandals involving divorce, adultery and sharp business practices have shocked the world, let alone the nation. Putting these latter day sensations into context, we can see that over the years, in times when the royal family and the nobility enjoyed a much greater degree of power and prestige, scandals were no less frequent. We can only speculate how outraged and amazed the general public must have been when figures set up as role models revealed their flaws.

ELIZABETH BARTON was born in Aldington in Kent in 1506 and very early in her life she developed the symptoms of epilepsy and mental disorders. As a teenager she became a servant for Thomas Cobb, who looked after the estate of William Warham, then Archbishop of Canterbury. The turning point in Elizabeth's life came in 1525 when she fell ill and went into strange hallucinogenic trances. When she recovered she was able to go into these trances at will, and during them she was able to make prophecies and political comments. Soon the Archbishop was informed and in the following year two monks were despatched, led by Edward Bocking, with orders to admit Elizabeth into the convent at Canterbury. It was believed by many that she acted as a spokesperson for the Virgin Mary and in this guise she attracted many pilgrims and the interest of important religious figures, including Sir Thomas More.

It was not long before Elizabeth's statements brought her into direct conflict with Henry VIII, particularly given the fact that she warned the monarch not to divorce Catherine of Aragon. Later, in 1532, Elizabeth met the king and tried to persuade him not to marry Anne Boleyn.

In the event, Henry married Anne in January 1533 and his marriage to Catherine was annulled in the following May. By now Warham had been replaced by Thomas Cranmer and he arranged Elizabeth's arrest and interrogation. She admitted at the time to having faked the trances and the visions.

On 25 September 1533 Bocking was arrested, and promptly implicated everyone associated with Elizabeth. Elizabeth and her associates were tried by the Star Chamber and were later forced to make public confessions at St Paul's Cross. In January 1534

Elizabeth and her accomplices were sentenced to death and the act was carried out at Tyburn on 21 April 1534.

Throughout her short career Elizabeth was considered by many to be literally the voice of God. There is considerable doubt about whether her confessions were authentic. Many Catholics still believe that Elizabeth's only crime was to remind Henry VIII about the sanctity of the marriage vows that he had taken. There was no real trial and it is strongly believed that whatever the truth behind Elizabeth's abilities was, her execution was carried out for purely political reasons. Her execution attracted a huge crowd, the majority of which was convinced of Elizabeth's authenticity despite the confessions.

* * * * *

Simple acts of herbal or faith healing by **Jilly Duncan** sparked off a series of witchcraft trials between 1590 and 1592, which culminated in an accusation that a group of witches had conspired to kill King James VI of Scotland. Jilly Duncan was denounced for using her healing abilities by David Seaton and was tortured unmercifully until she admitted that she and several others, including **Agnes Sampson**, **Effie MacLean**, **Barbara Napier** and the schoolteacher, John Fian, had conspired to bring about the death of the king.

As far as the authorities were concerned, Agnes, an elderly midwife, was considered to be at the centre of the plot. She eventually made a full and detailed confession, after protracted and severe torture. She confessed that they had thrown a cat with a dead man's limbs tied to its paws into the sea in order to ensure that the king's ship would sink on its voyage to Denmark to collect his future bride. They also burned a wax image of the king and even tried to obtain some of his clothes so that they could smear them with poison from a toad. The most damning proof of Agnes's involvement was that she could repeat exactly what the king had said to his bride on their wedding night.

The unfortunate Agnes, largely on account of her vivid imagination, was hanged with the rest of the conspirators. At the time the case caused a sensation on both sides of the border and seemed proof positive that witchcraft was a real and malignant force. James was to use his experiences during the North Berwick witch trial as a template for writing anti-witchcraft tracts and developing severe legislation against witches when he became king of England.

* * * * *

Frances Howard, the daughter of Lord Thomas Howard, Earl of Suffolk, was to find herself at the centre of what is arguably the greatest court scandal in British royal history. She was born in 1591 into a family that had increased its power and prestige helping to defeat the Spanish Armada in 1588. Her father was well-respected and when James I came to the English throne in 1603 the family continued to enjoy royal patronage.

Frances had been born at Audley End near Saffron Walden and at the age of 15 she married Robert Devereux, the Earl of Essex. But, at the king's insistence, Robert returned to Oxford to finish his studies with a view to joining the army. Frances was left alone in the royal court and had an affair with the Prince of Wales. She then turned her attentions to another of the king's favourites, Robert Carr, Viscount Rochester. It is believed that Carr was one of the king's lovers and it is certain that he had had a long-term sexual relationship with Thomas Overbury.

There was, however, a storm cloud on the horizon, in the shape of the return of the Earl of Essex. Frances was now 18 and the marriage had not yet been consummated. She refused to have sex with her husband. Luckily for Frances, Essex contracted smallpox and for the time being his sex life was probably not high on his list of priorities. Meanwhile, the illiterate Carr had persuaded his friend Overbury to write passionate letters on his behalf to Frances and this caused inevitable friction between the two men. Frances could not bear the prospect of her husband demanding his conjugal rights and employed Dr Simon Forman and Anne Turner to supply her with a poison to kill her husband. To back up this plan she visited a Norfolk witch called Mary Woods and promised to give her a diamond ring and £1,000 if she could kill the Earl of Essex. It seems that neither of these plans came to fruition and eventually, with little prospect of his wife ever consummating their marriage, Robert Devereux agreed to a divorce.

This left Frances free to marry Robert Carr, but they did not account for the effect that this would have on Sir Thomas Overbury. Overbury was well connected and he had the ear of the king, but James I sided with Carr and offered Overbury a diplomatic post abroad. Frances was sure that Overbury would come back and haunt their lives and managed to persuade Carr to convince Overbury that he should turn down the king's offer. The king was furious and had Overbury put in the Tower of London. Frances was not content with this and knew that the only way to have Carr to herself was to ensure that Overbury was dead.

Frances managed to have Sir Gervase Elwes made Lieutenant of the Tower and used an agent called Weston to administer the poison to Overbury. It seems that Elwes was in a quandary and did not know who lay behind the attempts to kill Overbury. He managed to intercept and destroy most of the poisoned food. Frances then contacted William Reeve and paid him £20 to steal poison from his master, Dr Paul de Lobell, the physician at the Tower. Reeve procured mercury and the gullible Overbury, thinking it was a medicine, took it and died an agonising death on 15 September 1613.

France's divorce had come through on 16 May 1613, on the grounds that her husband was inexplicably impotent with her but not with other women. Frances and Carr married shortly after Overbury's death; Carr still remained a frequent visitor to the king's bedchamber. Unfortunately the king was beginning to tire of Carr and turned his attentions to George Villiers, who was later to become the Duke of Buckingham.

In 1615 William Reeve confessed on his deathbed that he had poisoned Overbury. The king was livid when he was informed and he confined Frances and Carr to their apartments in the court and had Elwes, Weston and the chemist, James Franklin, who had supplied Anne Turner with the poisons, arrested and hanged. All of the conspirators had been tortured and confessions wrung out of them before they were executed. The evidence against Frances and Carr seemed conclusive. Carr then played his trump card and threatened to make it public that he had a sexual relationship with the king if he and Frances were brought to trial. Therefore, bizarrely, when the trial opened at Westminster Hall the king had two men standing behind Carr, ready to smother him with a cloak should he utter a word about their relationship.

The pair were found guilty of murder and sent to the Tower to await their execution. For some reason the king decided to spare their lives; his loyalties lay more with Carr than with Frances, who had scandalised the nation by her activities. Feelings ran so high that on one occasion, when the queen was travelling through London in a coach, it was attacked by a mob in the mistaken belief that the coach contained Frances and her mother.

Frances and Carr were incarcerated in the Tower until January 1621, when they were released into the care of Frances's brother-in-law, Lord Wallingford. They were instructed to stay at his home, Grey's Court, in Oxfordshire and not to leave. For the next 11 years they were forced to live together, Carr now acutely aware of France's murderous tendencies and the fact that she had had Overbury poisoned, had attempted to kill her first husband and, more importantly, had ruined his career and his relationship with the king. Carr was released from this purgatory in August 1632 when Frances died of cancer. Carr died an obscure and bitter man in 1645.

* * * * *

Just 18 years after Lady Frances Howard died **Nell Gwyn** was born in Hereford. At some point Nell came to London and was initially employed as an orange seller. She later became an actress and it was at the King's Theatre, now known as the Theatre Royal, Drury Lane, that she first came to the attention of King Charles II.

Nell may well have become Charles II's mistress prior to 1670, but this date confirmed all of the gossip that had been surrounding them when she gave birth to his son. Characteristically Nell called her son 'Bastard' until Charles II acknowledged him as his son. He was then renamed Charles Beauclerk and was made a baron and later an earl and finally the 1st Duke of St Albans. They had a second son who was born on Christmas Day 1671 and they called him James, but the child unfortunately died in Paris at the age of eight.

The couple's favourite haunt was Bestwood Lodge, to the north of Nottingham, and they spent many days each year riding around and hunting there. It seems that Nell liked to lie in bed until late each morning and in order to break her out of this habit Charles offered her a wager. He told her that if she could get up and ride around the whole Bestwood Lodge estate before breakfast, then he would give it to her. An amazed Charles, the following morning, stepped outside and saw Nell galloping towards him; she had won the wager and to prove that she had covered the full distance she had dropped white handkerchiefs along her route. The estate became the home of the Duke of St Albans.

When Charles II died in 1685 one of his deathbed wishes was 'Let not poor Nellie starve'. His brother, James II, was keen to honour the late monarch's final plea and paid off the £3,774 mortgage on the Bestwood Lodge estate.

Life was not good for Nell after the death of Charles; her health was poor and her finances precarious, as she spent a great deal of her money on trying to cure herself of

her various illnesses. She died in 1687 at the age of 37 and was buried next to her mother, Eleanor, in the graveyard of St Martin-in-the-Field.

Nell was one of at least 15 mistresses of Charles II and her two children had at least 12 other half-brothers and sisters. Charles had started his harem back in 1648 when he met the Welsh beauty, **Lucy Walter**. In 1649 she gave birth to Charles's first child, James, who was to become the Duke of Monmouth. After finding her implicated in a plot in 1650 Charles dismissed Lucy and for the next eight years she plied her trade as a prostitute until dying of syphilis in 1658.

Another notable mistress was **Moll Davis**, who was a singer and dancer on the London stage. The wife of Samuel Pepys described Moll as being 'The most impertinent slut in the world'. She had met Charles in 1667 and quickly became his mistress. Shortly before her daughter was born the following year she gave up the stage but by then Charles was already seeing Nell Gwyn. Nell was successful in disposing of Moll by cooking for her on the day that she knew Moll was to spend the night with the king. She laced Moll's food with laxatives and after a disastrous night with the king, Moll was dispensed with but given a £1,000 a year pension.

Nell was not, however, alone in attracting the interests of the king. He was also seeing **Louise de Keroualle**, whom Nell called 'Squinter Bella' or 'Weeping Willow', on account of the fact that the king had confided in Nell that she always cried in order to get a present from him. Nevertheless, Louise, who was maid of honour to the Duchess of Orléans, became Charles's official mistress in 1671 and after she gave birth to Charles Lennox in 1672 she was made the Duchess of Portsmouth and her son the Duke of Richmond. Louise seemed to be quite a resilient woman, fighting off a number of rivals seeking the attentions of the king.

One of the many mistresses that Louise was able to see off was **Barbara Villiers**, who later became the Countess of Castlemaine and the Duchess of Cleveland. Barbara was already heavily pregnant with Charles's son when he returned from Portugal with his future queen, Catherine of Braganza. Barbara's son was born on 18 June 1662 and the fact that the father was Charles II was not a closely kept secret. In fact when the queen visited her at Hampton Court the shock was so great that she started bleeding from the nose and then fainted.

When a second son was born in 1663 Charles was certain that the child was not his, and he felt the same way about another child born in 1667. It seems that Barbara was not content to simply be the faithful mistress of the king and was sleeping with several other men. When Barbara left the court and moved to Paris in 1677 she was to have another four children, making her total seven, with at least six different fathers. Regrettably for her husband, none of the children were his.

Nell Gwyn, however, is credited with the belief that she was the only one of Charles's mistresses that really loved him and moreover was faithful to him. On one occasion the Duke of Buckingham tried to seduce her and so she punched him. Nell had come a long way from her first job at the age of seven when she poured drinks for customers in a brothel. Her critics claim that both she and Moll Davis were women who lived on the very edge between their acting careers and outright prostitution. Nell was much criticised and mocked both during and after her life but she never showed any sign of being overawed by the company that she kept.

Nell Gwyn, mistress of Charles II.

* * * * *

While Barbara Villiers, the namesake of the Duke of Buckingham, George Villiers, was sleeping with Charles II and various other men, and the Duke of Buckingham himself was trying to seduce Nell Gwyn, **Madam Mary Butler**, the Duke of Buckingham's mistress, was developing troubles of her own.

On 13 October 1688, a year after the Duke of Buckingham had died, Mary Butler, who was also known as Mary Strickland, was indicted at the Old Bailey for forging a bond. In itself forgery was not necessarily big news, neither was it a question of her associations; it was the amount that the bond had been written for that stunned everyone at the time. Mary had forged this document in the name of the Worshipful Sir Robert Clayton, who was a knight and alderman of the City of London. The amount was a staggering £40,000.

The bond stated that Mary was entitled to £1,200 per annum, with interest, and that after the death of Sir Robert, Mary should be paid a lump sum of £20,000 within six months. By all accounts the bond looked the part: it had a seal and had been witnessed by four people. It had in fact been created on Mary's orders by a man called Lucas who worked in Bishopsgate Street. She admitted that the bond was a forgery and despite calling notables to attest to her previously good character, the jury found her guilty of forging the bond and she was fined £500. Unfortunately for Mary she was penniless and she would therefore have to remain in Newgate Prison until the fine had been paid. It was never paid and she died, still incarcerated, in 1692.

* * * * *

The Countess of Bristol.

It is amazing that given all the partner-shuffling that went on in the upper echelons of British society, that it took so long for one of them to find themselves married to two people simultaneously.

The Countess of Bristol was the daughter of Colonel Chudleigh from Devon and her trial for bigamy, which began on 15 April 1776 at Westminster Hall, attracted so much attention that even the queen and other members of the royal family came to watch.

Her family was not a rich one, although comfortable enough. Her father had died when she was young and her mother did everything in her power to ensure that her daughter would be well-educated and connected. By good fortune she attracted the attentions, at the age of 18, of Mr Pulteney, who was a member of the opposition in the House of Commons and well-connected with George III. Through his efforts she was made maid of honour to the Princess of Wales and this new position brought the young Miss Chudleigh enviable new contacts.

She had attracted the attention of the Duke of Hamilton, but her aunt had introduced her to the Honourable Mr Hervey, the son of the Earl of Bristol. At length Miss Chudleigh and the Duke got engaged and agreed to marry when he returned home from a tour abroad. They promised to write to one another as often as possible, but neither could have counted on the continued interference of the aunt.

Gradually Hervey convinced her to accept his hand in marriage; largely on account of the fact that she had not heard from the Duke because her aunt had been intercepting his letters. They married secretly in Hampshire but the new Mrs Hervey knew immediately that she had made a mistake and never slept with her husband after the first night. To outward appearances they were simply friends. Their one night together produced a child, a boy, but he died soon after birth.

Shortly after the Duke of Hamilton returned to England and beat a path to Miss Chudleigh's door, desperate to know why she had not written to him. He was intercepted by Mrs Hanmer, the aunt, and was told that his fiancée had changed her mind and that he should not trouble her any longer.

Although her marriage was a sham, Mrs Hervey eventually returned to her court responsibilities but was continually dogged by the fear that Captain Hervey would disclose their marriage. It seems that she did tell the Princess of Wales and a plan to deal with the situation was hatched. The clergyman who had married them was dead. All that remained was their names in the marriage register. At some point either Mrs Hervey or someone working on her behalf tore out the relevant page from the register and it was considered that there was no other evidence that she had ever married Captain Hervey.

Shortly after this Hervey's father died and he became the Earl of Bristol. Mrs Hervey was torn between accepting the title of Countess of Bristol and continuing to deny that the marriage had ever taken place. Again it appears she paid a visit to the chapel in which she had been married. She had kept the page that had been torn out, which she now reinserted.

Ever-changing, soon after, she fell in love with the Duke of Kingston. She approached her husband and asked him whether he would be prepared to give her a divorce; he refused. At length he agreed and as he was unable to substantiate the fact that the marriage had ever taken place, the claim was considered to be null and void. The Earl had also met another woman with whom he felt that he could live a much happier life.

Convinced that the nightmare was over, she married the Duke of Kingston, the wedding being attended by several dignitaries and being publicly solemnised. The Duchess of Kingston spent several happy years enjoying her title and the glamour it brought, and all appeared to be going well for her. Her husband, however, was not a well man and she used to take him around the country hoping that a change of air would help improve his health. Eventually it became obvious to the Duchess that her husband was close to death. She knew that he had made a will leaving everything to his nephew when he died and she swiftly drew up a second will, which left everything to her providing she remained unmarried after the death of her husband. Mr Field, her solicitor, refused to get involved in this subterfuge as it was clear that the Duke would not know what he was signing.

The Duke died very soon after this attempt by the Duchess to change his will and she fled immediately to Rome and lodged in the palace of one of the Cardinals.

Meanwhile, back in London, a Mrs Craddock, who had witnessed her marriage to the Earl of Bristol, visited Mr Field and told him that unless he organised a substantial payment to her then she would tell all she knew. Field refused to be threatened so Mrs Craddock went to see Mr Evelyn Meadows, one of the sons of the late Duke of Kingston's sisters, Lady Frances Pierpoint, who had been left out of the inheritance. This provided the slighted young man with the opportunity to get his own back on the Duchess of Kingston. Accordingly, he had an indictment served on Mr Field as the Duchess's representative.

While in Rome the Duchess visited Mr Jenkins, a representative of a banker in Rome. He held her funds for her but Meadows's people had already got to him and Jenkins avoided meeting her. Not to be trifled with in such a way, the Duchess pulled two pistols out and threatened the servants, saying that if Jenkins did not come and see her immediately she could not be held responsible for her actions. Jenkins caved in and the Duchess now had funds to enlist help.

The Duchess then left Rome, headed for Calais and then on to Dover and Kingston House, where she found her true friends rallying around her, including the Duke of Newcastle, Lord Mountstuart and Mr Glover. By now the papers were full of the story and everyone was eagerly awaiting her explanations at Westminster Hall.

Proceedings opened on 15 April 1776 and among the spectators were the queen, the Prince of Wales, the Princess Royal, other members of the royal family, foreign ambassadors and sundry members of the British nobility. The case was to be heard by the Lord High Steward and the Duchess, after being asked how she pleaded to the charge of bigamy, said firmly 'Not guilty My Lords.'

The case wrangled on until 22 April when the prosecution completed their case. In her defence she claimed that she had never felt herself to be legally married to Mr Hervey. She claimed she could prove that the Archbishop of Canterbury himself had told her that she was at liberty to marry the Duke of Kingston and that as far as all of her peers were concerned, including the royal family, she was the Duchess of Kingston. In the event, later in the day, the judges found her guilty of bigamy.

Paradoxically, when she claimed 'privilege of peerage' as her defence against possible imprisonment, the judges accepted this and discharged her after she had paid a fine. To all intents and purposes she was no longer the Duchess of Kingston but was the Countess of Bristol. Although a party had been arranged for her by her friends in anticipation of victory in court, she drove straight to Dover and boarded a yacht to Calais. There was trouble for her to sort out in Rome; she had left a Spanish Friar in charge of her palace and possessions in Rome, but he had sold everything and eloped with an English girl who worked there. Having done her best to retrieve as much of her property as possible, she then returned to England to find that the Duke of Kingston's will had been proved in court and her access to much of the estate had been blocked.

She purchased a mansion in Montmartre in Paris; by all accounts she had never seen the place and when she was pushed into completing the purchase in an unusually short period of time, she discovered the reason. At great variance to the description of the building, it was in a pitiful state of repair, but it was now hers so she brought a law suit against the previous owners. While waiting for the case to appear in a Paris court she went to St Petersburg, where she set up a brandy distillery. On her return to Paris the case was still not concluded to her satisfaction and she began plans to acquire an even bigger house. This one was owned by the brother of the French king and the Countess put all her energies into becoming his mistress.

She secured the property, called St Assise, for the sum of £59,000; it was an incredibly good purchase as it had extensive grounds and, more importantly, literally thousands of wild rabbits. In the first week she killed and sold 300 guineas worth of rabbits and set up a regular trade as a rabbit merchant.

When the legal judgement on the house in Paris finally came through on 26 August 1796, the court had found against her and this seemed to be the last straw. She flew into a fit of rage and died in her sleep that night from internal bleeding.

* * * * *

The marriage between the German **Caroline of Brunswick** and the future King George IV, then Prince of Wales, began inauspiciously when they first met on their wedding day in 1795. Caroline had been born in 1768 and seemed to be a brash, precocious young woman with a strange sense of humour and few feminine charms. She had made life difficult for her mother and father, always being wild, ill-disciplined and apt to tell lies. They were delighted, however, to off-load her on the unsuspecting Prince of Wales. Technically he was already married to the Catholic widow, Maria Fitzherbert, but he had massive debts, and his father not only wanted to find him a woman whose family could wipe out the debts, but also one who would be a more suitable provider of heirs.

When Lord Malmesbury came to collect Caroline for the wedding he was shocked by what he saw. She was short, coarse, undignified and had several other odd habits. Uppermost was the fact that she neither washed very often, nor changed her underclothes and stockings. The lord quickly realised that something would have to be done to knock the edges off this rough diamond. Lady Jersey was deployed to turn Caroline into a potential queen.

The Prince of Wales met Caroline for the first time on their wedding day, 8 April 1795, at the Chapel Royal at St James's Palace. It is said that his first reaction was to whisper into Lord Malmesbury's ear and say 'I am not well, pray get me a glass of brandy.' Caroline, on the other hand, shouted in a loud voice 'Is the Prince always like that? I find him very fat and nothing like as handsome as his portraits.' This was to set the scene for their whole marriage and indeed on their wedding night Caroline claimed that her new husband spent the better part of it snoring in a chair near the fire.

Despite their apparent dislike of one another Caroline gave birth to a daughter, Charlotte, on 7 January 1796. The Prince was bitterly disappointed and had wanted a son. He proclaimed that he felt so bad about it that he believed he was going to die. So convinced was he that he wrote a will leaving everything to Maria Fitzherbert and left express instructions that Caroline should have nothing to do with the upbringing of his daughter.

Caroline, soon after the marriage, had returned to her normal laundry and bathing routines and the prince could not bear to sit, let alone eat or sleep, in the same room as her. He lived in one of the wings of Carlton House and the princess in another. At length they decided to remain married but live separate lives, and consequently Caroline moved to Montague House on Blackheath.

Despite the fact that Caroline repulsed the Prince of Wales, the same could not be said for the innumerable naval officers that enjoyed parties at Caroline's home. It is believed that she had affairs with both Admiral Sir Sidney Smith and a frigate commander called Captain Manby. Indeed, several servants claimed to have seen her sharing her bed with the two men. Caroline had a distinct dislike of English women and consequently all her parties were restricted to male guests. She even told a friend 'I have a bedfellow whenever I like'. People thought her coarse as she would often hitch up her skirt when dancing and wear exceedingly low cut dresses.

Not all English women spurned her: indeed, Lady Charlotte Douglas, a neighbour, befriended her. Sometime into their friendship Charlotte fell pregnant and Caroline rather foolishly decided to play a trick on her. She mirrored Charlotte's growing belly with cushions stuffed up her own dress and started eating all manner of strange food, including onion rings for breakfast. At the appropriate time Caroline gave 'birth' in the shape of a child that she had acquired from Mrs Austin, the wife of an unemployed dock worker from Deptford. Her prank was about to misfire. The prince received word that his wife had given birth to a child and wanted to know who had fathered it. Charlotte had been told the truth after Caroline had had her laugh at her friend's expense, and now told the prince that Caroline had been sleeping with Sir Sidney Smith, among others.

In 1806 a Royal Commission finally cleared Caroline of adultery and she saw this as her opportunity to re-establish herself at court. This also gave her the opportunity to see her daughter, but by the time Caroline arrived back, just in time to take part in King George III's birthday celebrations, she did not exactly cut a figure to impress her husband. She had put on a great deal of weight, dressed inappropriately and showed far too much cleavage.

Up until this point, despite Caroline's reputation, the general public had continued to be supportive of her against her husband. This was all to change when Princess Charlotte, her daughter, at the age of 16, fell in love with an officer in the Dragoons. Lieutenant Hess was believed to be the Duke of York's illegitimate son and despite the dangers Caroline approved of the match. She even agreed to let them meet in her apartments at Kensington Palace, providing them with a bedroom where she had turned back the covers on the bed. After having let them in to the room, she locked the door. It was fortunate for both her and her daughter that Lieutenant Hess never took advantage of the situation and the Prince of Wales never knew.

By February 1811 the Prince of Wales's father, the king, had become so ill that the prince assumed the role of Regent. He took full powers the following year but kept Caroline at a great distance.

The Whig Party had been given assurances by the prince that they would become the government as soon as he became king. But in a letter written by Caroline, detailing her grievances against her husband, it became clear to them that they had been fooled. Indeed, at the insistence of his new mistress, Lady Hertford, he had given this role to the Tories. The Whigs saw Caroline as an opportunity to seize power and consequently they mobilised all of the support that they possibly could in her favour. The Prince of Wales struck back by calling another investigation into the morals of his wife, but it effectively cleared her once more, and only served to rally more people to her cause.

In July 1813 Caroline took her daughter's side when she broke off her engagement to the Prince of Orange. Under considerable pressure from the Prince of Wales, she allowed Charlotte to return to her father. Caroline and Charlotte were never to meet again.

Caroline decided that there was little to be gained by staying in England and, with the young William Austin in tow, her 'son', they travelled to Brunswick then

Switzerland and Italy. Even though she was 46 years old Caroline was determined to live a full life. When Lady Bessborough encountered her in Genoa, she wrote:

> I cannot tell you how sorry and asham'd I felt as an Englishwoman. The first thing I saw in the room was a short, very fat, elderly woman, with an extremely red face in a girl's white dress, but with shoulder, back and neck quite low down to the middle of her stomach; very black hair and eyebrows, which gave her a fierce look and a wreath of light pink roses on her head.

While in Milan Caroline had initiated a relationship with an Italian called Bartolomeo Pergami. The majority of her household were now members of his family and even the long-suffering Lady Charlotte Campbell, her lady-in-waiting, finally resigned and returned to England. Caroline bought Bartolomeo the title of Baron de la Francine and a villa on the shore of Lake Como for herself. She and her new lover and his family toured around Sicily, where they were only just able to convince her of the rashness of climbing Mount Etna. They then moved on to Tunis and then to the Holy Land. There she made Bartolomeo the Grand Master of her newly created Order of St Caroline.

Everything changed while Caroline was en route to Rome. George III was dead and her husband was about to be crowned king of England. She hastened towards England and was intercepted by Lord Henry Brougham at Saint Omer in France. He had brought with him a deal which offered Caroline £50,000 per year if she would only to renounce her claim to the throne. Characteristically she refused, and despite Brougham's pleas to return to England quietly, and sort the situation out with her husband, she made it her business to return to English soil in style.

Dover had been alerted to her imminent arrival and there was a vast crowd waiting to meet her. She was honoured with a 21-gun salute and the crowd were also said to have chanted 'Long Live the Queen and Long Live King Austin'.

When her husband found out the details of her arrival he was angered, and before hiding up in Windsor he set the wheels in motion for yet another investigation into his wife's moral behaviour. This time he could not afford the outcome to be in her favour. On every step of her journey abroad he had ensured that spies were available to feed back information about her immoral activities. The investigation was to be carried out in the House of Lords.

The king had been advised not to attempt to divorce Caroline but to find some other means to deny her the crown. His Prime Minister had found the solution, the 'Bill of Pains and Penalties'. If it could be proved that Caroline had committed adultery, then an Act of Parliament could be created to deny her the right to become queen and to effectively annul the marriage. The hearing ground on for 40 days and the country was spellbound throughout, as every detail of Caroline's behaviour was revealed.

Several Italian witnesses were brought forward and testified that they had seen Caroline cavorting with Bartolomeo in nothing more than her pantaloons. On other occasions they had seen Caroline asleep with her hands resting on his groin. Even more shockingly they had danced naked together wearing just fig leaves in mockery of Adam and Eve. When it was alleged that Caroline must have had sexual relations with Bartolomeo, Caroline could stay silent no more. She stood up and in a thunderous voice which echoed around the chamber, declared that this could not be so as while Bartolomeo had been fighting in Napoleon's army his penis had been shot off with a musket ball.

On Friday 10 November 1820 the hearing concluded with a vote. Against all odds 108 peers of the realm voted in Caroline's favour, with 99 siding with the future king. Caroline and her supporters were triumphant; the future king retreated to Windsor with his tail between his legs. It was a popular decision; reinforced by Caroline's decision to go to St Paul's to give thanks to God that justice had been accorded to her. Her procession drew an enormous crowd and almost universally the public were behind her.

The brooding, desperate and deeply unhappy husband remained holed up in Windsor. He had to find a way to prevent her from becoming the queen of England. The Privy Council leapt to his aid and told him that they had decided that because of the long period of time that he and Caroline had spent apart, that he had the right to refuse to allow her to be present at the coronation.

Caroline's popularity was short-lived. She moved into Brandenburg House and drank heavily. She made repeated attempts to get her husband to agree that she should attend the coronation. Every time he refused. Against all advice she climbed into a carriage on the morning of 19 July 1821, dressed in white satin and with ostrich plumes in her hair, and made for Westminster Abbey. When she arrived the guards were on strict orders to bar her entry and the doors were slammed in her face. Desperately she cried 'I am your Queen will you not admit me?' The reply came: did she have a pass? One of her entourage piped up and said 'I present you your Queen, surely there is no need for her to have a ticket?' The Prince of Wales became George IV alone.

Shortly after the coronation, on a visit to Drury Lane Theatre, Caroline fell ill. She faded fast, probably as a result of cancer, but before she died she told her friends that she had no regrets. Her daughter, Princess Charlotte, should have the last words on her life. She was once quoted as having written 'My mother was wicked but she would not have turned so wicked had not my father been much more wicked still!'

* * * * *

Lady Caroline Lamb was born in 1785, the daughter of Lord Duncannon and Lady Henrietta. When Caroline was nine years old her father became the 3rd Earl of Bessborough and at the age of 20 Caroline married William Lamb, Lord Melbourne's son. Her new husband had great political ambitions and became an MP in 1806. Although Caroline bore William two children, only one survived, and was still sickly. By her own admission the marriage was over and she craved the attention of other men. Indeed, of this period of her life she said 'I behaved a little wild, riding over the downs with all the officers at my heels'. She had also had an affair with Godfrey Webster, who was well-known for his sexual adventures.

Sometime around 1814, having read his poetry, she became determined to meet Lord Byron. When she saw him for the first time at a ball she wrote 'That beautiful, pale face will be my fate'. She later met him again at Holland House and from then on they were inseparable. The Duchess of Devonshire, her aunt, said of her niece 'She is, as usual, doing all sorts of imprudent things for him and with him'. Caroline adored Byron and

The poet Byron, pursued by Lady Caroline Lamb.

literally worshipped him. In a few short months he tired of her but Caroline was not to be dissuaded.

For the next few years she could only pursue him with letters and then her obsession began to become more acute. She had somebody spy on Byron and on one occasion she dressed up as a tradesman in order to gain access to his house.

All of this was causing chaos and scandal and it was having a marked affect on the rest of her family. Caroline ran away and tried to get between Byron and his new mistress, Lady Oxford. She was devastated when he married Annabella Milbanke and on another occasion she forged Byron's signature to obtain a portrait of him. Later she manufactured a meeting with him at a ball and attempted to commit suicide when he would not talk to her. This was all too much for Byron and he left England for good; he was later to die in Greece.

Caroline's husband, despite the urgings of his family, stayed with her, but there was more shame and shock in store when she published a novel, *Glenarvon*, with Byron as its central character. It also contained thinly disguised character assassinations of her family and major society figures. Although the book was a best seller, it was the final straw and she was virtually ruined. She was, however, to meet Byron one last time.

After suffering an illness she was taken out in a carriage to catch some fresh air and the driver stopped as a funeral cortège passed along the street. The procession was that of Lord Byron.

Despite her frantic lifelong obsession with Byron, she famously described him in her diary as 'mad, bad and dangerous to know'.

Her Grace, the Duchess of Devonshire.

* * * * *

Jane Digby was born in 1807 and in her prime was considered to be one of the most beautiful women in England. Digby was an aristocrat through and through; she was high-spirited and probably lived one of the most scandalous lives of the 19th century. She was better than her male counterparts at almost everything, from literature to horse riding. By the time she was 13 it was clear that the only way that the family could calm her mischievous spirit was to get her married off as soon as possible.

In the spring of 1824 Jane met the 35-year-old widower, Edward Law, who was the 2nd Lord of Ellenborough. Despite his dashing appearance and eligibility, Jane's decision to accept his marriage proposal was an absolute disaster. As far as Jane was concerned Ellenborough was only interested in two things; firstly having a woman with an eye-popping cleavage on his arm at functions, and secondly, having a means to produce a son and heir. In the event he paid her little attention, and after only three years of marriage Jane began to look for a more receptive and attentive man.

For a long period of time she had felt attracted to her first cousin, George Anson, who was a scholar working for the British Museum. Luckily, just at the right time, while he was cataloguing the books in the Digby family home at Holkham Hall in Norfolk, she had the opportunity to seduce him.

Returning to London Jane attended several balls with her husband and on one evening she was introduced to the new Austrian attaché, Prince Felix Schwarzenberg. The prince fascinated Jane and as far as she was concerned, he was the most perfect example of manhood.

It did not take long for them to tumble into bed with one another. The prince already had a reputation and during the summer of 1828 he and Jane were often seen together.

Jane's husband, meanwhile, seemed to be more interested in furthering his political career than taking any notice of the fact that he had been supplanted as Jane's bedfellow. The potential for scandal had not escaped the Austrian Ambassador, Prince Esterhazy. He was concerned that if Ellenborough kicked up a fuss it could cause irreparable damage between England and Austria. The ambassador told Schwarzenberg to find another woman; any woman other than Jane. When Schwarzenberg obliged Jane proceeded to tell everyone she knew that she had been abandoned by her dashing Austrian lover. The ambassador considered the situation and at length ordered Schwarzenberg home. It was, however, too late; Jane was already carrying his child and had planned with Schwarzenberg to leave her husband and move to Vienna with him.

The situation was fast becoming a political nightmare; on the one hand Ellenborough, his family and the Digbys faced public disgrace if Jane left for Austria. On the other hand Schwarzenberg's political career would be finished if it was seen that he had stolen an Englishman's wife. Ellenborough decided that he needed to salvage as much of his reputation as he could and divorced Jane. The Digbys desperately tried to persuade Jane to beg Ellenborough's forgiveness; she refused.

On 31 August 1829 Jane sailed for the continent a divorced woman. She had arranged with Schwarzenberg that she would live in Basle. Her daughter, Mathilde, was born in the November and when Schwarzenberg was assigned to the Paris Embassy he took Jane with him. Because of their situation the couple found themselves socially excluded but Jane fell pregnant once more and gave birth to a son who died very soon after the birth. Any hopes that Jane had of marrying Schwarzenberg died with the child, as he had already been linked with a number of other notable beauties in Paris and had arranged to be transferred to a post in Bavaria. Jane had nowhere to turn apart from her mother, Lady Andover. On no account did her mother wish her to return to England; she had an alternative. The family had strong connections in Munich and it was there that Jane fled with her daughter.

It did not take long for Jane to attract the attentions of King Ludwig I of Bavaria. She was also being courted at the same time by Baron Karl Venningen. It was a perfect situation; the baron could take her to all of the places where she could not be seen on the king's arm. However perfect the situation may have been for Jane, the baron could not cope with her seeing the king, or constantly harping on about Schwarzenberg.

Everything changed when Jane fell pregnant; the baron proposed and she accepted. This did not stop her from still having a relationship with the king and the baron tried everything in his power to put distance between the two of them. He moved Jane to Weinheim, north of Heidelberg, but after several weeks of agitation Jane convinced him to take her back to Munich. It is unclear what happened to the baron's child. Jane was not very maternal and although she was to have six children in her life, she only ever kept one of her sons with her and he died when he was six years old.

One evening Jane was attending a carnival ball where she met the fascinating Greek aristocrat, Count Spiridion Theotoky, known as Spiro. He was 24 and his family owned considerable estates on the island of Corfu. The Greek immediately fell in love with Jane. Jane was not prepared to make the same kind of mistakes that she had made when she first started seeing Schwarzenberg. This time any liaison would be kept strictly out of the public eye. Consequently, she would wait until her husband and the household were asleep before saddling up a horse and riding out in the middle of the night to make love with the count. Jane and the count did make one attempt to elope together but the baron had been tipped off and gave chase to their coach. He pulled his Greek rival out of the carriage and challenged him to a duel. The baron managed to wound the count during the duel, but the victory did not douse the flames of passion between the count and Jane. In 1839 she eloped with the count to Paris, leaving behind her two children and her husband. As far as her family was concerned this was the last straw; she was struck from their wills and her name was rarely mentioned again.

The spring of 1841 found the couple at Tinos on Corfu. The count's father was the governor of the island. They wished to marry but Jane was still married to the baron. Before setting off to the Aegean they had persuaded a Greek Orthodox priest in Marseilles to dissolve Jane's marriage and so it was that when Jane met her father-in-law, she could be introduced as Countess Theotoky. They lived on the island happily for three years, enjoying life and a whirl of social engagements, until Spiro was called to Athens by King Otto.

The king wanted Spiro to become his aide, and when the king caught sight of Jane he fell madly in love with her. Queen Amalia hated Jane as both she and Spiro strongly believed that Otto was having an affair with her. Spiro got his own back by having a string of affairs of his own.

In the summer of 1846 the Count and Countess Theotoky planned to spend the time in their villa in the town of Bagni di Lucca in Italy. They took their son with them and tragedy struck. The young boy leaned over a balcony and fell to his death three stories below at the feet of his mother. This was the end of her and Spiro's relationship; only their son had sustained them through their tough time in Athens.

Jane did return to Athens in 1849 but by then King Otto had given Spiro's job to a Greek-Albanian brigand chief called General Cristodoulos Hadji-Petros. He had been the leader of the Pallikari, or 'the brave ones', who had been instrumental in winning the Greek War of Independence against the Turks. By the time Jane met him he was nearly 70 years old but obviously still something of a looker, as Jane fell in love with him. When he was made Governor of the Province of Lamia Jane sold her house in Athens and followed him to this mountainous area. This was a life that Jane had never encountered. Life was hard, rough and almost peasant-like and so far removed from everything that she had ever known, yet she loved the fiery old man and desperately wanted to marry him.

Her relationship, once it had become known in Athens, rocked the royal family. Despite the fact that the king knew that Christos supplemented his government's salary with highway robbery, the reports that he was openly keeping a mistress led people to demand that he should be sacked. In the event, Christos seems to have had far less attachment to Jane than she had to him as he openly admitted in a letter to the queen that he was living with Jane because of her money and not because he loved her.

This was Jane's cue to make another move. She had decided some time earlier that she would travel to Syria to buy horses and accordingly, at the age of 46, she set sail for Beirut on 6 April 1853. One of the men that she met very early on her buying trip was a young Bedouin sheik called Saleh. He was in his twenties and she fell in love with him. She yearned for somewhere that she could be accepted and felt that life in the desert could provide her with everything that she had been looking for all of these years. In order to cut all of her ties with her past she decided to return to Athens. Everyone was horrified that she was intending to marry a Bedouin. She ignored all their pleas and advice and returned to Saleh only to find that he had replaced her with a much younger woman.

Jane was devastated but decided to stay in the region and now headed for Damascus. She wanted to see the ancient ruins of Palmyra and asked the British Consul how this could be best achieved. He told her that the area was controlled by the Mesrab Arabs and accordingly the youngest son of the sheik was sent to talk to her. The young man was much taken with Jane and not only agreed to help her in any way he could, but actually accompanied her on her journeys.

He asked her to marry him but Jane was still distraught from her experiences with Saleh. The persistent young man, Medjuel el Mesrab, could not put Jane out of his mind and before she returned to Damascus he had finally persuaded her to marry him.

Jane returned to England for the last time in the autumn of 1856. Her family was still scandalised by her behaviour; after all, as far as they were concerned she had brought their name into disrepute, had three living husbands and was now married to a Muslim. A few bridges were repaired but Jane, still ostracised by the majority of society, left England after six months, never to see her family again.

She returned to Medjuel with guns and ammunition for the tribe and a flock of Norfolk turkeys. She lived out the rest of her life halfway between the nomadic life of the Bedouin and her more sedentary European roots. For her 73rd birthday Medjuel bought her a horse so that they could continue to ride alone together in the desert. Unfortunately in August 1881 Jane caught dysentery and on her deathbed persuaded Medjuel to bury her in the Protestant cemetery in Damascus. He was true to his word and later that day he sacrificed a camel in her honour and to her memory.

* * * * *

Two remarkable women found themselves operating as courtesans in Paris in the mid-19th century. They were both called Eliza, and although one would retain her true name, they would both leave their humble roots behind and live fast, incredible lives beyond the imaginings of their peers.

Eliza Emma Crouch was born in Plymouth in 1835, the daughter of the music teacher and writer, Frederick Crouch. It was the sales of her father's ballad *Kathleen Mavourneen* that paid for Eliza's education. By the time she returned from a convent school in Boulogne she was, by all accounts, a beautiful young woman with striking red hair who yearned to become an actress. It was, perhaps, her naivety that drove her into a life of prostitution.

On a visit to London she accepted a dinner invitation from a man who claimed to be a diamond merchant. Somehow she found herself in bed with the man at the end of the evening and when she woke up the following morning he had left £5 beside the bed. With these first earnings she took a room near Covent Garden and persuaded Robert Bignell, a theatrical impresario of ill-repute, to book her to perform at the Argyll Rooms. It seems obvious that they became lovers and he took her to Paris as his wife, although they had not married. It was in Paris that Eliza adopted her stage name, **Cora Pearl**. Her perfect figure brought her plenty of singing work and a constant line of admirers. Cora seemed to be very adept at getting them to spend money on her and she developed a taste for Cartier jewellery.

Cora attracted the attention of the Duc de Rivoli, who moved her into a house, provided her with servants and paid for all of her luxuries. She had become something of a gambler too and Rivoli paid off all her debts. Cora did not seem content with just the one man and also took up with Prince Achille Murat, who was 17 years old at the time. He bought her horses and later a stable, staffed by English grooms in yellow uniforms.

By 1862 Cora had firmly established herself among the society elite of Paris and numbered among her lovers were the Prince of Orange, who was the heir to the Dutch throne, and two of the Emperor's relatives, the Duc de Morny, his half-brother, and his cousin, Prince Napoleon.

Her golden period, however, lasted between 1865 and 1870. She was freely spending all of her lovers' money, and in particular, Prince Napoleon's. He had fallen desperately in love with her and, in addition to buying her a magnificent home on the Rue de Chaillot, he had spent over two million francs on the furniture. As far as the Prince was concerned Cora could do no wrong, and he even agreed to pay off her 70,000 franc debt at Monte Carlo. He also bought her a second home in the Rue de Bassins.

One of Cora's most magnificent triumphs occurred when she appeared semi-naked in the role of Cupid in a comic opera on 26 January 1867. What little she did wear was studded with diamonds and it is said that one French nobleman offered to buy her boots for 50,000 francs and to pay twice that amount if Cora was still wearing them.

July 1870 brought about the collapse of the French Second Empire, and the Prussian siege of Paris. Cora rose to the occasion and turned her home in the Rue de Chaillot into a hospital. She worked day and night tending the French wounded and it is said that she tore up all of her fine clothes for use as bandages. The end of the war in 1871 left France a very different place and the French monarchy was in exile.

Cora turned her attention to Alexandre Duval. He paid off all of her debts for her and brought about the ruin of his family's chain of hotels and restaurants. When the money was gone Cora lost interest in him, so he shot himself on her doorstep. In the event Duval actually recovered, but the details of his affair had created a sensation in Paris. Reluctantly Cora left Paris and headed back to London. Her reputation had preceded her and even though she managed to scrape enough money together to pay a month's advance for a suite in the Grosvenor Hotel, they discreetly turned her away.

For a brief time she stayed in a house in Mayfair, and then decided to tour Europe, visiting all the major casinos on the way. If she had had any illusions about having luck in these gambling establishments she was mistaken, and she returned to Paris in 1874 virtually penniless. She was forced to sell her house in the Rue de Chaillot and then her jewels. Eventually all of the rich furniture and other household possessions bought for her by Prince Napoleon found their way into an auctioneer's sale. She was reduced to living in the back streets of Paris.

Broken financially, and with her looks gone, she died a pauper's death on 8 July 1886. Someone, however, had learned of her death and although the aristocratic man was never identified, he gave a local undertaker a great deal of money to ensure that Cora's funeral and burial would reflect the magnificent life which she had led in her heyday.

* * * * *

Eliza Alicia Lynch only ever wanted a man who loved her and would protect her. It is improbable that she ever planned to become a Parisian courtesan. Her life had its ups and downs, but the woman who had begun life as a poor, Irish immigrant, fleeing the potato famine, later died in London with an estate conservatively valued at £300,000.

Eliza was born in 1836 and after the family had fled to France in the hopes of starting a new life, she married a French officer at the tender age of 15. Xavier Quatrefages, her new husband, was posted to a dangerous Algerian outpost and after three years of suffering hardships on the edge of the French empire, she returned to Paris alone. Her marriage had not given her either the lifestyle or man that she yearned for and with little other option open to her she launched her career as a courtesan.

Luck now smiled upon Eliza and she was eventually introduced to Princess Mathilde. Her clients tended to be rich foreigners visiting Paris or embassy officials. On her calling card, which was left in all of the best hotels around Paris, she simply described herself as 'Madame Lynch, instructress in languages'.

Eliza had picked up French and Spanish very easily and would entertain men over a game of cards at her new home in Paris. It was there that she met Francisco López. As looks went he was not much of a catch; his front teeth were missing and those that remained were heavily stained by cigar smoking and he had a broad nose and a pear-shaped head. But he was the eldest son of the president of Paraguay. More importantly, he was extremely rich and, within a few days, was infatuated by Eliza.

López had plans to become an emperor. Eliza soaked up all his tales and plans and even agreed to return with him to Paraguay. But before all of this they went on a whirlwind tour of Europe and López showered Eliza with gowns, furs and diamonds. López's father continually sent messages to his eldest son to return home and the couple finally boarded a ship bound for South America on 11 November 1854. The couple were well-prepared. López had a wardrobe filled with magnificent military uniforms and Eliza had brought with her all the trappings of a European monarch. When they landed in South America reality began to dawn on Eliza, as she faced not only a vastly different climate, even worse than the one that she had endured in Algeria, but also the matter of a 1,000-mile trip upriver to the capital Asunción. For the first time Eliza saw South American wildlife such as crocodiles, but there was worse to come and any illusions that she had had about the palace and the city that she was to make her home were shattered.

Asunción was a dump, according to Eliza, and after her first sighting of the palace she determined to convince her lover that it should be rebuilt from scratch. As for the president and his family, from the moment they clapped eyes on Eliza, they spurned her. Old Carlos Antonio simply grunted and Francisco's mother and his two sisters were openly hostile. Already Eliza was known as 'The Irish Strumpet'.

Despite the disagreeable welcoming committee, Francisco loved Eliza dearly and did his best to protect her from the sharp tongues of his family. In any case, Francisco had great delusions about his future. He likened himself to Napoleon and believed that he had equal military ability and presence. Francisco had a terrible reputation among the nobility of Paraguay; he loved the company of young virgins and many families sent their innocent daughters abroad to prevent them ending up in Francisco's bed. As evidence of his cruel and rapacious nature, Francisco presented one young bride, who had refused to submit to his advances before her marriage, with the dead body of her bridegroom. As if this was not enough, Francisco also frequently visited brothels. Eliza adopted a practical solution to this problem and chose mistresses for him.

By the time Eliza was 32 she had given birth to six of Francisco's children and was now living in a palace decorated in pink and white. She was still spurned by the local nobility and foreign visitors alike and she was hated by women. But then Francisco's father died and from then on she became the empress in her own eyes. Despite his father's pleas on his deathbed that Francisco should not turn to war, his first acts were to imprison everyone who had ever shown signs of dissent or disrespect to himself or Eliza. No one was safe from the new delusions that the couple had. Admittedly Paraguay had a strong army but acts such as making the new British Ambassador walk through the capital, rather than arrive in a state procession, did little to cement friendly relationships. Francisco had a dream; he wanted to create a vast empire that would encompass Argentina, Uruguay and Brazil. He began by attempting to marry the daughter of the Emperor of Brazil. Dom Pedro knew exactly what Francisco was like and turned down the request, but in Francisco he had made a bad enemy.

In support of Francisco Eliza was made Minister Without Portfolio and she saw that the way to fulfil Francisco's dreams was to set all of the other countries around Paraguay at one another's throats. By now everyone in Paraguay knew that Eliza's commands carried the same weight as Francisco's. They seized a Brazilian gold fleet and threw their troops into an attack on Brazil. Eliza and Francisco were triumphant when the Brazilians were caught off guard. Fate was about to turn against them, however, and Brazil, Argentina and Uruguay signed a treaty and began a five-year war against Francisco and Eliza.

Eliza took the opportunity to collect all the fine jewels and possessions owned by the nobility of Paraguay, claiming that they were needed to fund the war effort. She was already sending treasures back to Paris, including four cases of gold coins. Paraguay was on the verge of collapse and Eliza knew it, but she did not, as yet, abandon Francisco. On the contrary, she joined him at his military headquarters. Eliza sat by and watched Francisco's brother-in-law being tortured for the theft of the gold coins that she herself had removed from the treasury.

By 25 July 1868 Paraguay was virtually fully occupied by the forces ranged against them. Eliza and Francisco were almost fugitives in their own country. The Brazilians caught up with them on 1 March 1870, and in a last, desperate struggle, Francisco was shot dead. Eliza had tried to escape but was captured, but before being taken away she dug a grave for Francisco with her bare hands, covering the spot with stones. The Brazilians took her and the majority of the royal family back to the Paraguayan capital. They were aware that the Paraguayans would kill Eliza if they got their hands on her. The situation was diffused to the relief of both the Brazilians and Eliza when she agreed to board a ship bound for Europe.

Whatever her reputation had been like in South America, she presented herself in London as a much-wronged and misunderstood ruler, whose husband had been brutally murdered. For some time she tried to retrieve money that had been deposited by Francisco all around Europe. The vast majority of it, however, had disappeared. She briefly returned to Paraguay once more and received a mixed reaction. Many had accepted her legitimacy while others wanted her put on trial for the ruin she had brought to Paraguay.

Eliza died on 27 July 1886. Her death certificate described her as the widow of Francisco S. López. Her remains were taken back to Paraguay nearly 100 years later and she was proclaimed a national heroine.

* * * * *

Albert Edward, the future Edward VII, was born in 1841 and privately educated at all of the best establishments in England. His ability to attract some of the most well-known and outrageous women of his time was to bring enormous grief and heartache to the royal family. It is believed that even while still at Cambridge he had an affair with an Irish actress and got her pregnant. His father, Prince Albert, rushed to Cambridge to sort the situation out and in doing so caught a chill which brought about the end of his life. Edward's mother, Queen Victoria, never forgave him.

One of his first acknowledged mistresses was **Lillie Langtry**, an actress and beauty who had been born on Jersey in 1853. She first met Edward in 1877 after John Everett Millais painted an enchanting portrait of her. Lillie was an educated woman who had married a wealthy widower called Edward Langtry. By the time she met Edward he had already been married to Princess Alexandra for 14 years and had had several adulterous relationships with other women whose names never became public.

It was in May 1887 that Lillie and Edward met at a supper party at the home of the explorer Sir Allen Young. From the outset they were indiscreet and Lillie accompanied Bertie, as he was known, to functions at Balmoral, Buckingham Palace, Sandringham, Paris and the Riviera. The newspapers were full of stories, particularly scandalised by the fact that Bertie presented Lillie at court.

In 1879 her otherwise quiet and undemanding husband was rumoured to be planning to divorce Lillie. Rather foolishly the newspapers picked up the story and even went so far as to mention that one of the co-respondents would be the Prince of Wales. It was to cost the newspapers dearly. Lillie's husband sued them and one of the newspaper editors was sentenced to 18 months imprisonment. Truth being far stranger than fiction, Lillie finally divorced her husband and he ended up an alcoholic destitute in a lunatic asylum in Chester in 1896. He had paid the full price for his involvement with Lillie, or 'The Jersey Lillie' as she had become popularly known.

As if this was not enough to put Lillie into the limelight, she used Bertie's contacts to get her acting roles on the London stage, but by the late 1880s Lillie had been replaced by **Daisy Brooke**, the Countess of Warwick, as Bertie's preferred mistress.

When Queen Victoria died in 1901 no fewer than three of Bertie's mistresses sat in Westminster Abbey and were also present when Bertie became Edward VII. Daisy, too, had been replaced, this time by **Alice Keppel**, who was to bear Edward a daughter, Sonia, who was the great-grandmother of Camilla Shand Parker-Bowles, the mistress of the current Prince of Wales. Alice Keppel began her relationship with Bertie in 1898 and Sonia was born in 1900. Alice was already married to Colonel George Keppel, who she had married in 1891, and their daughter, Violet, who was born in 1894 would later

Lillie Langtry, actress and mistress of Edward VII.

become the lover of Vita Sackville-West. Alice continued as Bertie's mistress until his death in 1910. She died in 1947 and the long-suffering George passed away two weeks later.

Lillie faded into the background disgracefully and she is perhaps best remembered by what George Bernard Shaw once wrote of her 'I resent Mrs Langtry. She has no right to be intelligent, daring and independent as well as lovely. It is a frightening combination of attributes.' Lillie died in France in 1929, her last stage appearance having taken place in 1917.

Bertie had a voracious sexual appetite and at some point in the 1870s he began an affair with **Sarah Bernhardt**, who was the illegitimate daughter of a Jewish milliner and a law student. Prior to hitching up with Bertie she had been the mistress of Prince Henri de Ligne, a member of the Belgian royal family. It is believed that her son, Maurice, was his. Sarah acted on the British stage and this is where she drew the attention of Bertie. It is believed that she was even present at his coronation. On one occasion during her acting career she convinced Bertie to appear on the stage with her. His role did not require a great deal of acting skill as he played a corpse. Sarah died in 1923, having had most of her right leg amputated following a fall. Some 30,000 mourners were present at her funeral.

Bertie was also associated with **Jennie Jerome**, the mother of Winston Churchill. She married Randolph Churchill in 1874, shortly before Winston's birth, but she had formed a close association with Bertie. Even after their affair was over they remained close friends. Her husband died in 1895 from syphilis and Jennie had affairs and took other husbands considerably younger than herself. In 1901 she married George Cornwallis-West who was only two weeks older than her son. Later, in 1918, she married Montague Porch who was three years younger than Winston. Jennie was another of the Prince of Wales's former mistresses that attended the coronation when Bertie became king.

Equally as scandalous and perhaps potentially ruinous was **Harriet Moncreiffe**'s relationship with Bertie. Officially she was Lady Mordaunt as she was the wife of Sir Charles. They had moved to his Warwickshire mansion, Walton Hall, in December 1866 and Harriet soon became closely associated with the Prince of Wales and his circle of friends.

Harriet's daughter, Violet, was born on 28 February 1869; the girl was blind, and probably out of guilt, Harriet confessed to her husband that she had committed adultery with Lord Cole, Sir Frederick Johnstone and the Prince of Wales. Inevitably there was to be a divorce case, probably one of the most acrimonious and bitter cases of the 19th century. Despite Harriet's admissions there was little hard evidence and Sir Charles's counsel was determined to put the three men through the wringer in court. The Prince of Wales himself was examined for seven minutes, answering questions regarding the nature of various letters that Sir Charles had discovered written by him to his wife. In order to undermine Bertie's reputation before he even appeared in court, the letters had been leaked to *The Times* and published.

Among all of the scandals that Queen Victoria had faced as a result of her errant son, this proved to be one of the most dangerous. There was a very real fear that Bertie's adultery, brought into such clear public view, would undermine the very security of the

throne, particularly given that there was a great deal of Republican sentiment in Britain at the time.

At a crucial point in the trial a counter-claim was made by Harriet's defence counsel, claiming that she had been mentally deranged and therefore was not responsible for her actions. The 'Warwickshire Scandal', as it became known, ran on and on and the public eagerly consumed every word that was reported.

Eventually Harriet was allowed to be sent as a private patient to the home of Dr Andrew Wynter in Chiswick. In 1871 she found herself in the private mental asylum of Dr Tuke; he concluded that Harriet had the mind of a child.

The acrimonious divorce proceedings continued and eventually Sir Charles managed to divorce his wife in November 1875. Two years later, as the plain Miss Moncreiffe, Harriet moved into a new asylum under the care of Dr Benbo; she was never to be released and finally died in 1906.

There were more scandals for Bertie; he was involved with several other women and notably, before his accession to the throne, he would often visit the Parisian nightclub, Cabaret of Hell. Here he would be greeted by naked women who would stand beside a doorway that was dressed as the Devil's mouth.

* * * * *

Bertie's grandson, also an Edward and the Prince of Wales, was destined to become king of England, but his association with a mistress forced him to abdicate the throne in 1936. He was king between January and December that year. Although it had become

Wallis Simpson, the American divorcée who caused Edward VIII to abdicate, with her lover.

public knowledge that he intended to marry a twice-divorced American, his speech on 11 December 1936 to explain to his subjects and the Empire why he had chosen love above duty remains evidence of one of the greatest royal scandals in British history:

At long last I am able to say a few words of my own. I have never wanted to withhold anything, but until now it has not been constitutionally possible for me to speak.

A few hours ago I discharged my last duty as King and Emperor, and now that I have been succeeded by my brother, the Duke of York, my first words must be to declare my allegiance to him. This I do with all my heart.

You all know the reasons which have impelled me to renounce the throne. But I want you to understand that in making up my mind I did not forget the country or the empire, which, as Prince of Wales and lately as King, I have for twenty-five years tried to serve.

But you must believe me when I tell you that I have found it impossible to carry the heavy burden of responsibility and to discharge my duties as King as I would wish to do without the help and support of the woman I love.

And I want you to know that the decision I have made has been mine and mine alone. This was a thing I had to judge entirely for myself. The other person most nearly concerned has tried up to the last to persuade me to take a different course.

I have made this, the most serious decision of my life, only upon the single thought of what would, in the end, be best for all.

This decision has been made less difficult to me by the sure knowledge that my brother, with his long training in the public affairs of this country and with his fine qualities, will be able to take my place forthwith without interruption or injury to the life and progress of the empire. And he has one matchless blessing, enjoyed by so many of you, and not bestowed on me – a happy home with his wife and children.

During these hard days I have been comforted by her majesty my mother and by my family. The ministers of the crown, and in particular, Mr Baldwin, the Prime Minister, have always treated me with full consideration. There has never been any constitutional difference between me and them, and between me and Parliament. Bred in the constitutional tradition by my father, I should never have allowed any such issue to arise.

Ever since I was Prince of Wales, and later on when I occupied the throne, I have been treated with the greatest kindness by all classes of the people wherever I have lived or journeyed throughout the empire. For that I am very grateful.

I now quit altogether public affairs and I lay down my burden. It may be some time before I return to my native land, but I shall always follow the fortunes of the British race and empire with profound interest, and if at any time in the future I can be found of service to his majesty in a private station, I shall not fail.

And now, we all have a new King. I wish him and you, his people, happiness and prosperity with all my heart. God bless you all! God save the King!

Edward VIII – 11 December, 1936

Bessie Wallis Warfield, better known as **Wallis Simpson** was born on 19 June 1896 in Pennsylvania. She was something of an extrovert and socialite. Her first husband was a US Navy Lieutenant called Earl Winfield Spencer Jnr. She married him in Baltimore in Maryland in 1916 but this marriage was dissolved in 1927, a year before she married for a second time. Her second husband was also an American, living and working in London. Ernest Aldrich Simpson provided her with all of the opportunities to mix with the smart social set that she had craved. She met Edward at a country house party in 1931 and it quickly blossomed into a love affair. Edward had never married and was in his mid-thirties when she met him.

1936 was to be a traumatic year for them both. Wallis had desperately been trying to get her divorce from Simpson finalised, but with the death of George V on 20 January, they were fast running out of time. With such close associations with the future monarch, a constitutional crisis emerged, when neither Edward's family, nor the Houses of Parliament or the Church of England, would countenance him marrying a twice-married foreigner, who was still not divorced. Hoping that somehow the situation could be resolved, Edward acceded to the throne, but the storm clouds gathered around them. Under intense personal and political pressure, Edward VIII voluntarily abdicated on 10 December 1936, delivering his famous speech to his subjects the day after Parliament's endorsement of his decision.

Edward's younger brother took the throne as George VI and gave Edward the title Duke of Windsor. Wallis's divorce became final on 27 April 1937 and on 3 June they married in France. Wallis was never accepted as the Duchess of Windsor and for the rest of their lives they lived in France. During World War Two they took refuge in the Bahamas where Edward acted as governor.

In her autobiography *The Heart Has Its Reasons,* published in 1956, Wallis tried to explain from her perspective how their love had overruled all thoughts of duty. Although she briefly visited England in 1967 she was only to return once more in 1972 to attend Edward's funeral. He had died in Paris on 28 May. Wallis returned to France and lived the life of a recluse until she died on 24 April 1986. Time had healed many of the wounds and displeasure of the establishment and her body was buried next to Edward's at Windsor Castle.

* * * * *

Whether the American Wallis Simpson could be considered a true victim of the British establishment or not, in 2001 the American Thomas Cressman was in every sense of the word. He was the lover of the former aide to the Duchess of York, **Jane Andrews**, and lived a jet-set lifestyle, frequently travelling back and forth across the Atlantic. Andrews had worked for Sarah Ferguson, as her aide and dresser, for nine years until 1997, and since then had tried several jobs, but none seemed to match up to the one she had really loved. Cressman went away for a stag weekend and Andrews looked through his emails, discovering, to her horror, that he had several sexually explicit messages from a woman in Las Vegas. Andrews had been trying to convince Cressman to marry her for some time and saw this as an opportunity to force the issue. After she had forwarded the emails to Cressman's parents, she awaited his return. She confronted Cressman and gave him the marriage ultimatum. Again, he refused. There are two different explanations for what happened next, but both end with the same tragedy.

According to Andrews, she had taken a knife to bed with her to protect herself against Cressman. He attacked her in the night and tried to rape her and, in an attempt to ward him off, he fell on the knife. Forensic evidence proved otherwise, as it was shown that Andrews had battered him with a cricket bat and then stabbed him.

After disappearing from the scene, Andrews tried to convince friends that she knew nothing of Cressman's death and even attempted to commit suicide. She was found near Plymouth and charged with Cressman's murder. The prosecution counsel said of Andrews that:

> She realised that their relationship was simply not going to last and her hopes of marriage to him were evaporating. As the hope went out of the relationship, so the anger and jealousy rose up in her and led her to take a terrible revenge on the man she loved. Here we have a usually friendly and decent woman who was so transformed and burnt up inside that she killed.

The jury seemed to agree with the prosecution and on 16 May 2001 Jane Andrews was found guilty. In his summing up Judge Hyam said:

> In killing the man you loved you ended his life and ruined your own. It is evident that you made your attack on him when you were consumed with anger and bitterness. Nothing could justify what you did. After you struck him, first with a cricket bat and then stabbed him with a knife, you left him to die without remorse. It is true that your flight was obviously unprepared and that the attack took place, perhaps only with a few minutes of premeditation, but there is only one sentence which I can place upon you and that is one of life imprisonment.

* * * * *

Jane Andrews's former employer, Sarah Ferguson, has been continually in the public and media's eye since her marriage to Prince Andrew. Tales of divorce and adultery have dogged the majority of Queen Elizabeth II's children; Princess Anne, the current Prince of Wales and other notable members of the royal family, including Princess Margaret, have been through divorces and affairs. More recently Prince Edward's wife, Sophie, was exposed by the press as cynically using her regal relations to secure business for her public relations company. Scandal will no doubt always be attached in some way to the royal family and the nobility.

CHAPTER FOUR

PISTOLS AND PETTICOATS

It should come as no great surprise that many women masqueraded as men in the armed forces or operated successfully as pirate entrepreneurs in a time when very little attention was given to the question of recruitment. Medical examinations, for example, were virtually unheard of and it was therefore possible to disguise oneself as a man and with a degree of cunning and good luck, operate successfully in the male role without any real fear of discovery. Against the backdrop of the pitiful state in which women would find themselves if their husbands or fathers chose a life at sea or in the armed forces, joining their male colleagues was a viable option for determined women. Men would not be paid their full money until they had been released from service. This left households without any clear income for many years. Some of the women found themselves forced into a position where they had to seek their own fortune by any means. Others found themselves thrust into a situation where simply revealing themselves as being female would expose them to great danger.

Given the primitive conditions on board ships, and the privations suffered by soldiers posted to the far-flung colonies around the world, it is not surprising that when women revealed themselves, or were exposed, they caused enormous interest and shock.

GRACE O'MALLEY was born into the powerful O'Malley family in 1530. Her father was Owen 'Black Oak' O'Malley, the chieftain of Umhall Uachtarach. The family had traded with Scotland and Spain from their base in Ireland for nearly 400 years. At 16 Grace married Donal O'Flaherty and bore him three children. Soon, however, Grainne Mhaol, as Grace had become known, began to eclipse her husband. She would use her family's galleys to waylay merchant shipping.

From an early age Grace had wanted to go to sea herself, and it seems that her nickname dates back to the time when she cut off her hair in order to look like a boy to convince her father that a life on the sea was for her. As a young woman she had accompanied her father to Spain and on the return trip they were attacked by the English. Despite her father's instructions to stay below, Grace had attacked one of the English sailors, enabling her father's men to turn the tables on the English and escape. Grace, however, could not avoid English interests in Ireland. Her family's position and power were based on what the English considered to be pagan and tribal law. Provided the Irish submitted to the English, their position would be protected in exchange. Unfortunately, during this period Grace's husband was said to have murdered his step-nephew, and it fell to Grace to protect the clan against the English. Indeed, on one such occasion, Grace organised the defence of their castle after her husband had been killed fighting a rival clan. To all intents and purposes Grace became an outlaw as the English had placed their own man in control of her clan.

With 200 men she established a sea base on Clare Island and controlled all the shipping in the area. Later she remarried Richard Burke in order to gain control of his castle near Newport. A year after her marriage she divorced Burke after locking him out of his own castle and taking it over with her own men. Despite this it appears that the couple remained together for another 17 years until he died.

While at sea off the coast of Algeria at the age of 37, Grace fought off pirates the day after she had given birth to Richard Burke's son. It was not long before the English turned their interests towards Grace once more and in 1574 they lay siege to Rockfleet Castle. After an 18-day siege Grace attacked the English and forced them to retreat. Two or three years later, however, she finally pledged her loyalty to the English crown.

It seems that the lure of piracy was too much for Grace and she continued to organise raids against shipping. She was captured in 1577 and given an 18-month prison sentence in Dublin Castle. The judge described her at the trial as being 'a woman that hath impudently passed the part of womanhood and been a great spoiler and chief commander and director of thieves and murderers at sea'. Whether the prison sentence was as short as this is unknown and the various reports suggest that she either escaped or promised to turn in her own ex-husband, who was believed to be involved in organising an uprising.

By now the political situation had changed once more and the English were determined to dispense with the troublesome Irish nobles. In 1586 Sir Richard Bingham, the Governor of Connaught, managed to capture Grace and proposed to hang her. Bingham released Grace in exchange for her son-in-law and although she lacked resources, she then began to gather troops to fight the English. After the murder of her son, Owen, Grace attacked her other son, Murrough, who had sided with the English and burnt his town. Reluctantly Grace realised that the power of the English was so great that in time she would inevitably lose. She also realised that there was little to be gained in corresponding with Bingham about a treaty or a truce.

In July 1593 she began a correspondence with Queen Elizabeth I in order to explain her position. It is clear that Grace was very politically aware; she explained that she had taken to raiding because this was the only way that she could feed her people. She also pledged 'During her life to invade with sword and fire all your highness's enemies wheresoever they are or shall be without any interruption of any person or persons whatsoever'. Elizabeth was wary to begin with but agreed to meet Grace at Greenwich and concluded peace with her. Bingham was forced to release Grace's son, Tibbott, and lost his job two years later. Grace was as good as her word and her troops fought against the Spanish-backed rebels between 1598 and 1600.

Soon after, however, Grace had fallen back into her old ways and there is a report that the English attacked one of her galleys after it had been on a raid. Grace died in Rockfleet Castle in 1603 and it is possible that she was buried in the Cistercian Abbey on Clare Island in a family tomb.

* * * * *

Operating openly as a woman was not an option available to the majority of females that sought fame and fortune on the seas or in the army. **Charlotte de Berry** was born in 1636 and had always wished to go to sea. When her husband joined the navy she, too, boarded ship disguised as a man. It seems that at one point her true identity was revealed on board ship off the African coast. After suffering a sexual assault from the captain, Charlotte organised a mutiny and took over the vessel. She achieved her revenge by personally cutting off the captain's head with a knife. Taking the captain's place in charge of the ship, she and her crew became pirates and enjoyed success for some years, attacking unwary merchant vessels.

* * * * *

The amazing lives of **Ann Bonny** and **Mary Read** are inextricably linked as they were both pirates, cutthroats and women with incredible resilience and strength. Ann Bonny was the illegitimate child of Mary Brennan and William Cormac and was born in Kinsale in Ireland in 1697. Her father was a lawyer and it seems clear that his wife was more than suspicious that he was the father of their servant's daughter. Indeed, she planned a trap for him by sacking Mary Brennan and then pretending to be the servant awaiting the return of her lover by lying in Mary's bed ready for William to arrive home. William duly obliged by stripping off and getting into bed beside who he thought to be his mistress. Whether he realised his mistake or whether his wife told him that she was not Mary Brennan is unknown. The outcome was that William was jailed for his adultery and when released he stood by Mary and his child and they sailed to America and settled in Charleston where they established a plantation.

Mary married Cormac, and she and Ann enjoyed a much more stable life, but this did not stop Ann from falling in love with a pirate called James Bonny. She married him and they eloped to the Bahamas. It seems that Ann was not a stay-at-home wife and their home in New Providence was not the place for Ann to while away the days and weeks that her husband was at sea. She met a man called John 'Calico Jack' Rackham who had been a well-known pirate but had recently been given a king's pardon. When James Bonny arrived back from his voyages it was clear that his position had been usurped by Calico Jack. He sought the aid of the governor while Calico Jack offered to buy Ann from Bonny. Ann and her new man ran away to sea and both adopted the guise of male pirates.

Within a short period of time Ann gained a reputation on board ship of being one of the fiercest pirates in the crew. In fact a shipmate accused her of being a woman and she stabbed him through the heart to keep him quiet. During this time Ann felt herself strangely attracted to another pirate on board. To her astonishment she discovered that this handsome man was not male at all but was another woman called Mary Read.

Mary Read was also illegitimate and had probably followed her mother's lead in dressing up in men's clothes. Her mother had disguised Mary as her deceased son in order to fool the family into giving her some inheritance money. Mary had followed this through, becoming Mark Read, as whom she enlisted as a cabin boy in the British Navy. Later, during the War of the Spanish Succession (1701–4), she served as a foot soldier and a dragoon in the British Army. Sometime around 1698 she had fallen in love with a fellow soldier and married him and moved to Holland, where they established a coaching inn called the Three Horseshoes, near Breda. Her husband died of a fever and Mary donned men's clothes once more to become a sailor on a Dutch ship. While the ship was en route to the Caribbean it was attacked by the notorious pirate, Charles Vane, who worked with Calico Jack. Mary quickly established a reputation as being a good fighter and Calico Jack gave her Vane's ship. Soon Rackham, Bonny and Read were all on board the same ship and it was only after she had revealed her true identity to Ann that they became firm friends. Indeed, Rackham had threatened to cut Mary's throat, believing her to be a love rival. He, too, was brought in to the secret of Mary's true gender and the two women effectively ran the ship, *Revenge*, for him.

By October 1720 Ann had given birth to a baby while the ship was docked in Cuba and the English were on the trail of pirates in their attempt to control the seas around the Caribbean. Off the coast of Jamaica, Rackham's ship was attacked by one of the governor of the Bahamas' pirate-hunting vessels, the *Barnet*. As the English boarded, Rackham and the majority of the crew cowered in a drunken stupor beneath the decks, while Ann and Mary tried to fight them off. In the event the English took the ship and transported the pirates to Jamaica for trial. They were all sentenced to be hanged but both Mary and Ann claimed that they were pregnant. Rackham was hanged on 17 November 1720 and Mary's lover, believed to be a Dutchman, was released because he managed to prove that he had been forced to become a pirate. Mary herself, shortly before giving birth to her child, succumbed to a fever, miscarried and died at the age of 37 on 28 April 1721, still in prison in Jamaica. Ann escaped execution and apparently gave birth on 25 April 1721. By then her father had caught up with her and paid over a considerable sum of money for her release.

Ann and her son John moved to Virginia where Ann married again in December and had eight other children. She may have rejoined James Bonny or taken up with another unknown man. She is particularly remembered for her comments to Rackham on the eve of his execution. She told him 'I am sorry to see you here, Jack, but if you'd have fought like a man you needn't hang like a dog'.

* * * * *

Mary Read was not alone in carving out a successful career as a soldier. **Phoebe Hessel** was born in Stepney in 1713. She joined the Fifth Regiment of Foot or the Northumberland Fusiliers at the age of 15, disguised as a man. Phoebe fought as an English soldier at the Battle of Fontenoy, on 11 May 1745, and also served in Montserrat. Both Phoebe and her lover were wounded and when they returned to England she may have given birth to as many as nine children over the following years. At the incredible age of 108, Phoebe died, after two marriages, in Brighton in 1821.

* * * * *

Phoebe had several contemporaries who either fought for the English or in rebellions against them. One of the most extraordinary stories is that of **Hannah Snell**. Hannah was born in Worcester on 23 April 1723 and moved to London in 1740. She married, at the age of 20, James Summs, on 6 January 1744. Shortly afterwards Hannah Snell became James Gray. It appears that she enlisted in Carlisle, or at least was stationed there, on 23 November 1745. In the following September she gave birth to a daughter, Susannah, who unfortunately did not live even a year, as by 23 October 1747, as James Gray, Hannah boarded HMS *Swallow* in Portsmouth and set sail to Lisbon. The following January Hannah sailed with the ship to Gibraltar and then on to India, arriving at Fort St David on 28 July.

Hannah was part of the British attempt to capture the Indian town of Pondicherry and after two abortive attempts she joined the retreat on 30 September and was transferred to HMS *Eltham* with the rest of her regiment. She arrived in Bombay on 25 October.

In 1749, after repairs to the ship, Hannah was again at Fort St David in May. She was involved in the attack on Devicotta on 12 June, where it appears that she received a wound in the groin. She was then sent to a hospital to recover. By 25 May 1750, at the age of 27, she was back in Portsmouth with her regiment and after receiving her back pay, admitted to her fellow soldiers on 2 June 1750, 'Why gentlemen, James Gray will cast off his skin like a snake and become a new creature. In a word, gentlemen, I am as much a woman as my mother ever was, and my real name is Hannah Snell.'

For nearly three years she had fought with great resilience and courage with her regiment. She had endured storms, mud and danger in India and, what is more, she had been injured on several occasions and had been wounded. Her colleagues were as one in convincing her to request a pension. While the Duke of Cumberland was reviewing troops in St James's Park on 16 June 1750, he was approached by Hannah who told him of her service in the Royal Marines. The press were full of stories of her bravery and life in the army. She sold her story to Robert Walker, a London publisher, and embarked on a short career on stage in London, Bristol, Bath and other venues around the country. A biography was published in July 1750 and by the November the army had begun to realise that they could not ignore public sentiment or the fact that she had served diligently in defence of the Empire. Her wounds were examined at the Royal Chelsea Hospital on 21 November and, as a result, she was granted a lifetime pension for her military service.

After her brief spell in the limelight, Hannah disappeared from public view and married Richard Iyles with whom she produced two sons, Thomas and George. She outlived her first husband and remarried Richard Habgood at the age of 49. At the age of 68, in 1791, Hannah was admitted to the Bedlam Asylum where she died on 8 February the following year.

Over the years there has been considerable controversy regarding the details contained in her ghost-written biography against official army records. It seems that at the time whoever wrote Hannah's biography had not been averse to bending the truth. What is certainly true is the fact that Hannah did serve as a Royal Marine in Frazer's regiment for up to five years. When her story was made public, it not only caused an immense sensation, but it also rocked the establishment to its core. The British Army was forced to accept that Hannah had done much of what she had claimed.

* * * * *

It is also recorded that **Ann Mills** fought as a British soldier or marine in around 1740 on board the frigate HMS *Maidstone*. The Scottish rebellions provided other women with the opportunity to don men's clothing and fight either for the Hanoverians or the Jacobites. **Lady Anne Macintosh**, who was also known as Colonel Anne or Anne Farquharson of Invercauld, was married to Lord Macintosh, a prominent Hanoverian. Lady Anne, however, was a Jacobite and she funded and organised the raising of rebel troops from 1745–6. It seems that being in opposite camps did not adversely affect their husband and wife relationship as on more than one occasion either one of them was captured and released into the custody of the other.

* * * * *

Meanwhile, **Jean Cameron** of Glendessary, also a Jacobite, raised her own small army of 300 men and was reported as being present at the major Jacobite muster on 19 August 1745. **Margaret Murray**'s husband was one of Bonnie Prince Charlie's officers and she accompanied them on campaign. She appears to have made herself particularly useful and resilient in stealing horses and money to support the army. **Lady Lude**, another Jacobite, was not prepared to sit by and accept that her ancestral home, Blair Castle, should become a garrison for Hanoverian troops. She is credited with the honour of having fired the first shot at the garrison when the Jacobites launched their assault to reclaim the castle from the Hanoverians.

* * * * *

The 1760s saw three women in various services in the British forces. **Hannah Whitney** confessed that she was a woman in 1761 after having been a marine for five years. It seems that she finally admitted her subterfuge after having been locked in a cell. HMS *Amazon*'s captain discovered that he, too, had a female marine who had served on board ship for nine months under the name of William Prothero. The 32-gun ship's crew finally discovered the truth on 20 April 1761. In November of 1762 **Jane Meace** accepted the king's shilling when a recruiting party of marines arrived at the Plume of Feathers in Uttoxeter. She enlisted as John Meace but was discovered the morning after when the marine party had shared a room together in the inn. As they prepared to leave they had made her try on a marine tunic and a careless hand had discovered that their new comrade-in-arms had breasts.

* * * * *

It seems that the British Navy or the Army could still be fooled. The 81st Highland Regiment recruited a female volunteer in 1779 and **Margaret Catchpole**, after having served as a sailor for a number of years, was finally discovered in 1797.

* * * * *

Several Irish women were directly involved in the Irish Rebellion of 1798. **Mary Doyle** from Castleboro gallantly marched with the rebel army and fought at the Battle of New Ross. She fearlessly criss-crossed the battlefield, looting fallen government troops for weapons and cartridges and may well have died when the town was burned to the ground shortly after the battle. **Suzy Toole** was the daughter of a blacksmith from County Whitlow by the name of Phelim. She joined her father who had fallen in with the rebels and distributed ammunition and acted as a spy against the English. **Madge Dixon** accompanied her husband, Thomas, who was the son of a publican from Castlebridge, onto the high seas during the rebellion. On one occasion back in Wexford she had ridden to the home of Colonel le Hunte and broken into the house and taken an orange fire screen which she believed to be evidence that the landowner was an Orangeman. Still astride her horse, she exhibited her discovery to an assembled crowd and demanded that they follow her back to the house to lynch the colonel. It was only as a result of the timely intervention of local leaders that the man was saved.

* * * * *

Perhaps one of the strangest stories was recounted on 21 August 1865, following the death of a Dr James Barry. The story appeared in the *Manchester Guardian*:

> An incident is just now being discussed in military circles so extraordinary that, were not the truth capable of being vouched for by official authority, the narration would certainly be deemed incredible. Our officers quartered at the Cape between 15 and 20 years ago may remember a certain Dr Barry attached to the medical staff there, and enjoying a reputation for considerable skill in his profession, especially for firmness, decision and rapidity in difficult operations. The gentleman had entered the army in 1813, had passed, of course, through the grades of assistant surgeon and surgeon in various regiments, and had served as such in various quarters of the globe. His professional acquirements had procured for him promotion to the staff at the Cape. About 1840 he became promoted to be medical inspector, and was transferred to Malta. He proceeded from Malta to Corfu where he was quartered for many years… He there died about a month ago, and upon his death was discovered to be a woman. The motives that occasioned and the time when commenced this singular deception are both shrouded in mystery. But thus it stands as an indisputable fact, that a

woman was for 40 years an officer in the British service, and fought one duel and had sought many more, had pursued a legitimate medical education, and received a regular diploma, and had acquired almost a celebrity for skill as a surgical operator.

Although the gender of Dr James Barry proved to be something of a bombshell as far as the British Army was concerned, she had aroused the suspicions of the Count of Las Cases, who had met Barry on 20 January 1817. The doctor had accompanied another officer to visit the count's son. The count was convinced that the man, purporting to be an 18-year-old, was a woman, but had been impressed with the doctor's credentials nevertheless. Barry had told him that she had obtained her medical diploma at the age of 13 and had operated successfully as a doctor at the Cape for a number of years.

* * * * *

No doubt there were many more women who chose a life in the Armed Forces or on the seas in order to escape poverty and drudgery at home. As the 19th century moved to a close, it probably became increasingly difficult for women to masquerade as men, given the slightly more sophisticated methods of recruiting soldiers and sailors. There must have been some women who managed to fool the recruiting officers and flourished in their role as a man in a male-dominated environment. It is probably the case that the Horse Guards and the Admiralty gradually became much better at hiding the truth.

CHAPTER FIVE

PASSING
STRANGERS?

Many women who kill unrelated people have either perpetrated the crime for greed or for jealousy. It is interesting to see just how many women are capable of carrying out the crimes alone. But in a good number of cases, they are part of a wider conspiracy that inevitably involves men.

THE CASE of **Mary Norcott** and her son, Arthur, was considered at the time, in 1629, to be so important that Sir John Maynard, one of the Commissioners of the Great Seal of England, recorded it. He wrote:

> The case, or rather history of a case, that happened in the county of Hertford, I thought good to report here, though it happened in the fourth year of King Charles I, that the memory of it may not be lost, by miscarriage of my papers, or otherwise. I wrote the evidence that was given, which I and many others did hear; and I wrote it exactly according to what was deposed at the trial, at the bar of the King's Bench.

Joan Norcott, the wife of Arthur and daughter-in-law of Mary, had been found dead in her bed. It was at first assumed, at the coroner's inquest, that she had committed suicide. She had, apparently, gone to bed with her child, as on the night in question Arthur had not been at home. Her mother-in-law, John Okeman and his wife Agnes had found Joan the next day; the knife was sticking in the floor and her throat had been cut. According to the testimony of the witnesses, they had been asleep in other rooms of the house and they confirmed that no person could have entered the dwelling without their knowledge.

Neighbourhood rumour after the death and the subsequent funeral caused the authorities to think again about the cause of death. They ordered Joan's body to be exhumed 30 days after burial, not in order to carry out a post-mortem, but to carry out a process known as 'Touching of the Body'. The four defendants, Mary, her son, Arthur, and John and Agnes Okeman, were taken to the burial place for the exhumation. As the body was taken from the grave it was then placed on the ground and each of the defendants, in turn, had to touch the body.

According to Sir John Maynard's account, Agnes Okeman 'fell to her knees and prayed to God to show some token of her innocency'. The body, then, it would appear, shocked all of those present:

> … Whereupon the brow of the dead began to have a dew, or gentle sweat, arise on it, which increased by degrees, till the sweat ran down by drops on her face. The brow changed to a lively colour, and the dead opened one of her eyes and shut it again; and this opening of the eye was done three several times. She likewise thrust out the ring – or wedding-finger three times, and pulled it in again, and the finger dropped blood from it on the grass.

It was assumed by the court that if Joan had not killed herself and the witnesses had claimed that no other person had entered the house, then it could only be assumed that they must be the murderers.

To prove that Joan had not committed suicide it was deposed:

> Firstly that she had been found in the bed to be lying in a composed manner, the bed-clothes nothing at all disturbed, and her child by her in bed. Secondly, that her neck was broken, and she could not possibly break her neck in the bed if she first cut her throat, nor contra. Thirdly, that there was no blood in the bed, saving a tincture of blood on the bolster whereon her head lay, but no substance of blood at all. Fourthly, that from the bed's head there was a stream of blood on the floor, which ran along till it ponded in the bending of the floor in a very great quantity; and that there was also another stream of blood on the floor at the bed's foot, which ponded also on the floor to another great quantity, but no continuance or communication of blood, at either of these two places, from one to the other, neither upon the bed; so that she bled in two places severally. And it was deposed, that upon turning up the mat of the bed, there were found clots of congealed blood in the straw of the mat underneath. Fifthly, that the bloody knife was found in the morning sticking in the floor, at a good distance from the bed; and that the point of the knife, as it stuck, was towards the bed, and the haft from the bed. Lastly, that there was a print of a thumb and four fingers of a left hand.

Joan's husband, mother-in-law and John and Agnes Okeman were brought to trial. Okeman was acquitted but the other three were found guilty of murder. Despite their cries of 'I did not do it' Arthur and Mary Norcott were hanged in 1629 while Agnes Okeman, because of a pregnancy, was not executed. Sir John Maynard had enquired if they had confessed anything while at the gallows but the executioner had reported that he 'could not hear that they did'.

* * * * *

Another tragic family tale began on 16 August 1660, when William Harrison disappeared and was presumed murdered. He was employed to collect rent on behalf of

Lady Campden in Gloucestershire. Harrison was 70 years old and, after having spent the day away from home collecting rents, he did not return at his usual time of 9pm. His wife sent out their servant, John Perry, to find him, but he disappeared that night as well and was not encountered again until the following morning by Edward Harrison, William Harrison's son.

Edward met Perry on the road to Charringworth, where he believed his father to have been the previous day. Perry had already been to Charringworth and William was not there, so they both went to Ebrington and confirmed that William had visited a house there the previous evening. William's next logical visit would have been Paxford but he had not been seen there. They later discovered that a woman had found a hat, band and comb, which belonged to William Harrison, on the road towards Campden. Edward and Perry immediately thought that William had been waylaid and they feared that he had been murdered, particularly as there were signs of blood on the items that had been found.

Many locals joined the hunt for William Harrison but no sign of him was found. Mrs Harrison, meanwhile, had begun to suspect Perry and referred him to a Justice of the Peace. Perry carefully described his unexplained absence, saying that he had left Campden shortly before 9pm and had gone towards Charringworth. Here he had encountered William Reed and had decided to return with Reed to Campden as it was getting dark. He rested for about an hour in a hen roost and then got lost in a mist as he walked towards Charringworth. He decided to sleep under a hedge that night and when he woke up at dawn he walked into Charringworth, where he met Edward Palisterer, who had paid William Harrison £23 rent the previous afternoon. Another man, William Curtis, confirmed that Harrison had been in the town the previous day although he had not actually seen him himself. Perry had headed back to Campden at about 5am, where, on the road, he had met Edward Harrison.

The hunt for the body continued and Perry languished in jail and suddenly, on Friday 24 August, he decided to change his story. He first told the Justice of the Peace that it was his belief that William Harrison had been murdered. When pressed he admitted that his mother and brother had murdered Harrison. The reason he gave was their extreme poverty and to his eternal shame he had colluded with them to waylay his master in the certain knowledge that his pockets would be full of rent money. He even described how his brother had strangled Harrison and then thrown the body into the waters of Wallington Mill. He admitted that he had also planted the hat, band and comb on the road in an attempt to fool the authorities into believing that highwaymen had attacked his master.

Joan Perry and her son, Richard, were arrested and examined on Saturday 25 August. They both denied any knowledge of the incident. For some reason John had also told the justices that his mother and brother had burgled Mr Harrison's house and stolen £140 the previous year. They were all indicted for the robbery and the murder of William Harrison, despite the fact that no body had been found. They all admitted to the burglary the previous year but only John confessed to the conspiracy to murder William Harrison. He even accused his mother of trying to poison him while he was in prison.

When their trial came up before the Spring Assizes they all pleaded not guilty, John claiming that his confession had been made during a period of temporary insanity. Unfortunately they were all found guilty and hanged on a hill near Campden.

The sad story has an incredible twist, because two years later, William Harrison, who was not, in fact, dead wrote a letter to Sir Thomas Overbury, the magistrate of the County of Gloucester:

FOR Sir THOMAS OVERBURY, Kt.

HONOURED SIR, – In obedience to your commands, I give you this true account of my being carried away beyond the seas, my continuance there, and return home. One Thursday, in the afternoon, in the time of harvest, I went to Charringworth, to demand rents due to Lady Campden, at which time the tenants were busy in the field, and late before they came home, which occasioned my stay there till the close of the evening. I expected a considerable sum, but received only three and twenty pounds. In my return home, in the narrow passage amongst Ebrington furzes, there met me one horseman, and said, 'Art thou there?' and I, fearing he would have rode over me, struck his horse on the nose. Whereupon he struck at me with his sword several blows, and ran it into my side, while I, with my little cane, made my defence as well as I could. At last another came behind me, ran me into the thigh, laid hold on the collar of my doublet, and drew me to a hedge near to the place, when another came up. They did not take my money, but mounted me behind one of them, drew my arms about his middle, and fastened my wrists together with something that had a spring lock to it, as I conceived; they then threw a great cloak over me, and carried me away. In the night they alighted at a hayrick, which stood near a stone-pit, by a wall side, where they took away my money. About two hours before daybreak, as I heard one of them tell the other he thought it to be then, they tumbled me into the stone-pit. They stayed, as I thought, about an hour at the hayrick; when they took horse again, one of them bid me come out of the pit. I answered, they had my money already, and asked what they would do with me. Whereupon he struck me again, drew me out, put a great quantity of money into my pockets, and mounted me again after the same manner; and on the Friday, about sunset, they brought me to a lone house upon a heath, by a thicket of bushes, where they took me down almost dead. When the woman of the house saw that I could neither stand nor speak, she asked them whether they had brought a dead man. They answered No; but a friend that was hurt, and they were carrying him to a surgeon. She answered, if they did not make haste, their friend would be dead before they could reach one. There they laid me on cushions, and suffered none to come into the room but a little girl. We stayed there all night, they giving me some broth. In the morning, very early, they mounted me, as before, and on Saturday night they brought me to a place where were two or three houses, in one of which I lay all night on cushions by their bedside. On Saturday morning they carried me from thence, and about three or four o'clock they brought me to a place by the seaside, called Deal, where they laid me down on the ground; and one of them staying by me, the other two walked a little off to meet a man, with whom they tackled, and in their discourse I heard them mention seven pounds; after which they went away together, and after half-an-hour returned. The man, whose name, as I afterwards heard, was

Wrenshaw, said he feared I should die before he could get me on board. They then put me into a boat, and carried me on shipboard, where my wounds were dressed. I remained in the ship, as near as I can reckon, about six weeks; in which time I was indifferently recovered of my wounds and weakness. Then came the master of the ship and told me, and the rest who were in the same condition, that he discovered three Turkish ships. We all offered to fight in defence of the ship, and ourselves, but he commanded us to keep close, and said he would deal with them well enough. A little while after we were called up, and when we came on the deck we saw two Turkish ships close by us; into one of them we were put, and placed in a dark hole, where how long we continued before we were landed I know not. When we were landed they led us two days' journey, and put us into prison where we remained four days and a half. Eight men next came to view us, who seemed to be officers; they called us, and examined us of our trades, which everyone answered: one said that he was a surgeon, another that he was a weaver, and I said I had some skill in physic. We three were set by, and taken by three of those eight men who came to view us. It was my chance to be chosen by a grave physician of eighty-seven years of age, who lived near to Smyrna, had formerly been in England, and knew Crowland in Lincolnshire, which he preferred before all other places in England. I was there about a year and three-quarters, and then my master fell sick on a Thursday, and sent for me; and calling me as he used, by the name of Bell, told me he should die, and bid me shift for myself. He died on Saturday following, and I presently hastened to a port, almost a day's journey distant, when I addressed myself to two men who came out of a ship belonging to Hamburgh, which, as they said, was bound for Portugal within two or three days. I inquired of them for an English ship; they answered there was none. I entreated them to take me into their ship; but they durst not, for fear of being discovered by the searchers, which might occasion the forfeiture not only of their goods but also of their lives. At length they took me on board, and placed me below in the vessel, and hid me with hoards and other things, so that I lay undiscovered, notwithstanding the strict search that was made in the vessel. On arriving at Lisbon in Portugal, as soon as the master had left the ship, and was gone into the city, they set me on shore moneyless, to shift for myself. I now met four gentlemen discoursing together; after a while one of them came to me and spoke to me in a foreign language. I told him I was an Englishman. He then spoke to me in English, and told me that he was an Englishman himself, and born near Wisbeach, in Lincolnshire. I then related to him how I had been carried away, and my present condition; upon which he took me along with him, and by his interest with the master of a ship bound for England, procured my passage, and commended me to the master of the ship, who landed me safe at Dover, from whence I proceeded to London, where being furnished with necessaries, I came into the country. Having arrived at Crowland, I was told of the unhappy fate of my servant Perry, and his mother and brother. What caused John so falsely to accuse them and himself, I know not. He has not only brought his blood upon his own head, but that also of his innocent mother and brother. For I never saw either of them that evening; nor do I know who they were that carried me away after that rude and barbarous manner.

Thus, honoured sir, I have given you a true account of my great sufferings and happy deliverance. Your Worship's, in all dutiful respects, William Harrison.

* * * * *

Sarah Swift and her confederates proved to be ineffectual murderers despite the severity of their attack on their victim. The fact that the Reverend John Talbot survived long enough to positively identify the ring leaders is amazing considering his injuries.

Apparently Sarah and six men decided to rob and murder Talbot, following him around from 4pm in the afternoon of Friday 2 July 1669. Talbot was the preacher at St Alphage in the Wall and the curate for the church in Laindon in Essex. It seems that the would-be murderers followed him from the London church, through Grays Inn, onto Old Street and then waylaid him in the fields near Shoreditch. It was about 11pm. Talbot had feared that he was being followed and when his assailants made their move he tried to force his way through a hedge and into a garden. But they grabbed him and threw him to the ground, removing 20 shillings and his own knife from his pocket. One of them then cut his throat near his windpipe and stabbed him in the chest. They then stripped him of his clothes and left him for dead.

The commotion had woken the dogs in the area, whose barking brought their owners to the scene. A posse followed the disappearing group of attackers. The first was caught lying in a clump of nettles and he was rendered unconscious by one of the pursuers, who smacked him over the head with a pewter pot. The captive turned out to be a confectioner called Stephen Eaton.

Meanwhile, the Revd Talbot was carried to the Star Inn near Shoreditch church and a doctor was called. The watchman dragged Eaton in front of Talbot and, to the confectioner's amazement, the man was still alive and positively identified him. Eaton wrote out a quick confession, implicating five other men and Sarah Swift. He was then taken before Justice Pitfield who sent him to Newgate.

One by one all of the other assailants were rounded up and Talbot was able to identify all of them. Talbot's condition seemed to improve over the next few days and he was tended for a week by Dr Hodges. Talbot had a fever until the following Friday but then rallied to such an extent that he wished to attend church. He was dressed but after a couple of hours, he began coughing so badly that he burst his jugular vein. He passed away in the early hours of the Monday morning.

The authorities had managed to get a statement from Talbot before he died and it was clear that Sarah Swift had been the leader and the instigator of the attack. He had claimed that Sarah had called out several times 'Kill the dog, kill him.' In the event Sarah Swift, Stephen Eaton the confectioner and George Roades, a broker, were all found guilty of robbery and murder.

One of their other accomplices, Henry Prichard, was reprieved due to lack of evidence from Talbot against him.

Talbot had written several letters to friends in his last week and these were produced as evidence that the murderers had followed him for around seven hours before setting upon him near Shoreditch. Before they were executed on Wednesday 14 July 1669 at

Tyburn, both Eaton and Roades confessed to their crimes, but Sarah Swift went to the gallows unrepentant of her barbarous conspiracy to rob and murder the clergyman.

* * * * *

For the time, the trial of Michael and **Catherine van Berghen** and Geraldius Dromelius, for the murder of Oliver Norris, showed how even-handed the English court system could be. When they were tried for murder half of the jury was made up of 'foreigners' to reflect the fact that all of the defendants were Dutch.

The van Berghens ran a public house in East Smithfield in 1700 and one of their customers was Oliver Norris, who is described as a 'country gentleman' who was, at the time, lodging at an inn near Aldgate. He visited the van Berghen's pub at about 8pm and continued drinking until 11pm. Gradually he realised that he had had enough to drink and asked the van Berghen's maidservant to call him a coach. Catherine intercepted the maid and told her to tell Norris that no coach was available. Norris then decided to walk back to Aldgate and he had only got a few yards when he realised that someone had stolen his purse. He returned to the pub and confronted the van Berghens with stealing his money. They denied it and threatened to throw him out on the street. Norris refused to go away and sat down claiming he would not leave the premises until his money had been returned. The van Berghens sent in their servant, Dromelius, to threaten him but this simply turned into another verbal quarrel. Suddenly Michael van Berghen burst into the room and smashed Norris over the head with a poker. Dromelius finished the man off with a knife. The van Berghens and Dromelius then stripped Norris's body and the two men threw his corpse into a ditch leading into the Thames. Catherine remained in the pub and cleaned up the floor and put Norris's clothes into a hamper. When Dromelius returned he took the hamper over to his lodgings in Rotherhithe.

Norris's body was found the following morning and a witness soon came forward, claiming to have seen Michael and Dromelius near the spot where the body had been found in the early hours of the morning. The authorities searched the van Berghen's pub and although Catherine had done her best to dispose of any evidence, some blood was found behind the door. Dromelius was not in the pub and the van Berghens told the authorities that he no longer worked for them. The maidservant who had been told to lie to Norris the previous night came forward and recounted the arguments that had occurred. A waterman came forward and told the authorities that he had taken Dromelius to Rotherhithe. When his lodgings were raided Dromelius was taken into custody.

The three defendants were quickly found guilty by the half-and-half jury and were executed on 10 July 1700 in East Smithfield, close to the spot where the murder had taken place. Michael and Dromelius's bodies were hung in chains between Bow and Mile End and Catherine was buried in a pauper's grave.

* * * * *

We would now call **Deborah Churchill** a habitual criminal, as throughout her 31 years she was continually in and out of prison, until finally, she turned to murder. Churchill was born near Norwich and seems to have come from a fairly respectable family. It is not clear exactly how she came to fall into her way of life. Her first husband, John Churchill, was a soldier in Major General Faringdon's regiment. She then married a man called Miller in Fleet Prison but it appears that she never lived with him. For around seven years, which had also prompted the divorce from her first husband, she had been living with Richard 'Bully' Hunt. If anything Hunt, who was a soldier in the Lifeguards, was the one true love of her life. She had, apparently, lived with Thomas Smith, a cooper, for about three months, and interestingly, he was hanged at Tyburn almost exactly a year after Deborah's execution. Smith was hanged on Friday 16 December 1709 for robbing the home of the Earl of Westmoreland. In the years running up to her final criminal act she was in and out of the prison at Clerkenwell at least 20 times. She was whipped for pick-pocketing, and forced to work hard for her bread and water.

Some time in February 1708 she was walking along Drury Lane with Hunt, William Lewis, John Boy and Martin Were. She took some offence from Were and they began arguing in the street. Madam Churchill, as she preferred to be known, then instructed Hunt, Boy and Lewis to kill Were. They murdered him somewhere between the King's Head Court and Vinegar Yard.

The four of them were quickly rounded up and after a short trial were condemned to death on 26 February 1708. While the three men met their date with death at Tyburn, Deborah claimed that she was pregnant. She was held in Newgate for 10 months, and after no child had appeared, she was called back to court and sentenced to hang at Tyburn at the age of 31 on Friday 17 December 1708.

* * * * *

Grace Tripp was just 19 when she was executed at Tyburn on 17 March 1710. Grace was from Barton in Lincolnshire and was working as a servant in the house of Lord Torrington. She colluded with a man called Peters to rob Torrington's house. The conspirators agreed that Grace would leave a door open and Peters would enter the house at an appointed time and she would help him burgle the house and then make off with him. Unfortunately the plan went disastrously wrong.

Torrington's family were not in the house and the only other person present was the housekeeper. While Grace and Peters were loading their ill-gotten gains into a sack, the woman appeared and Grace held the candle while Peters cut the housekeeper's throat. They stole 30 guineas from the housekeeper's room and then left via the front door.

The authorities caught up with them very quickly and Peters made a full confession, implicating Grace and making her appointment with the hangman inevitable.

* * * * *

Jane Housden was already a convicted coiner before she met up with highwayman William Johnson. Johnson had been a butcher in Northamptonshire and in London but both businesses had failed. He then worked for the garrison at Gibraltar before returning to England and becoming a highwayman. He was caught once, convicted and then reprieved.

Johnson and Housden met and worked together, but Housden was once more accused of coining and was awaiting trial at the Old Bailey. Johnson arranged to visit her and was told by the head turnkey, Mr Spurling, that he could not see Housden until the trial was over. Hearing Housden's shouted instructions Johnson calmly pulled out a pistol and shot Spurling dead.

Unfortunately for the pair, neither of them could get out of the Old Bailey, and they were both promptly arrested for the murder. Rather like many partners in crime, even when they faced the executioner on 19 September 1714 they were unrepentant and oblivious to the public outcry that their crime had created.

They never asked for forgiveness and seemed happy to be hanged together, partners to the end.

* * * * *

Sarah Malcolm was born in County Durham in 1711 and after the bankruptcy of her father she travelled to London to find work. After having been employed at a public house in Boswell Court, called the Black Horse, she obtained employment as a laundress at the home of Lydia Dunscumb, who lived in the Inns of Court. Her new mistress was 80 years old and lived in the house with Elizabeth Harrison, aged 60, and Ann Price, aged 17, both of whom were the old woman's other servants.

Sarah had intended to rob the old woman for some time and coveted Duncumb's wealth as a means by which to convince her boyfriend, Alexander, to marry her. As Sarah was later to claim, although she had planned the robbery, she had not intended to carry it out herself. She also later claimed that her boyfriend, Alexander, and his brother, along with a woman called Martha Tracy, actually carried out the robbery and she simply acted as a lookout.

In the event, what we do know is that the robbery took place on Saturday 3 February 1733 and that before the house was ransacked Mrs Dunscumb was strangled in her bed, as was Elizabeth Harrison. The only other possible witness, the young Ann Price, had had her throat cut in her bed.

It did not take the authorities too long to discover that Sarah Malcolm was the only person absent from the household. They found a bloodstained silver tankard and Sarah was arrested and sent to Newgate. When she was searched by a Mr Johnson at the jail he found a considerable amount of money hidden in her clothing. Sarah admitted that this had come from the robbery and apparently said 'I'll make you a present of it if you will say nothing of the matter'. Johnson promptly gave the money to the authorities and told them what Sarah had said to him. She openly admitted during her imprisonment that she had organised the robbery, but that the other three had carried it out and perpetrated the murders.

It is not clear exactly what became of Alexander, his brother and Martha, but it does not appear that they were ever charged with the offence. In the event, Sarah Malcolm was found guilty of robbery and murder, but steadfastly refused to confess her crimes to the very end. As she was taken in a cart to Fetter Lane where the gallows had been erected, she wept and wrung her hands, constantly telling anyone who would listen that she had not committed the murders. After she had been given her last rites she fainted and when she was brought round she cried 'Oh my mistress, my mistress! I wish I could see her!' She was hanged on 7 March 1733 on the gallows that had been erected between Mitre Court and Fetter Lane, still protesting her innocence.

* * * * *

Another woman who found the unpleasant prospect of hanging too much for her delicate constitution was **Elizabeth Jeffries**, who was executed in Epping Forest on 28 March 1752. Elizabeth had been taken in by her uncle, who was a fairly rich man living in Walthamstow. Since her uncle had no children of his own, he was quite happy to adopt Elizabeth and make her the sole beneficiary of his estate. The only stipulation was that she must not show any signs of bad behaviour as this would lead to her uncle writing her out of his will.

Elizabeth was desperate to get her hands on her uncle's money and was already plotting his death with her uncle's gardener, John Swan. It seems that the two of them were on intimate terms and discussed how they could do away with Jeffries. The ideal solution soon dropped into their laps.

Mr Jeffries had encountered a man called Matthews in Epping Forest. He had obviously taken to Matthews as he offered him work as Swan's assistant. After just four days Elizabeth approached Matthews with a deal that he found difficult to ignore. Elizabeth asked him whether he would like to earn £100, to which Matthews replied that he would, as long as it was 'in an honest way'. She told him to go and speak to Swan about it. Swan told him that he would give him £100 to murder Mr Jeffries. Matthews accepted the offer and Swan gave him half a guinea advance to buy two pistols.

It seems clear that Matthews never had any intention of carrying out the deed, as only a couple of days later he had already spent the half guinea, but not on pistols. The conspirators were due to meet at 10pm on the night of the murder and Matthews waited for an hour before Swan arrived. Another hour passed before Elizabeth Jeffries joined them. Swan then said 'Now it is time to knock the old miser, my master on the head'. Matthews admitted that he had spent the money and added 'I cannot find it in my heart to do it'. Elizabeth Jeffries was livid and told Matthews 'You may be damned for a villain, for not performing your promise!'

Unluckily for Mr Jeffries, Swan had taken the precaution of bringing two of his own pistols and they now told Matthews to swear that he would not reveal to anyone what was about to occur. Swan went upstairs and shot the old man and Matthews bolted. He crossed the ferry and headed for Enfield Chase. He could hear Elizabeth Jeffries shouting for help, claiming that a robber had entered the house and shot her uncle.

The authorities could find no evidence that anyone else, apart from Elizabeth and Swan, had been in the house, and initially arrested them both. They were then released and Elizabeth believed that the investigation was over and she took possession of her uncle's estate.

The authorities were still looking for Matthews and he readily confessed what had happened on the night of the murder. This prompted the re-arrest of Elizabeth and Swan and the former soon made a full confession.

They were taken from the prison at 4am on 28 March 1752, Elizabeth fainting several times before they reached the gallows in Epping Forest. She was hysterical by the time the hangman placed the noose around her neck. She and Swan were hanged together and her body was given back to her family for burial. Swan's corpse was left hanging in chains in the gibbet.

* * * * *

The last words of **Mary Edmondson** before she was executed on Kennington Common on 2 April 1759 for the murder of her aunt, Mrs Walker, were:

> It is now too late to trifle either with God or man. I solemnly declare that I am innocent of the crime laid to my charge. I am very easy in my mind, as I suffer with as much pleasure as if I was going to sleep. I freely forgive my prosecutors, and earnestly beg your prayers for my departing soul.

With that, she was dispatched.

The events which led to her execution had occurred only a few weeks before. Mary Edmondson was the daughter of a farmer from Yorkshire and was living with her aunt, a widow, in Rotherhithe. By all accounts she had lived there for two years and had been the perfect niece.

On the fateful evening Mary had spent some time with her aunt and their friend, Mrs Toucher, and had accompanied the woman partway home before returning to her aunt's house. No sooner had Mary entered than she cried out 'Help! Murder! They have killed my aunt!' She then ran to the next-door neighbour and together with some men that had come out of a nearby pub, went into her aunt's house and found the unfortunate woman lying on her side with her throat cut. One of the gentlemen, a Mr Holloway, exclaimed 'This is very strange; I know not what to make of it; let us examine the girl.'

There was a cut on Mary's arm and she explained that four men had come in through the back door and grabbed her aunt around the neck and had told her that they would kill the both of them if they uttered a word. The leader, who Elizabeth claimed was a tall man, dressed in black, responded to her aunt's scream by cutting the woman's throat. Mary then claimed that she had tried to get away and her arm had been injured as she attempted to get out through a door.

Holloway and the others thought that this was nonsense and there was no sign of a struggle or burglary. Mary claimed that a number of things had been stolen but these were later found hidden under a loose floorboard in the privy. When the men accused Mary of murdering her aunt, she fainted and then went into a fit. She was taken into a neighbour's home and bled and when the coroner's inquest brought a verdict of wilful murder, Mary found herself committed to the New Jail in Southwark.

She languished there awaiting the next Surrey Assizes, being moved to a prison in Kingston shortly before her trial began. There was no direct evidence that Mary had carried out the murder, but the jury seemed convinced. She wrote several letters to her parents, clergymen and other people, protesting her innocence. It was all to no avail. By 9am on Monday 2 April 1759 the sentence had been carried out.

* * * * *

It seems very clear that **Maria Theresa Phipoe** was a strong and aggressive woman and that she used her strength on more than one occasion to get exactly what she wanted.

Just two years before her death she had been sentenced to 12 months in Newgate on 23 May 1795. The crime is almost unbelievable, given its vicious and determined approach.

Maria had apparently lured a man called John Cortois into her house. She already knew that he had a considerable amount of money and was determined to get a piece of it. Somehow Maria managed to tie him to a chair and then told him that she would cut his throat if he didn't write her out a promissory note for £2,000. John seems to have taken the threats very seriously, as he signed the note. But this brought him even closer to death. Maria told him that she wasn't sure how she would kill him and threatened him with arsenic, a pistol and a knife. Somehow John managed to wriggle free and, after grappling with Maria for some time, during which his fingers were badly cut, he made good his escape. The fact that Maria was only sentenced to a year for her crime seems to be as a result of a legal technicality. But, what is clear, is that no sooner had she been released, than she involved herself in many other similar criminal acts before resorting to murder.

By 1797 Maria was living in lodgings in Garden Street, London, and her neighbours were awoken by the sounds of groaning one night. When they came to investigate Maria barred their entrance to her lodgings and told them that her landlady had been fitting but that everything was now under control. When one of the neighbours peeped in through the door they could see the landlady, Mary Cox, lying on the floor with blood all over her. One of them called for a doctor while another one pushed the door open and saw the bleeding woman and screamed 'Murder!'

Mary Cox was not dead and in the confusion managed to slip out of the room and get to her kitchen. By now a beadle and a doctor had arrived. Mary told them that Maria had attacked her. When Maria was asked 'For God Almighty's sake, what have you done to the woman below?' Maria answered 'I don't know; I believe the Devil and passion bewitched me'. The beadle then noticed a knife and part of a finger on a table. He said to Maria 'Is this the knife you did the woman's business with?' Maria said 'Yes' and when asked whether it was her finger Maria told the man that Mary Cox had cut it off.

Meanwhile the doctor had been looking at Mary and there were five stab wounds in her neck and throat and more in her chest and stomach. Soon afterwards she succumbed to her injuries and died. Before her death she had told a magistrate that she had bought a gold watch, a china coffee cup and several other things from Maria for £11 and when she had gone to pick up the coffee cup, Maria had stabbed her in the neck.

This evidence was enough to condemn Maria as the jury only took 20 minutes to consider their verdict. A huge number of spectators were present when she was executed on Newgate Street, within sight of the Old Bailey, on 11 December 1797. Over a third of the crowd were women.

* * * * *

It is probably the case that if **Maria Manning** had married 50-year-old Irishman, Patrick O'Connor, instead of Frederick George Manning, she would not have been driven to murder, and Patrick would not have found himself her victim.

Maria Manning was born Maria de Roux in Switzerland in 1825. She was Swiss-French and in her late teens moved to London to become the maid of Lady Blantyre, the daughter of the Duchess of Sutherland. In 1846 she met Patrick O'Connor, who was a custom house officer in the London docks. They were much taken with one another and had it not been for the appearance of Frederick George Manning, who worked for the Great Western Railway, they would probably have married. Maria clearly weighed up the two men before choosing Manning. He had a regular job and also claimed that he would inherit a great deal of money from his mother. O'Connor, on the other hand, on the face of it, was a good earner but drank a great deal. What she did not know was that

Maria Manning, murderer of Patrick O'Connor.

he had a considerable amount of money in railway bonds and that he was a part-time money lender.

In any event, Maria chose Manning and after they married Frederick gave up his job and they managed a pub, the White Hart Inn in Taunton. It was a disaster and Frederick was sacked. They came back to London to run a beer shop in Hackney. No sooner had Frederick and Maria returned to London than she rekindled her sexual relationship with O'Connor. She had realised that she had married the wrong man and it is not clear whether Frederick knew anything about her relationship with O'Connor, but certainly the three of them became friends.

Frederick and Maria were living in Bermondsey and Maria had just heard the devastating news that her husband was unlikely to inherit very much from his mother after all. They had taken in a lodger who was a medical student called Massey. Over a period of months Frederick continually asked Massey about drugs and whether someone under the influence of either laudanum or chloroform could sign their own name, where the weakest parts of a skull were and whether an airgun was capable of killing a man.

Matters seem to have come to a head around 23 July 1849, when two events occurred. Firstly Massey was told that his lodgings were no longer available, but before that he had witnessed a delivery of quicklime. On 8 August Maria took delivery of a large shovel and a couple of days after that O'Connor was invited to come to dinner. He turned up with a friend, which ruined the Mannings' plans. Maria apparently took O'Connor aside and told him that if he came to dinner the following night then she would be on the menu for dessert.

O'Connor duly obliged and the last two sightings of the Irishman were when he crossed London Bridge, on his way to the house, and later, smoking a cigar at the back door of the Mannings' house. Maria welcomed O'Connor with a good deal of affection and as she wrapped her arms around his neck, she grabbed a pistol and shot him in the head. Unfortunately this did not kill him and Frederick, in his own words, finished off the deed. 'I never really liked him, so I battered his head with a ripping chisel'. The Mannings then buried O'Connor's body in quicklime under the flagstones of the kitchen.

The following morning Maria went round to O'Connor's lodgings with his keys and took a wad of notes, gold watches, chains and his valuable railway bonds. She returned the next day and ransacked the lodgings for more loot. She then dispatched Frederick to sell some of the bonds, masquerading as O'Connor.

Two of O'Connor's workmates arrived at the Mannings' house on 12 August. The Mannings admitted that O'Connor had eaten with them on 8 August but denied that he had been at their house on the 9th, the day of the murder. The workmates were certain that he had been, as O'Connor had told them that he would be 'dining with Maria' that night.

This visit obviously spooked the Mannings and Maria fled with the money and the shares and headed for Edinburgh. She left two trunks under the name of Smith at London Bridge Station. Frederick, meanwhile, was told to sell the household effects and head for a relative of Maria's called Bainbridge in Jersey. He achieved the sale very quickly, left London via Waterloo and boarded a boat bound for Jersey.

O'Connor's friends had tipped off the police and during their enquiries a woman matching Maria's description was said to have been seen ransacking O'Connor's lodgings. They then went to the Mannings house and it did not take them long to notice fresh mortar between the flagstones of the kitchen floor. From beneath it they exhumed O'Connor's body. Warrants were promptly issued for the arrest of both Frederick and Maria Manning.

Maria had made the mistake of trying to sell some of O'Connor's railway bonds, claiming to be Scottish. Her French accent gave her away and she was arrested in Edinburgh and taken to London. Frederick, meanwhile, had been moving around Jersey with his money gradually running out. He was drinking heavily and it probably came as some relief to him when he bumped into a man who knew him. The man promptly told the police and Frederick was arrested on 21 August and taken back to London. Apparently his first words were 'Is the wretch taken? She is a very violent woman, I have been afraid for my own life.' Maria, meanwhile, had been blaming Frederick for the murder.

Their trial opened at the Old Bailey on 25 October 1849 and after two days the jury took just one hour to find them both guilty. Maria apparently stood up as soon as the verdict was delivered and said 'You ought to be ashamed of yourselves! There is no justice and no right for a foreign subject in this country.' She claimed that she would never have killed O'Connor and if she had chosen to kill anyone it would have been her husband, who had made her life 'a hell on earth'.

Maria tried every trick to avoid the death sentence. She wrote to Queen Victoria, claiming that her husband had murdered O'Connor and that she had known nothing about it until the following day. Her efforts were in vain, however, as in front of up to 50,000 people, believed to be the largest ever crowd at an execution, she and Frederick were hanged on 13 November 1849.

Maria's execution had two other notable effects. The first was that after she had been seen mounting the scaffold in a black, satin dress, the fabric went out of fashion for nearly 20 years. Secondly, Charles Dickens was present at the execution and was shocked to see people sitting in the specially constructed seating around the gallows, gawping at the events through binoculars. He was later to write in *The Times*:

> When the day dawned, thieves, low prostitutes, ruffians and vagabonds of every kind flocked on the ground, with every variety of offensive and foul behaviour. Fightings, faintings, tumultuous demonstrations of indecent delight when swooning women were dragged out of the crowd by the police, with their dresses disordered, gave a new zest to the general entertainment. I am solemnly convinced that nothing that ingenuity could devise to be done in this city, in the same compass of time, could work such ruin as some public executions and I stand astounded and appalled by the wickedness it exhibits.

* * * * *

The sensational case of **Jessie M'Lachlan** only goes to prove that the class system was very much alive in the latter part of the 19th century. It condemned the servant who was probably only guilty of knowing what had really happened, and freed the man who almost certainly carried out the crime.

James and John Fleming lived in Glasgow. James, the father, was a heavy drinker and ageing disgracefully with an eye for his female servant, whereas John seems to have been a perfectly normal accountant. John was always keen to leave the town house they occupied in Sandyford Place at the weekends in order to get some peace from his bad-tempered father.

So it was that John left for his villa in Dunoon on Friday 4 July 1862. Whatever happened over the next couple of days has always been unclear, but certainly when he reappeared on the Monday morning, he found his father, James, alone in the house. James, by all accounts, was a rather frisky old man and had constantly tried to get into the bed of their 25-year-old maid Jessie M'Pherson. James told his son that he had not seen Jessie since the previous Friday but John found that her room was locked. After he found a second key, he discovered, to his horror, that Jessie's almost naked body was lying, covered in blood, on her bed. It appeared that she had been hacked to death with a cleaver. Although there was no sign of a break-in, most of Jessie's clothes were gone, as was some of the family silver, and there were bloody footprints around the bed. Some of his father's shirts had blood on them and there were signs of bloodstains on the kitchen floor.

Reluctantly John told the police his fears after they had been called to investigate the matter. They promptly arrested James. He adamantly denied any wrongdoing and two days later the missing silver turned up at a pawnbrokers. The pawnbroker contacted the police and he told them that it had been pledged by Jessie M'Lachlan.

She had also worked as a servant at the Fleming's home and when she was arrested she initially told the police that she had been instructed to pawn the silver by James Fleming, who was short of money. The police discovered that the footprints next to the bed matched M'Lachlan's.

James was released and M'Lachlan was arrested. She was brought to trial in September and there was, indeed, a good amount of circumstantial evidence. However, many present, including her defence counsel, were certain that Jessie was holding something back. The judge clearly thought her guilty and was extremely biased in his summing up. The jury followed his lead and found M'Lachlan guilty and before the judge passed sentence M'Lachlan was given an opportunity to make a statement.

She described how she had come to visit her friend, Jessie M'Pherson, on the Friday evening. She was shocked to see that the girl had a serious wound on her forehead. M'Pherson explained to her that James had attacked her with a knife after she had turned down his sexual advances. M'Lachlan was determined to go and fetch a doctor and had left her friend in the kitchen alone. She had not even managed to get out of the house before screams brought her back to the kitchen, where she saw James Fleming attacking M'Pherson with a meat cleaver. There was nothing M'Lachlan could do and her friend was dead. M'Lachlan agreed to help Fleming make it look like her friend was the victim of a bungled burglary, which is why she had pawned the silver on his behalf.

In the event the judge dismissed her statement as 'A tissue of wicked falsehoods' and sentenced her to death. There was an enormous public outcry and thousands signed petitions about the unfair way in which M'Lachlan had been treated in court. Reluctantly the authorities agreed to commute her sentence to life imprisonment and on 5 October 1877, after 15 years in prison, Jessie M'Lachlan was finally released. She immediately emigrated to America, where she died on 1 January 1899. She always stood by her story and simply said that she had been foolish to agree to hide the murder carried out by James Fleming.

* * * * *

Marguerite Diblanc was a strong Belgian woman who had fought in the streets of Paris in 1871 with the revolutionaries. In 1872 she was working as a cook for Marie Riel, the bad-tempered mistress of Lord Lucan, who had led the disastrous 'Charge of the Light Brigade'. Marie Riel was in her late forties and at nearly thirty herself, Marguerite was clearly of the opinion that she had chosen the wrong employer.

Their arguments came to a head in March when Riel sacked Marguerite. She gave her a week's wages but Marguerite refused to leave as she claimed she was entitled to one month's pay. Reluctantly the two compromised that Marguerite would stay on as cook and work out the month's notice.

At the end of March Marie Riel's daughter, the actress Julie Riel, left for a short holiday, after a run at St James's Theatre. This left the disagreeable French woman and the strong-willed Belgian in the home alone. It did not take them long to begin rowing again.

Marie Riel was expecting a visitor on Sunday 7 April and went down to the kitchen to see if Marguerite had everything ready. She found the kitchen empty as Marguerite was still working upstairs. Riel was livid and the two of them had a violent argument which concluded with Marguerite being ordered out of the house. Marguerite would not go quietly and it seems that she tried to strangle Riel and then hit her. She was not to know at the time that this blow had killed her employer.

The gravity of the situation must have hit Marguerite because when Eliza Watts, another servant, arrived at the house, she dragged Riel's body into the coal cellar. She managed to get Eliza out of the way for a short time, giving her enough opportunity to move her employer's body into the pantry, which, as it also contained the safe, was always kept locked. It is not clear whether Riel was still alive when she was dragged into the pantry, but the presence of a rope around her neck, which Marguerite had used to drag her body, later pointed to this as being the method which finally extinguished Marie Riel's life.

Marguerite had the presence of mind to remove money from the safe and then continue as if nothing had happened. Eliza came back and later, at 4pm, Marie Riel's guest arrived. Marie Riel had last been seen walking her dog at noon and the guest waited impatiently for the hostess. Eventually she left and soon after Marguerite put on her satin dress and told Eliza that she was going to church. In fact she caught the boat train to Dover and then went on to Paris.

Julie Riel found her mother's body the following day and it was Marguerite's French accent that helped the police track her down. She had caught a cab to Victoria and a station clerk clearly remembered a 'French' woman buying a ticket for the overnight boat train. The French police were informed and reluctantly they allowed Marguerite to be extradited to stand trial at the Old Bailey.

The jury found her guilty of murder but asked the judge to consider the fact that Marguerite had been severely provoked to commit the murder. The judge ignored their pleas and sentenced Marguerite to death. In June 1872 Marguerite was reprieved and her sentence commuted to life imprisonment.

* * * * *

Kate Webster is arguably one of the most reviled murderesses in British criminal history. She killed the retired school teacher, Julia Thomas, in 1879. Kate had an astonishing criminal record and in 1875 she had been sentenced to 18 months for no fewer than 36 lodging-house robberies.

Her story, however, begins back in Killane, County Wexford, in 1849, when she was born to poor but respectable parents. Her criminal career began as a small child and she was well-known for her stealing. By the time she reached her early teens she had stolen enough money for a one-way boat trip to Liverpool. Her first prison sentence came at the age of 18, when she was sentenced to four years for pick-pocketing. On her release she moved to London, where she took up a post as a char woman and prostitute. She was in and out of prison for a number of boarding-house robberies. She would take lodgings and then sell everything that she could from the house before disappearing. Also, at some point, she lived with a man and gave birth to a son. What is certain is that by the time she was released from prison in 1877, both her boyfriend and her son had abandoned her.

In January 1879 Kate moved to Richmond and sometime in late February she became a maid to Julia Thomas, a wealthy old woman who lived at 2 Vine Cottages, Park Road. She had not long been in the employment of Mrs Thomas when, on 2 March 1879, she ambushed the old lady at the top of the stairs. She clobbered Mrs Thomas and then threw her down the stairs and strangled her.

It is how she dealt with the body that makes Kate Webster a notorious and hated figure. She dragged Thomas's body into the kitchen and lay it on the table. She then removed the head with a meat saw and proceeded to dismember the rest of the body with a carving knife. Having achieved her purpose, she waited until the following morning, when she boiled up a large copper pan of water and began to systematically boil the body parts. Over the next few days the neighbours complained of the unpleasant smell while Mrs Thomas bubbled away in the copper pan.

Kate then adopted her employer's name and wore her jewellery and dresses. She explained to friends, Ann and Henry Porter, who had not seen her for six years, that she had married, been widowed and been left a considerable amount of money by an ageing aunt. The story was plausible enough, and she convinced their son, Robert, to help her take a heavy box to Richmond Bridge. They stopped off at a pub, where Kate left Robert alone for 20 minutes. She disappeared with a carpet bag, and when she came back it was no longer with her. It was later believed that the carpet bag had contained Mrs Thomas's head.

Kate had also disposed of the box, by heaving it into the river. It was found next day at Barnes Bridge and when the police were called it was discovered that the box contained the boiled human remains. The newspapers were full of the story, but what they did not know was that Kate had been selling Mrs Thomas's body fat as 'best dripping' to her neighbours in Richmond.

Kate forged ahead with the disposal of the rest of Mrs Thomas's possessions and agreed with John Church to sell all of her furniture for £68. He arrived to pick it up on 18 March and inquisitive neighbours were told by Kate that Mrs Thomas had instructed her to sell the furniture on her behalf. The neighbours were not convinced, particularly as Kate could not tell them where Mrs Thomas was. The situation was beginning to slip out of Kate's hands; an argument ensued and Church became suspicious and wanted his money back.

Before the police could be called Kate managed to flee to Liverpool and board a boat back to Ireland. The Irish police arrested her in Killane on 28 March. Meanwhile, the police in London had discovered, to their horror, that there were bloodstains, charred bones and human fat in the kitchen of Mrs Thomas's house. Robert Porter identified the box as being the one that he had helped Kate carry to Richmond Bridge.

From the outset Kate denied any knowledge of Mrs Thomas's murder and then tried to implicate Henry Porter and John Church in the murder, telling the police that she had fled to Ireland because she feared that the two men would murder her next. Church was arrested, but luckily for him he had an alibi.

Her defence counsel at the Old Bailey trial which opened on 2 July tried desperately to convince the jury that Porter and Church had manipulated Kate and that she knew nothing of their plans. The jury was not convinced and found her guilty of murder. The judge sentenced her to death. She even tried to claim that she was pregnant but a medical examination proved this to be a lie.

Shortly before her execution Kate Webster again claimed that she had nothing to do with the murder and that it was, in fact, carried out by her child's father, who had told her to blame Church. On the eve of her execution the truth finally emerged when all her appeals and statements had been ignored or disproved. She told a prison chaplain, Father McEnrey, 'I am perfectly resigned to my fate and am full of confidence in a happy

eternity. If I had a choice I would almost sooner die than return to a life full of misery, deception and wickedness.'

Kate Webster was hanged in Wandsworth Prison on 29 July 1879. The day after her execution Mrs Thomas's possessions, including the knife, chopper and meat saw, were sold off at an auction in Richmond. Mrs Thomas's home remained empty for some time as no one was prepared to live in a house where such a foul murder had taken place.

* * * * *

When Thomas Pierrepoint hanged **Louie Calvert** at 9am on Thursday 24 June 1926, she was the first woman to have been hanged at Strangeways Prison since 1886. Louie was well-known to the local police. In 1925 she was 33 years old and had a string of convictions for theft and prostitution. She had also been implicated in the death of John Frobisher, whose body had been found in a canal on 12 July 1922. Significantly, as it was to turn out, his body had been found minus his boots, which confused the police at the time.

By 1925 Louie was working as a housekeeper for Albert Calvert in Railway Place, Leeds. It seems obvious that they were sexually intimate, as Louie claimed to have fallen pregnant with Albert's child. Honourably, Albert married her but then began to worry why Louie was showing no signs of pregnancy. Close to the time when Louie claimed that the child was about to be born, she persuaded Albert that she was going to stay with her sister in Dewsbury. She confirmed her arrival with a telegram, but had, in fact, returned to Leeds.

She took a job as a maid for the 40-year-old widow, Lily Waterhouse. Louie agreed to work for the woman in exchange for her room and board. Over a period of time Louie stole Lily's silver and pawned it. Lily eventually noticed that her possessions were slowly disappearing and went to the police.

Meanwhile, Louie had agreed to adopt a newly born child from an unmarried teenage girl. The day after Lily had been to see the police, on 30 March 1926, neighbours were alarmed to hear banging noises coming from Lily's house. They saw Louie leaving the house with a baby and she explained to them that the noises had been her collapsing the child's cot. She also went on to explain that the other strange noises were Lily crying because Louie had decided not to work for her anymore.

A couple of days later the police paid a visit to Lily's house in order for her to sign the complaint that she had made against Louie. They could get no answer and enquired of neighbours whether they had seen Lily. The police officer was told about the noises and, using a spare key from one of the neighbours, gained access to the house. He found Lily strangled to death on her bed; her body had been battered.

Louie had returned to her husband and the police had little difficulty in finding her. The link was made with the Frobisher case and when the police asked Louie to take her boots off they found that they had belonged to Lily Waterhouse.

Louie had had a very odd and complicated life. She had worked as a prostitute under the name of Louie Gomersal; she was a regular Salvation Army meeting attendee, under the name of Louie Jackson, and she did, in fact, have a six-year-old son called Kenneth. She had married Albert as Louie Jackson, and it seems that she had thought that she would have created a cast-iron alibi by disappearing to Dewsbury and eventually returning with a new-born child.

It may well be that Louie had already identified Lily as a potential theft victim but had not initially intended to murder her. Her undoing was allowing Lily to make a complaint to the police before she did away with her. When she was arrested, shortly after the murder, her multiple names and lifestyle began to unravel, although she initially claimed that Lily had given her the property to pawn.

On Wednesday 7 April she was remanded in custody for the murder of Lily Waterhouse and her murder trial was set for May. The case took just two days to be heard, between 5 and 6 May 1926. Louie was found guilty and instantly claimed that she was pregnant again. She was sent to Strangeways and underwent a medical examination which failed to prove conclusively that she was not pregnant.

Meanwhile, back in her home town of Ossett in Yorkshire, a petition was being arranged for her reprieve. This attracted 3,000 signatures. Her execution date was set for 24 June, but not before questions were asked about the case in Parliament.

Her final appeal was turned down on 22 June and only after that did Louie confess to murdering John Frobisher as well. She had been working as his housekeeper under the name of Jackson and when his body was found in the canal, medical examiners found that he had a wound on the back of his head, as well as a fractured skull. In the event, the coroner's inquest returned a verdict of misadventure, believing that Frobisher had fallen into the canal and struck his head in the process.

As for Louie, her motive was pure greed. She had stolen from both Frobisher and Waterhouse but, unusually, she had kept Frobisher's boots and was wearing

Waterhouse's shoes when she was arrested. It seems that the most likely motive for murder was that her thefts needed to be covered up and that she had probably been confronted by her two victims. Louie's legendary bad temper had got the better of her on both occasions.

* * * * *

Strangeways saw the hanging of another woman on 12 January 1949, when Albert Pierrepoint hanged **Margaret Allen** for the murder of 68-year-old Nancy Ellen Chadwick. In retrospect it is clear that Margaret Allen was suffering from severe depression, was in debt and had never really recovered mentally from the death of her mother in 1943.

Margaret was a very strange woman but then so too was the eccentric Nancy Chadwick. It is probable that they were lovers as it was obvious to all that knew Margaret that she was a lesbian. She was 42 and a heavy smoker, with short hair and a masculine appearance. She habitually wore men's clothing and was known by everyone as 'Bill'. Margaret was the 20th of 22 children.

She claimed that she had undergone a sex change operation and she spent nearly all of her time playing darts and drinking in pubs. Her closest friend was Annie Cook, who had once gone on holiday to Brighton with Margaret, but had apparently turned down her friend's sexual advances.

Nancy Chadwick was last seen walking along Bacup Road in Rawtenstall. It was known by popular gossip that she carried a great deal of money in her knitted shopping bag. It is probable that Margaret encountered the old lady and demanded money from her and then something went wrong. When Nancy's body was found in a sack on Bacup Road in the early hours of the morning of 28 August 1948, by a bus driver, the police discovered that her head had been battered in with a hammer.

Margaret was one of the first people to be interviewed by the police. She told them that she had seen Nancy when she came out of the pub. She knew about a secret pocket in Nancy's clothing that the old woman used to hide money. The police were suspicious from the very beginning and when they searched Margaret's house they found blood on the walls of the kitchen; more blood on floor cloths, and then, Margaret confessed:

> I'll tell you all about it. I was in a funny mood and she seemed to insist on coming in. I just happened to look around and I saw a hammer in the kitchen. On the spur of the moment I hit her with the hammer. She gave a shout and that seemed to start me off more. I hit her a few times. I don't know how many. I put the body in my coal house.

More forensic evidence was found in Margaret's cellar and on her clothes.

When she came to court Margaret was still dressed as a man, and in the short five-hour trial her defence counsel unsuccessfully tried to claim that Margaret had suffered from temporary insanity. The jury rejected this plea and took just 15 minutes to find her guilty. She was sentenced to hang and her friend, Annie Cook, desperately tried to organise a petition to save her. It attracted little more than 150 signatures.

When she was hanged on 12 January 1949 Margaret was the first woman to have been hanged in Britain for 12 years. On Annie's last visit to her condemned friend Margaret said to her, 'It would help if I could cry but my manhood stops my tears'.

* * * * *

Edith Chubb was a much more fortunate woman as her depression, although causing her to resort to murder, ended up saving her life. Edith lived in Broadstairs in Kent and it was a packed household. The home contained not only her husband and five children, but also her mother-in-law and her sister-in-law. At the age of 46 Edith had all of this to contend with, and in addition she held down three 12-hour night shifts as a cleaner at a local hospital. Edith's ability to handle all of these pressures finally gave way on 6 February 1958.

That evening her sister-in-law, the unmarried Lillian Chubb, who worked in a Margate department store, failed to return home from work. The family could virtually set their clock by Lillian's departures and arrivals, but on the following morning there was still no sign of her. Edith herself rang the police and told them that her sister-in-law had gone missing.

The police began by searching the local area around their home in Broadstairs and did not take long to discover Lillian's strangled corpse, pushed under a hedge not far from the house. The body was sent to Professor Francis Camps to carry out a post-mortem examination. He discovered that shortly after death Lillian's body had been placed in a seated position. This immediately alerted the police, who had found a wheelchair in the Chubbs' garden shed. They had also discovered by this time that no one had seen Lillian leaving for work. Edith had also, in the past day or two, paid off some debts belonging to her husband and herself, which they tied in with the fact that Lillian's handbag was missing.

The police returned to interview Edith and she almost immediately broke down and confessed to murdering her sister-in-law. As she would later recount to the court, she told the police that she had become sick to death of Lillian, who was rude, smug and demanding. Something had made Edith crack that morning, perhaps a final comment from Lillian as she left to go to work. In any event, Edith had grabbed Lillian's scarf and given it a hefty tug. Lillian had fallen over and hit her head and then Edith had panicked. She had retrieved the wheelchair from the shed, heaved Lillian's body into it and put her sister-in-law's corpse into the shed before she disposed of it under the hedge the following morning.

Edith came to trial at the Old Bailey on 30 April 1958. Her full confession obviously went in her favour, as did evidence from her doctor, which alluded to her depression and the fact that she was under continual pressure. The judge was much more scathing, but despite this the jury did not find her guilty of murder and returned a verdict of guilty of manslaughter. As a result the judge sentenced Edith to just four years in prison.

* * * * *

By the middle of the 20th century women were no longer always hanged for murder, but this did not prevent them from having to face the very real prospect of spending the rest of their lives in prison. What is also interesting is the fact that as the decades progressed, courts became more willing to consider the mental state of a woman murderer. Insanity, or temporary insanity, and in other cases depression, was a partially acceptable explanation for the crime. However, this did not mean that callous acts of premeditated murder escaped punishment, as there was still a feeling that women who resorted to murder were more guilty than their male counterparts, as they had betrayed their perceived role in society.

CHAPTER SIX

LOVE KILLS

Love can so easily become an obsession and as the playwright, William Congreve, once said 'Heaven has no rage like love to hatred turned, nor hell a fury like a woman scorned'. Rejection in love, regardless of social status or age, or even unrequited love, has proved to be a powerful motive for murder. Sometimes the jealousy wells up so suddenly that a murder has been committed almost before the murderess is aware of what is happening. Several of the cases, however, show long-term suffering and slights which eventually conspire to create the conditions where a premeditated and well-planned murder is the inevitable outcome.

ELIZABETH RICHARDSON found herself facing the hangman's noose at Tyburn on 21 December 1768. For some years Elizabeth had been able to subsist on the proceeds of occasional prostitution. At some point she was taken in by Mr Pimlot, a lawyer who had chambers in Symond's Inn, Chancery Lane, London. Whether Pimlot and Richardson had sexual relations is not known, but it seems that Elizabeth would have wished it to be so and felt protective of her new benefactor.

One Sunday evening Richardson arrived at Pimlot's chambers and as he was not there, she determined to wait for him. Pimlot was with friends in Fleet Street and returned to his chambers around midnight. He did not see Richardson, nor she him. It seems that the watchman, Mr Wilson, had not allowed Richardson to wait inside the chambers, but within half an hour of Pimlot retiring, Richardson reappeared and insisted that she should see him. The night-watchman was not keen as he was aware that Pimlot had already retired for the night. Richardson became aggressive and swore and finally broke one of the panes of glass in the window. Pimlot emerged at this point, desperately embarrassed, and turned the woman over to the watchman. On hearing this instruction Richardson produced a pen-knife of about two inches long and stabbed Pimlot on the left of his chest. The watchman grabbed Richardson and Pimlot pulled the knife out of his wound, telling the watchman to take the knife. Pimlot followed the other two to the watch-house and sat down in a chair, obviously feeling weak and shocked from the stab wound. When he unbuttoned his waistcoat there was a good deal of blood loss and Richardson said 'What have I done! Oh, Mr Wilson, it was I that did this shocking deed; instantly send for a surgeon, send for a surgeon! I have murdered my dear Pimlot.' It seems that at this point Pimlot expired and Richardson was taken away to prison. Meanwhile, a Mr Minors, a surgeon in Chancery Lane, was called to look at Pimlot's body. In the event Minors was asleep but two of his pupils came and confirmed that Pimlot was dead.

The following day Minors conducted a post-mortem and found that the blade had punctured the heart and that the wound corresponded to the blade that Richardson had used. A coroner's jury passed a verdict of wilful murder against Elizabeth Richardson and she was brought to trial at the next session at the Old Bailey. The trial seemed to be a foregone conclusion, and she was found guilty and hanged the Monday after her conviction. After her death the body was left at Tyburn until it was removed to the surgeon's hall to be dissected.

Whatever the relationship between Richardson and Pimlot, it seems clear that her desire to be admitted into his chambers was rooted in the fact that she had suspected he had brought back another woman. It is unlikely that the passion and the violence could be explained in any other way, implying that they had once shared a bed.

* * * * *

On 17 July 1794, **Anne Broadric** found herself indicted for the murder of Mr Errington. Errington was a divorced land-owning gentleman from Grayes in Essex. Some three years after his divorce he met Anne Broadric, who was considered something of a beauty. Broadric had agreed to leave her lover, Captain Robinson, and live with Errington as husband and wife, although in fact they never married. They lived together for three years until Errington's eyes moved to another somewhat more respectable lady who lived in the local area. He told Broadric that she should leave his house and never see him again, although he had made provision for her needs. It seems from a letter written by Broadric on 11 April 1794 that although physically she would need for nothing, Errington had seriously damaged her reputation and left her emotionally distraught:

Dear Errington,

That you have betrayed and abandoned the most tender and affectionate heart that ever warmed a human bosom cannot be denied by any person who is in the least acquainted with me. Wretched and miserable as I have been since you left me, there is still a method remaining that would suspend, for a time, the melancholy sufferings and distress which I labour under at this moment; and still, inhuman as thou art, I am half persuaded, when I tell you the power is in your hands, that you will not withhold it from me. What I allude to is the permission of seeing you once more, and, perhaps, for the last time. If you consider that the request comes from a woman you once flattered into belief of her being the sole possessor of your love, you may not perhaps think it unreasonable. Recollect, however, Errington ere you send a refusal, that the roaring of the tempest and lightnings from heaven are not more terrible than the rage and vengeance of a disappointed woman. Hitherto you can only answer for the weakness and frailty of my nature. There is a further knowledge of my

disposition you must have if you do not grant me the favour demanded. I wish it to come voluntary from yourself, or else I will force it from you. Believe me, in that case, I would seek you in the farthest corner of the globe, rush into your presence, and, with the same rapture that nerved the arm of Charlotte Corday when she assassinated the monster Marat, would I put an end to the existence of a man who is the author of all the agonies and care that at present oppress the heart of
Anne Broadric

During the next month Anne wrote several letters to Errington, but nothing she could say would entice him into even replying to her. She had made her threat, and now she proposed to carry it out.

On Friday 15 May, elegantly dressed, she proceeded to the Three Nuns Inn in Whitechapel and boarded a coach bound for Southend-on-Sea. She alighted outside Errington's house and walked through the gate and towards the door. Both Errington and his new wife saw Anne approaching. Mrs Errington wanted to deal with the situation herself but her husband insisted that he would handle it. In the event Mrs Errington convinced her husband and asked him to wait in the drawing room while she interviewed Anne in the parlour. Anne entered the house through the kitchen and was on her way upstairs to talk to Mr Errington when she was intercepted by his wife. Anne demanded to see Mr Errington but his wife said that he did not wish to see her. Anne replied 'I am not to be so satisfied; I know the ways of this house too well, and I will search for him'. With that she ran up the stairs and barged into the drawing room. No sooner had she established that Errington was in the room than she produced a brass-barrelled pistol which she pushed against his heart. With the last words of warning 'Errington, I am come to perform my dreadful promise' she shot him at point-blank range.

Errington's wife appeared at the doorway and promptly fainted. Miraculously, however, her husband was not dead and demanded to know why Anne had shot him. She made no answer but when servants flocked into the room she threw the pistol on the floor and said 'Here, take me; hang me; do what you like with me, I do not care now'. One of the servants called for a local surgeon, Mr Miller, to come and have a look at the wound in Errington's chest. The pistol ball had shattered three ribs and had somehow found itself lodged in the shoulder. Miller tried in vain to get the shot out of Errington's body and while he was doing this Mr Button, a magistrate, arrived. Firstly he asked Anne why she had shot Errington, to which she replied that she was determined that he should not live as he had seriously wronged her. Errington begged the magistrate not to arrest Anne and said that the wound was not fatal and that he wanted to drop any charges against her. In the event Button refused and arranged for Anne to be taken to Chelmsford jail. Unfortunately Errington's wound was far more serious than he had imagined, and while Anne was in prison he died, which prompted her to state that she bitterly regretted what she had done.

On Tuesday 19 May the jury at the coroner's inquest returned a verdict of wilful murder by the hands of Anne Broadric. Anne languished in prison until the trial opened on Friday 17 July and it seems that she was in a very pitiful emotional state, as when she was collected from the prison at 6am to be taken to the Shire Hall she had to be carried there in a chaise. This hearing only took around 10 minutes and was officiated by Lord Chief Baron Macdonald. From there she was conveyed to the bail dock in the criminal court. Anne wore mourning dress and was attended by three other women and a doctor. The indictment was read out to her, during which time she burst into tears. With several prosecution witnesses able to clearly identify Anne as the woman who had shot Errington, her only chance of avoiding the hangman's noose was to prove that she was not in control of herself when she had shot him. Several witnesses were called to support the fact that they believed that the events leading up to the shooting proved that Anne was insane. The jury, after having heard the evidence against Anne and the pleading of her defence counsel, retired to consider their verdict. Only a few minutes elapsed before they returned and delivered a verdict of 'not guilty'.

It was the view of the judges that two local magistrates should be given the responsibility of ensuring that Anne was well-cared for, given her mental condition. Unfortunately we do not know what became of Anne Broadric but she certainly did not face her end at the gallows.

* * * * *

The tragic story of **Elizabeth Martha Brown** inspired Thomas Hardy's *Tess of the d'Urbervilles,* in which a milkmaid finds herself in a love triangle and is driven to murder the man who seduced her. She finds herself condemned to death but liberated from the shame. Tess was modelled on Elizabeth Brown, a woman who lived at Birdsmoorgate, near Beaminster in Dorset. Hardy was present when the unfortunate woman was hanged in Dorchester on 9 August 1856.

Elizabeth had married John, who was 20 years younger than herself. He was employed as a carrier and local gossip believed that he had only married Elizabeth for her money. Gossip also maintained that John was not averse to casual affairs with any woman he could tempt into bed. John did not seem to be concerned enough that his wife might discover what he was doing, as it appears that he was perfectly prepared to bring women home with him and make love to them in his wife's bed.

On one such occasion in 1856 Elizabeth returned home to find John tucked up in her bed with another woman. Swiftly the woman was ejected from the house but later Elizabeth and John had a violent argument. At the critical point of the row John struck Elizabeth with a whip; she responded by striking him with an axe. We can only speculate what went through Elizabeth's mind as she saw her husband's inert body lying on the floor. She was determined, however, to try to cover up the act. Unlike many male murderers she did not seek to dispose of the body; she simply chose to fabricate an alternative reason for her husband's death. Since John worked with horses on a daily basis, she concocted the story that he had been kicked by one and had somehow managed to get into the house and died. She persisted with this story throughout the trial and only towards the end did she finally confess that she had dealt the fatal blow.

There was intense public interest in the case but this did not prevent the jury from returning a 'guilty' verdict. Public opinion did not count for much as far as the judge was concerned either, and he passed a death sentence. The Home Secretary himself refused to give Elizabeth a reprieve.

Elizabeth was incarcerated at Dorchester jail and brought out for her execution on the rainy morning of 9 August. There was a huge crowd waiting to see whether a last-minute reprieve would save Elizabeth. Some three or four thousand people had gathered, including Thomas Hardy, who said:

> I remember what a fine figure she showed against the sky as she hung in the misty rain, and how the tight, black, silk gown set off her shape as she wheeled half round and back. I saw they had put a cloth over her face, how, as the cloth got wet, her features came through it. That was extraordinary.

The prison chaplain was so emotionally traumatised by the impending execution that a young clergyman called Henry Moule was drafted in to give Elizabeth her last rites. So shocked was the nation that Elizabeth had been hanged for the murder of her philandering husband that many called for the abolition of the death penalty. It is also interesting to note how much Hardy's fiction mirrors Elizabeth's case. In many respects Elizabeth Martha Brown's life and death are forever immortalised by Thomas Hardy's much-read and interpreted Tess.

Although the Elizabeth Martha Brown case received a great deal of publicity and sympathy, captial punishment was not abolished until 100 years after her death.

* * * * *

In the summer of 1871 a hotel in Colditz in Upper Saxony, Germany, welcomed a Mr Mainwaring with his beautiful new wife. They occupied a suite of rooms for their honeymoon. During their stay they received letters post-marked from Ferrybridge in Yorkshire. A few days after their arrival another English woman arrived at the hotel, occupying two rooms on the same floor. Unbeknown to the staff or Mr Mainwaring, the new arrival was none other than his real wife. His wife remained incognito for a couple of days before she struck. Armed with a pistol she crept along the corridor to their bedroom, flung open the door and, finding her husband in bed with his new wife, shot him straight through the head.

The murderess, having completed her task, offered no resistance when local police officials arrested her and put her in prison. When they visited her cell the following morning they found her dead on the floor. Doctors were called to ascertain the cause of death and it was established that she had hidden poison in her clothing and had taken it at some point during the night. **Mrs Mainwaring**'s worst fears had been confirmed and having determined to kill her husband, she no longer had any reason to live herself.

* * * * *

The case of **Christiana Edmunds** is a classic case of unrequited love. In 1871 Christiana was a 42-year-old spinster and lived in Brighton with her widowed mother. One day, while she and her mother were walking along the seafront they encountered the handsome Dr Beard. She instantly fell for him and over the next few weeks Christiana made numerous appointments to see him at his practice. There was never anything wrong with Christiana but she was able to initiate a relationship of sorts with the doctor. Christiana was even introduced to the doctor's wife and became a family friend.

Meanwhile, Christiana and the doctor were corresponding in increasingly passionate terms. Christiana was determined to have the doctor for herself and on a March afternoon in 1871 she brought a box of chocolates to the Beard's house and insisted that the doctor's wife eat some over a pot of tea. Christiana had filled the chocolate creams with strychnine. Luckily for Mrs Beard she only took a single bite and then spat it out, but later she had severe stomach pains. Her husband had a dilemma; he believed that Christiana had tried to poison his wife but was frightened of the scandal if he made his thoughts known. After all, Christiana would have been sure to have kept some of his letters.

Beard forbad Christiana to see him or his family ever again. Christiana was not, however, to be denied and she determined to create a fictitious Brighton poisoner in order to persuade the doctor that his suspicions were unfounded as far as she was concerned. She bought more chocolates from John Maynard's shop on West Street but did not purchase them herself; she paid the 11-year-old Adam May to buy them on her behalf. These chocolates she replaced with the previously purchased bag, which she had already laced with strychnine, and sent the boy back to swap them. Over the next few days, using a number of different boys, she systematically contaminated a large amount of Maynard's stock. Christiana had purchased the strychnine from Isaac Garrett and returned on 15 April for more.

Over the next few weeks several people fell seriously ill in Brighton as a result of eating the contaminated chocolates from Maynard's shop. Christiana's first victim was the four-year-old Sidney Barker, who died in convulsions in his mother's arms on 12 June.

Christiana was already taking steps to cover her tracks and sent a young boy called Adam Smith to Garrett's pharmacy with a forged note from David Black, the coroner. The note requested that he give the boy his poison book to help him with his investigations. When he received it back a page had been torn out. Christiana even presented herself at the inquest of Sidney Barker and claimed that in the previous September she had been ill as a result of eating chocolates from Maynard's shop.

Christiana's plan, however, began to fall apart when the inquest jury returned a verdict of accidental death. But she was not finished. She wrote anonymous letters to Albert Barker, Sidney's father, urging him to sue Maynard. Christiana had been leaving the poisoned sweets in shops and on at least two occasions children had eaten the abandoned chocolates and had fallen ill. She poisoned two boys with a bag of chocolate creams and Emily Baker was given a bag of chocolates by Christiana when she came out of school and also fell seriously ill. More anonymous letters were sent by Christiana to Brighton notables, including the editor of the local paper. She was also sending cakes and sweets to various people through the post and had contacted the police on two occasions claiming that she had received parcels herself. Inspector Gibbs was sent to investigate and Christiana pointedly spat out an apricot, claiming that it was bitter, while he was there.

Gibbs was sure that he had found the poisoner and returned to her house on 17 August to arrest her. She was charged with the attempted poisoning of Mrs Beard, as, finally, the doctor had summoned up the courage to talk to the police. Her case was originally to be heard at the Lewes Assizes but because of the public outcry it was transferred to the Old Bailey. By the time the trial opened on 15 January 1872 the police had added the charge of the murder of Sidney Albert Barker.

The evidence against Christiana was overwhelming, but on the second day of the trial, new light was thrown on the Edmunds family. Christiana's mother Ann told the court that her husband had been admitted to an asylum in 1843 and had died in 1845. Her son, Arthur, was an epileptic and had been admitted to another asylum in 1860, where he died six years later. Her other daughter had once thrown herself out of a window and had died at the age of 36. Ann's own father had died of a fit at the age of 43. A specialist in mental illness was called, who described Christiana as being 'on the border line between crime and insanity'.

In the event the judge and the jury disregarded this evidence and, after just an hour's deliberation, the jury found her guilty and Judge Martin sentenced her to death. There was outrage, not at her crimes, but at the fact that a mentally ill woman, who could not be held responsible for her actions, had been sentenced to hang. Her sentence was finally commuted and she was sent to Broadmoor, where she died at the age of 79 in 1907.

* * * * *

Mary Eleanor Wheeler was born in 1866, but by 1890 she was living in Kentish Town under her assumed name of **Mary Pearcey**. It is believed that she took this name from a former lover. She was now living with Charles Creighton but she had fallen for a successful furniture remover called Frank Hogg. Unfortunately for Mary, Frank was already married to Phoebe and he often told her that he had only married Phoebe because she was pregnant. Frank and Phoebe Styles lived with his mother and sister in Prince of Wales Drive in London. Mary lived close by in Priory Road.

It is probable that Frank and Mary had already started their relationship before he married Phoebe, and on at least one occasion Frank had seriously considered leaving England to escape the two women he had become involved with. After the marriage Frank still paid regular visits to Mary, always complaining about how miserable his marriage was and often talking about committing suicide.

Mary was determined to have Frank for herself and on 23 October 1890 she sent a note to Phoebe which said 'Dearest, come round this afternoon and bring our little darling, don't fail.' Phoebe did not reply and did not turn up. On the following day Mary sent another note via a local boy and this time Phoebe and her 18-month-old daughter accepted the invitation.

The two women knew one another quite well and Mary had actually sat with Phoebe when she miscarried Frank's second child. Phoebe could not possibly have guessed Mary's intentions.

Later that day a policeman on patrol in Crossfield Road, Hampstead, found the body of a woman lying among a pile of rubble. The woman's skull had been crushed and her head had almost been cut from her body. There was also a bloodstained pram nearby. How the link was quickly made is unknown, but Clara Hogg, Frank's sister, was instructed to come to the mortuary to identify the body. She brought Mary Pearcey along with her. It may be there that suspicions were aroused because Mary became hysterical when she saw the body.

On 25 October an even more tragic discovery was made on waste ground near the Finchley Road, about a mile from the scene of the other brutal murder. It was the body of Frank Hogg's daughter; she had been suffocated.

It did not take the police long to discover that Frank and Mary were having an affair. They arrived at Mary's house and immediately saw enough evidence to convince them that something sinister had happened in the house. They found a poker, covered with hair and blood, and a bloodstained knife, and there was blood up the walls and on the ceiling of the kitchen. Throughout the search Mary sat playing her piano and singing. When Mary was later searched they found blood on her underwear. She denied seeing Phoebe on the 24th and then changed her story and told the police that Phoebe had come to borrow some money but had asked her not to tell anyone.

The police had had a very easy job. Mary was not an efficient murderess. The body had been easily identified because Phoebe's undergarments were monogrammed PH. They were also able to rule out Frank Hogg as being in any way involved in the murder. They had found a note in Mary's house, written by Frank on 24 October, which read: 'Twenty past ten. Cannot stay.' This tied in with neighbours having heard screams coming from Mary's house earlier in the day and then, later that evening, seeing Mary wheeling a pram away. It later emerged that the child was still alive when it left Mary's house but had been suffocated by the weight of its own mother's body, which had been dumped in the pram by Mary.

Mary's trial was heard at the Old Bailey on 1 December 1890. Her defence counsel tried to convince the jury that she had been driven to the murder by a jealousy which had made her insane. The jury were unconvinced, largely due to the fact that Mary had killed Phoebe in the house and then had the presence of mind to abandon the bodies elsewhere. What was never considered was the fact that she had made no attempt to remove evidence from her house, and the fact that she had behaved so strangely when she viewed the corpse with Frank's sister. She was hanged for the murders on 23 December at Newgate Prison. It later emerged that her father had been hanged almost exactly 10 years before. Mary's last request was for a mysterious advertisement to be placed in a Madrid newspaper. The advertisement read 'M.E.C.P. Last wish of M.E.W. Have not betrayed.'

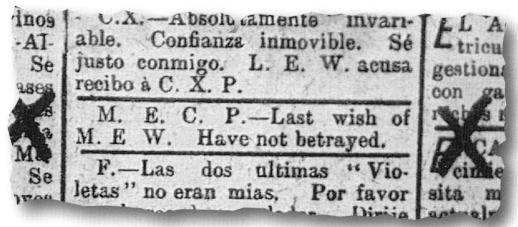

The strange newspaper advertisement, placed in a Madrid newspaper.

What was particularly striking about the case was the savagery of Phoebe's injuries. It drew close parallels with another contemporary case; that of the multiple murders in Whitechapel. The method of killing Phoebe matched exactly how it was believed Jack the Ripper killed his victims and, added to that, it was always believed that the Ripper killed in one place and then abandoned the body elsewhere.

* * * * *

The tragic tale of **Augusta Fulham** and Lieutenant Henry Lovell William Clark began at a regimental dance in Meerut, in British India, in 1910. Both were married, Augusta to a civil servant, Edward, and Henry to a nurse, Mary, who was somewhat older than himself and had borne him four children. Henry was 42 and a physician based in Agra. Augusta was a striking 36-year-old and their affair began with secret meetings and steamy love letters.

At Augusta's insistence Henry provided her with arsenic, which over a period of weeks she sprinkled on Edward's food. Edward was rushed into hospital and after a couple of days responded to treatment and was sent home, where he had a sudden relapse. This time he was sent to Henry's hospital in Agra and Henry Clark was able to deliver the final dose himself by giving Edward an injection. Henry even signed the death certificate, giving the cause of death as heat stroke.

Augusta and Henry's attention now turned to Mary Clark. Henry began poisoning her but his plans were foiled when she insisted on preparing her own food. More drastic action was required, which was arranged for 17 November 1912, when Henry hired four young men to break into his own home and murder his wife under the cover of a bungled robbery. Both Henry and Augusta had ensured they had alibis, but Inspector Smith was suspicious and questioned the Clarks' cook. He contradicted himself and finally confessed that on Henry's instructions he had let the four men into the house to murder Mrs Clark. More investigations by Smith revealed the link between Henry and Augusta. Foolishly Henry had not destroyed the hundreds of letters sent to him by Augusta, which referred to the planning of the murder of Edward.

Augusta was arrested first and admitted everything. Henry, still besotted with Augusta, and in the knowledge that she was carrying his child, was stunned just before the trial commenced when Augusta said 'He is the cause of all my trouble. He has poisoned and wrecked my life'.

Henry made a full confession at his trial and Augusta tried to place all of the blame on her lover. They both claimed that they had not intended to kill Edward and that they had only wished to make him ill enough to return to England. Henry said of the injection that he had only given it to Edward 'Out of pity, just to put an end to his misery'.

Augusta and Henry were found guilty of the murders and Henry was hanged on 26 March 1913. Augusta was indeed pregnant, and as a result she was reprieved, but after her child was born she died in May 1914.

* * * * *

Jealousy resulted in a triple murder in the Kent village of Matfield on a summer afternoon in wartime England. The victims were Dorothy Fisher, her 19-year-old daughter Freda, and their middle-aged maid, Charlotte Saunders. It was 9 July 1940 and when the Kent police made the gruesome discovery they called in the Flying Squad, led by Detective Chief Inspector Peter Beveridge. His first port of call was Walter Fisher's farm in Piddington in Oxfordshire. Walter and Freda had separated but from the very beginning the police realised that he still had a close attachment to his wife and daughter. Staying at the farm with Walter was **Florence Iris Ouida Ransom**, who preferred to be called Julia. It was clear to the police that she and Walter were lovers.

Fisher explained that Julia was a widow and that he had begun an affair with her shortly before the start of the war. Dorothy, his wife, had a Danish lover. They had lived together for some time, accommodating one another's new liaisons, but when their eldest daughter had got married Dorothy had moved to Matfield and Walter to Piddington.

Beveridge had already checked out the Danish man. Given the fact that he was an alien in wartime Britain it was especially difficult for him to move around the country, and the detective had already eliminated him as a suspect.

The servants at the farm were also interviewed and it became clear that they had little time for Julia. She had

Florence Ransom.

insisted that Walter take on extra staff, including a Mrs Guildford and her son, Fred. Unbeknown to Walter, Mrs Guildford was Julia's mother and Fred was her brother. Fred, it emerged, had been teaching his sister how to ride a bicycle and how to use a shot gun.

The police were able to begin to fit the pieces of the story together. They had found Dorothy Fisher's bicycle in a ditch at Matfield. They had also found a white pigskin glove in an orchard near where the bodies were found. Since Dorothy and Freda had been shot at close range, the police believed that they knew the murderer. It was surmised that the Fishers had taken this third person into the orchard to shoot rabbits and that the maid had been left in the house to prepare refreshments. The police had also turned up a number of witnesses, including a teenager from Matfield, who had seen a woman on a bicycle near the cottage on the day of the murders. He had described her as having auburn hair, a multi-coloured jumper and blue trousers. When Beveridge had first met Julia the description and the clothes were an exact match. A ticket collector at Tonbridge station also described a woman that he had seen getting off a train from London at about midday. She was carrying a long, thin parcel. He could also report that he had seen the same woman about four and a half hours later when she boarded the train back to London. There was even a taxi driver who came forward and said that he had dropped a woman matching the same description at Matfield, having picked up the fare from Tonbridge station.

Beveridge arrested Julia Ransom and several of the witnesses positively identified her. The glove also fitted her hand. A medical examiner discovered cuts and bruises on Julia's knees which circumstantially suggested that she had fallen off the bicycle and then abandoned it in the ditch.

In court her brother Fred confirmed that he had been teaching his sister how to use a shot gun and that she had borrowed it on 8 July 1940. She had returned it to him with instructions that it needed cleaning on 10 July, the day after the murder. The shot gun attack on the three women had been a frenzied affair and it appeared that Dorothy and Freda had been shot in the back. The murderer had continued to fire at the two bodies even after they were dead. As for Charlotte Saunders, she had been found dead on a path near to the cottage. Although she had been shot in the head, this was the only injury and the cause of death.

It was easy to surmise, therefore, that Ransom, in something of a frenzy, had pumped pellets into the bodies of Walter's family. Julia had made some attempt to make the killings look like the result of a bungled burglary and had ransacked some of the house, but it was later suggested that she was looking for mementoes kept by Dorothy and Freda of their husband and father.

When Ransom was put in the witness box at the trial she claimed to have no recollection of her movements on 9 July 1940. Whether this was true or a ruse to save her from the hangman's noose is unknown, but she was found guilty of the murders and sentenced to death. Before the sentence could be carried out psychiatric reports certified that she was insane and therefore could not be held responsible for her actions on that day. Consequently she was transferred into a mental asylum for life.

* * * * *

Shortly before the abolition of capital punishment the case of a woman whose crime was prompted by jealousy came to court. Her subsequent trial and execution seemed to pass the media by in comparison to the case of Ruth Ellis, some seven months later, and never captured the imagination of the public to the same extent.

Styllou Christofi was a 52-year-old Greek Cypriot who was hanged for the murder of her daughter-in-law just seven months before Ruth Ellis, the last woman to be hanged in England. Styllou had followed her son to England in 1953. In 1942 her son, Stavros, had left the poverty of the small, rural village in which he had been born by walking to

*Styllou Christofi,
hanged for the
murder of her
daughter-in-law.*

Nicosia. Here he worked as a waiter with the sole intention of saving enough money for the boat passage to London. By the time Stavros arrived in England he found himself in a position where well-trained staff were at something of a premium. Settling into a flat near Hampstead Heath with his girlfriend, Hella, he swiftly married and had three children. In the intervening 11 years since leaving his village he had barely seen his mother. This is, perhaps, what prompted Styllou to leave Cyprus, added to the fact that she had never seen her daughter-in-law or grandchildren. Equally, the situation was bleak in Cyprus. Successive olive crops had failed and it was agreed that Styllou should come to England, get a job and save up money in order to buy more land in Cyprus. Styllou left her husband, who she considered to be weak and unable to support her.

Styllou moved into the ground-floor flat in Hampstead in July 1953 to live with her

The body of Hella, strangled and burned by Styllou Christofi, as police sift through the remains

son Stavros and his German wife, Hella. It would have been a very different lifestyle for an illiterate woman from a peasant background. She found life very difficult in England, being unable to speak the language and not understanding the way her son and daughter-in-law ran their household. Not surprisingly, Styllou made life difficult for Stavros and Hella because of her entirely different perspectives on life. On two occasions Stavros found his mother alternative accommodation, but she caused so many problems for the owners of her lodgings that she never stayed for very long and returned each time to the Hampstead flat. She became increasingly jealous and critical of Hella, who worked in a fashion shop during the daytime, and one can only assume that Styllou's dominant nature caused indescribable conflict in the previously happy home.

Eventually Hella could take no more of her mother-in-law. She made plans to take the children for a holiday in Germany and made it clear to Stavros that when she returned Styllou should be back in Cyprus. Unfortunately for Hella, these plans never came to fruition.

On 28 July 1954, after Stavros had left for his evening job as a waiter at the Café de Paris in the West End, Styllou hit Hella over the head with an ash-plate from the kitchen stove. She then strangled her, soaked her body in petrol and set fire to her in the back garden. A neighbour, John Young, who was walking his dog at 11.45pm on that Wednesday, noticed the flames from the burning body and saw Styllou tending the fire. He assumed she was burning a tailor's dummy. He said 'All I could see was from the thighs down. The arms were raised and bent back at the elbow, like some of the models you see in shop windows. There was a strong smell of wax.'

Styllou herself raised the alarm at around 1am. She stopped a passing car driven by a Mr Burstoff, who was driving his wife home after closing up their restaurant, by shouting 'Please come. Fire burning. Children sleeping'. Mr and Mrs Burstoff went into the house and gardens and noticed the body; they called the police and when the officers arrived Styllou claimed that she had left Hella in the kitchen when she herself had gone to bed, but had woken up and smelled smoke. When she had gone to investigate, she had found Hella's body in the garden, smouldering away, and had attempted to save her by throwing water onto her face and body. When asked about the petrol smell she replied through an interpreter 'I did not make any use of petrol, but some few days previously some petrol spilled on the floor. I did not pay any attention to it. I stepped on it, and probably the smell was the result of that petrol. From this story I know nothing more.' The police officers, on searching the premises, found bloodstains in the kitchen, newspaper soaked in paraffin around the body itself and Hella's wedding ring wrapped in paper, hidden in Styllou's bedroom. In the dustbin outside the house the police also found one of the children's scarves, tied in a noose. Styllou had used this to strangle Hella.

Styllou was brought to trial at the Old Bailey on 25 October 1954. She pleaded not guilty but had been advised by her counsel to enter a plea of insanity. Styllou had apparently reacted strongly against this and had exclaimed 'I am a poor woman, of no education, but I am not a mad woman. Never. Never. Never.' In her defence she repeated the claims that she had gone to bed earlier than Hella and was awoken by the smell of smoke. She saw that Hella was missing and had run downstairs and seen a fire in the back yard. When she had investigated her daughter-in-law's bloody body was stretched out over the flames. She recounted how she had attempted to revive Hella and told that she had flagged down a car to help her. The police, however, had amassed a considerable amount of forensic evidence to suggest that Hella's death was far more complex. Even an attempt by the defence to prove to the jury that John Young could not have seen anything was something of a failure. They were all taken to Hampstead in darkness to look into the yard. This proved nothing one way or the other. The prosecution maintained that 53-year-old Styllou was a strong and powerful woman; her physical strength derived from her long years of toil on mountainsides in Cyprus. Forensic evidence suggested that she had repeatedly beaten Hella over the head with a cast-iron ash plate. The coroner reported that Hella's skull was fractured, that there were injuries to her face, bruising above the right ear and numerous scalp injuries consistent with heavy blows. Forensic investigation had also revealed that the ash plate was covered in Hella's blood. Chillingly, Hella was not dead as a result of this ferocious attack. Styllou had taken one of the children's scarves and made a knot in it and had then wrapped it around Hella's neck and throttled her to death. Styllou had made attempts to clean up the kitchen but the police had found blood on the lino and on the kitchen table legs. Styllou had then removed Hella's ring and hidden it in her room, after which she had attempted to set fire to the body in the yard. The trial lasted for four days and on 29 October the jury retired and after two hours returned a verdict of 'guilty'. The judge had no option but to sentence Styllou to be hanged.

The following month, on 30 November, the Court of Appeal dismissed Styllou's appeal against the conviction. There was even an attempt by several anti-capital punishment members of parliament to persuade the Home Secretary to cancel the execution on the grounds that Styllou was insane. With all avenues closed Styllou Christofi was executed at Holloway Prison on 13 December 1954.

The Home Secretary, Major Lloyd George, said of Christofi:

> If it appears to the Home Secretary in the case of a prisoner under sentence of
> death that there is reason to believe the prisoner to be insane, he must, under the

terms of Section 2 (4) of the Criminal Lunatics Act 1884, appoint two or more legally qualified medical practitioners to examine the prisoner and to enquire as to his sanity.

In view of the terms of the report by the Principal Medical Officer at Holloway Prison about Mrs Christofi, I appointed three distinguished and experienced doctors to conduct an enquiry in accordance with the statutory provision. The three doctors reported to me that the prisoner was not in their view insane, and they added that in their view she did not suffer from any minor mental abnormality which would justify them in making any recommendation on medical grounds relevant to the question of a reprieve.

It appears that no one was aware at the time that back in Cyprus in 1925 when Styllou was a young woman she had been acquitted of murdering her own mother-in-law. The death, it had been alleged, had been caused by Styllou ramming a burning torch down her mother-in-law's throat.

*   *   *   *   *

Like many of the women who have killed out of jealousy, the **Ruth Ellis** case illustrates that there is no great need for amazing detective work. It was clear from the outset that Ruth Ellis had gunned down David Blakely, but what was more stunning and scandalous was the reason behind her crime.

It was 9pm on Easter Sunday, 10 April 1955, when David Blakely and his friend, Clive Gunnell, emerged from the Magdala Tavern at the bottom of South Hill Park in Hampstead. They were heading for a party at Carol and Anthony Findlater's house in Tanza Road, a short distance away. As Blakely reached into his pocket for the keys to his car he

29 Tanza Road, Hampstead.

failed to notice Ruth Ellis standing in the shadows nearby with a revolver in her hand. She called out 'David'; he ignored her. She called out 'David' once more and this time Blakely turned and saw her pointing the gun straight at his chest. He attempted to hide behind the car but Ellis shot him twice, smearing his blood over the bodywork of the car. He screamed 'Clive' to his friend but Ellis said 'Get out of the way Clive'. As Blakely tried to escape she pumped three more shots into him, the last as she was standing over his dying body. Calmly Ellis then lifted the gun to her own head and pulled the trigger. The gun misfired and she lowered it and fired a shot into the pavement. Within seconds the street was filled with people, including an off-duty police constable, Alan Thompson. Ellis turned to him and said 'Fetch the police'. Thompson replied 'I am the police' and took the gun from her hand.

The story begins back in 1926 when Ruth Ellis was born on 9 October in Rhyl in Wales. Ruth was the fourth child of Arthur and Bertha Neilson. Her father was a professional musician and worked on transatlantic liners, operating in and out of Liverpool. Shortly before World War Two the family moved to Basingstoke and by 1941 they had moved to Southwark in London. Ruth began her working career as a machine minder in an Oxo factory, but at 17 she became a photographer's assistant and on her many assignments in the West End met and fell in love with a French-Canadian soldier. Unfortunately the man was married, but by the time he was posted back to Canada Ruth was pregnant with his son. With the help of her mother and elder sister Ruth was able to look for work as a model and often posed nude when required. At 19 she began working for Maurice Conley who owned a West End club and by all accounts he began putting trade Ruth's way. Ruth could earn more than £20 a week from her life on the edge of prostitution.

Ruth Ellis, the last woman to be hanged in England.

Carole and 'Ant' Findlater with Ruth and David in the Little Club.

During this time she met a Surrey dentist called George Johnston Ellis, a big-spending alcoholic. They married in November 1950 and moved to Southampton. However, her husband's drinking and her possessiveness meant for a violent marriage and it was over by the time their daughter, Georgina, was born in October 1951. Ruth moved back to London and she and Conley began working at the Steering Wheel Club in Brick Street, near Hyde Park Corner. By 9 October 1953 Conley had made Ruth the manageress of the Little Club in Knightsbridge. She and her children were living in a rent-free flat and Ellis was earning £25 a week.

She had met David Blakely and his friend Desmond Cussen in Brick Street and the two became regular clients at her new club. By November Blakely had moved into the flat with Ellis. Unfortunately Desmond Cussen had also fallen in love with Ruth Ellis but this was not the only problem. For the next two years Blakely and Ellis fell in and out of love with one another, punctuated by violence, heavy drinking and overwhelming jealousy.

Blakely had invested £7,000 in building a prototype racing car called 'The Emperor' and lived a glamorous, champagne-soaked life, despite his apparent lack of talent. Having got through the inheritance from his father, and an allowance from his stepfather, Blakely often borrowed from Ruth and caused considerable problems at the club. As a result, Conley sacked Ruth but it was Cussen who stepped in to save her and her children. He moved her into his flat in Devonshire Place and put much of his time and resources at her disposal.

Ruth's tempestuous relationship with Blakely continued and in the summer of 1954 it appeared that Blakely had finally disposed of his long-term fiancée, Linda Dawson, in order to marry Ruth. In less than three weeks Ruth discovered the ugly truth when she found love bites all over Blakely's back. They split up and then got back together again, and by January 1955 Cussen had acquired Ruth a flat in Kensington. Around this time Ruth fell pregnant with Blakely's child and despite the fact that her marriage to George was soon to be ended legally, Blakely did not offer to marry her. On the contrary, he beat her and punched her in the stomach, causing her to miscarry. By Easter they were back on good terms and they arranged to go to Blakely's friends, the Findlaters, on Good Friday, 7 April. Blakely left Ruth at Egerton Gardens, Kensington, and promised to return to take her to Hampstead that evening, but he never arrived. Instead he spent the evening in the Magdala Tavern telling his friends how much he wanted to break off his relationship with Ruth. The Findlaters had planned to have a party and Blakely decided to stay with them.

After the fatal shooting Ruth never once denied that she had deliberately travelled to Hampstead in order to kill Blakely. On 20 June she appeared at the number one court at the Central Criminal Court, at the Old Bailey, entering a plea of 'not guilty'. This plea was not entered because she wanted to deny having shot Blakely, but because she wanted the world to know why she had done it. Her potentially strong defence team had been paid for by the press but they were singularly unsuccessful in persuading Ruth to admit that she was demented with jealousy on that fateful weekend. Equally, the Findlaters did not think that there was anything strange about Ruth's repeated telephone calls to their house, or the fact that she had loudly demonstrated outside their home over that weekend. Inevitably, when the jury was finally sent out to consider their verdict, it took them just 14 minutes to return a 'guilty' verdict. Accordingly, Mr Justice Havers, the presiding judge, sentenced Ruth to hang on 13 July 1955. She was taken back to Holloway and refused her solicitor's pleas to appeal. Nevertheless they still wrote to the Home Secretary asking for the death sentence to be reduced to a prison term. Meanwhile petitions all around the country were being signed, including one with 50,000 names.

On a prison visit Ruth's brother, Granville, was asked by his sister to smuggle in a lethal drug so that she could kill herself. Instead he tried to discover how Ruth had got the gun and what her movements had been on that Easter Sunday. Ruth had always maintained that she had found the gun at the club. On the day before she was due to hang Ruth Ellis finally gave a sworn statement to her solicitors, telling them exactly what had happened. The statement revealed that she had been having an affair with Desmond Cussen and that they had been drinking in his flat and talking about Blakely. During the course of this conversation Cussen had given her a gun. On the previous day they had gone into Epping Forest for shooting practice. Cussen had even driven Ruth to Hampstead to kill Blakely. Cussen never admitted his role in the killing and it was only in this statement that Ruth implicated him.

The Magdala Tavern.

These revelations and the activities of her brother and solicitors came to nothing when Ruth was hanged at Holloway Prison at 9am on 13 July 1955. Her body was buried in the prison but her remains were exhumed and reburied at St Mary's Church, Amersham, Buckinghamshire in 1971. Shortly before the trial Ruth had written to Blakely's mother and had said 'I shall die loving your son. And you should feel content that his death has been repaid. Goodbye.'

* * * * *

Two tragic murder cases hit the headlines in 1980 and all three of the suspects in the trials must be considered to be victims in their own right. For their own different reasons they were driven to commit murder.

Wanda Chantler lived in a bungalow in the Welsh village of Pant Perthog with her husband Alan. They had built their home themselves and they loved the area and its seclusion and had brought up their two children in their isolated little world. After their sons had grown up they decided, foolishly, to sell up and move to Australia, where one of their boys had settled. It was a terrible mistake and by the late 1970s they were back in Wales. The Chantler's home was now owned by Roger and Josie Hartland. They too loved the house and had barely changed anything that the Chantlers had created.

Just three years after the transaction had been completed the Hartlands were stunned to see Wanda on their doorstep. She told them that things had not worked out in Australia and begged them to sell the bungalow back to her and her husband. Firmly, but politely, they told her that this was out of the question. Little did they know what was going on in Wanda's mind.

Her entire life had changed back in 1939 when at 17 her father had sent her from their home in Russia to a Berlin law school. When war broke out foreigners were rounded up by the Nazis and Wanda had found herself transferred into a prison full of young, fair-haired women. Initially they were not ill-treated but the camp doctors seemed especially interested in the inmate's health and physical appearance. Numerous medical tests were carried out on Wanda until it finally dawned on her that she had been transferred to a Nazi baby farm. We can only imagine the ordeals that she went through there until the end of World War Two when her husband Alan had rescued her. He had been among the Allied troops that had liberated the camp and he married Wanda and they moved to Britain together.

Clearly she had managed over the years to suppress what had happened in her subconscious mind, but now, she associated the Hartlands with the treatment that she had experienced 40 years before. She was consumed with anger and in her mind they were forcing her to relive a nightmare that she was unable to cope with. In her mind she could never be happy again until she was living back in her home.

Wanda enrolled at the Aberystwyth Rifle Club and learned how to fire weapons. Quickly she became very proficient and at the same time she wrote letters to the Hartlands. Gradually the words became more and more threatening and she even accused them of stealing family treasures that she had mistakenly left hidden under the bath. The Hartlands were getting very worried and contacted the police but since nothing had happened they took no action.

Alan was beginning to have his own fears about his wife's state of mind and believed that she was on the verge of a nervous breakdown. She only ever left the house to go to the gun club. He went to the police and told them that his wife was having mental problems and persuaded them to cancel her shot gun license. But as far as Wanda was concerned it was too late.

On Monday 16 June 1980, while Alan was doing the week's shopping, she slipped out of the house and drove to Pant Perthog. As she got out of the car she opened the boot and stuffed two air pistols into her belt and then brought out her double-barrelled shot gun. Calmly she walked up to the door and rang the bell. When the Hartlands looked through the door and saw Wanda standing there, armed to the teeth, they immediately rang Alan Chantler and shouted down the phone 'You've got to come quickly, she's got three guns'.

Roger Hartland was in the firing line; she shot him at point blank range. Josie Hartland fled out of the hall and into another room where she picked up another telephone and dialled 999. Precious seconds passed as she was transferred but before she could even speak to the police Wanda had shot her too and then finished her off with both barrels as she lay on the ground.

Wanda Chantler, on 24 October 1980, admitted that she had killed Josie and Roger Hartland and was committed to Broadmoor for an indefinite period. The judge, Justice Hodgson, clearly shocked by Wanda's story, was prompted to say 'Nobody could possibly have heard what we have here without feeling the most terrible compassion. In a sense, you are as much a victim of your Nazi experiences as the Hartlands were victims of that same horror.'

* * * * *

Annette and **Charlene Maw** were brought before Leeds Crown Court on 17 November 1980 for the killing of their brutal, alcoholic father, Thomas. The judge, Justice Smith, conceded that their life was 'a sad history' and went on to say 'it is also a very sad duty I have to perform because you deliberately and unlawfully stabbed and killed him'.

The two girls 'sad history' can be traced back to when they were small children. On numerous occasions they had seen their drunken and aggressive father beat their mother, Beryl, to a pulp more times than they cared to remember. They had lived in Bradford with their mother, father and younger brother, Bryn. Their mother had endured beatings that stretched back over 20 years, but it seems that she had always decided to stay with her husband for the sake of the children. As the court was to hear, Thomas Maw seemed to live to abuse his family. On one occasion, on his wedding anniversary, he and his wife had been driving home and he had stopped to proposition two prostitutes while his wife was still in the car. In full view of the two women he had punched Beryl squarely in the face when she had challenged him. He had killed the family rabbit in front of his children and then had made them eat it. On another occasion, when the children had found a frog in the back garden, he pushed a straw into its mouth and inflated the creature until it exploded.

On 27 March 1979 the turning point came. Typically, Thomas Maw was drunk. Annette and Charlene had begun to become targets of their father's aggression and both were determined that he would never touch them again. They knew what was likely to happen if their father continued drinking that night and so they decided to head off the situation by confronting him. They went into the front room and an argument broke out which led to Maw attacking Charlene. Annette sprang to her sister's defence and for the first time Maw experienced his family fighting back. The fight was not going the girls' way, and they attempted to find refuge upstairs, but their father grabbed Charlene on the stairs and she kicked him in the face. He lost his footing and they managed to make it into one of the bedrooms.

Maw hammered on the door until it caved in and they tried to calm him down but he launched another attack on them. The arrival of Beryl tipped the battle in favour of the two girls. She grabbed a mirror and smashed it over his head, rendering him unconscious.

The three women went downstairs to discuss what they should do next. Annette and Beryl wanted to kill him but Charlene favoured calling the police. In the event they decided to take the latter course of action, so Charlene put on her coat to go next door to make the telephone call. When she returned the three women went upstairs to see if Maw was still unconscious. As they crouched over him his hand shot out and grabbed Annette by the throat. Desperately Annette croaked 'Get a knife!' Charlene hesitated for a second and then ran down to the kitchen and brought up a cutlery knife. Annette jabbed it into her father's stomach but it snapped and she screamed 'A bigger one! Quick!' Again Charlene went down to the kitchen and this time she brought up the carving knife. Again Annette grabbed it and this time she plunged it into her father's neck. It severed his jugular and they were covered in his blood. His body twitched and the women's ordeal was over.

In court nine months later the murder charge was dropped and Annette and Charlene were found guilty of manslaughter. They were both sentenced to three years imprisonment. They appealed against the verdict but Annette's sentence was upheld and Charlene's imprisonment was reduced by six months. Their mother was not charged.

For many years the two girls and their mother had endured terror in their own home at the hands of their father. For the sake of their mother and in the event, for themselves, they had killed a monster who, in their eyes, deserved no mercy and certainly no love.

* * * * *

Christine English had tried almost everything to combat her moods of depression, loss of memory and insomnia. She suffered from what we now call pre-menstrual syndrome and this simply added a monthly trauma to her other problems. It seems that like many women she would suffer for at least a week a month from weight gain, blotchy skin, swelling, headaches and severe mood swings. Her boyfriend, Barry Kitson, was six years younger than her and used alcohol to drown his business troubles. For Barry drink was his great escape and after leaving his franchised bakery he would spend hours in the pub and then return to Christine and not be willing or able to listen to her problems. They seem to have had a tempestuous relationship, swinging from periods of tenderness and closeness to those of arguments and tension. Christine had tried transcendental meditation (TM), meditating for 15 minutes each morning in order to calm herself and gain some kind of balance. Meanwhile, Barry's drinking had begun to make him desperate and Christine offered him the opportunity to learn TM as it had helped her. He agreed, provided that she married him first.

When Christine and Barry awoke on the morning of 16 December 1980 the couple meditated together. As they sat over breakfast Barry announced 'I am going to meet another woman tonight'. For Christine this was a bombshell given the fact that she had begun to believe that they had finally found the way out of their troubles. She was determined to stop him at any cost.

As she sat at work over lunch Christine kept repeating to herself 'I am going to kill him. I am going to run him over and kill him'. By mid-afternoon Christine had told Barry's mother about what her son had said and what she intended to do about it.

When Barry arrived home that evening he was still determined to go ahead and meet this other woman. Christine kept repeating 'how can you do it, how can you?' to which Barry finally replied 'I have had enough of this. I am off.' Barry made for the Live and Let Live pub and it was not long before Christine had found him and tried to persuade him to come home. Barry was embarrassed at this public scene in front of his friends but determined to carry through his plans for the evening. Strangely, Christine said to him 'Well. If you won't come home, I'll drive you there.'

Christine still hoped that her presence would deflect Barry from his purpose. By the time she pulled up outside the pub where Barry claimed he had arranged to meet another woman, she was shaking with tension. After 30 minutes Barry emerged and got back into the car; Christine was triumphant. Either the other woman had failed to appear or Barry's attempts to chat someone up had not worked. By now Christine had a throbbing headache; she felt dizzy and had the sensation of bright lights being shined into her eyes. Nevertheless, she kept sneering at Barry and insulting him, until he finally grabbed her hair and slapped her as she was driving. Christine pulled the car over and began to fight back. She really wanted him to pay for what he had put her through.

They continued slapping and punching one another then suddenly Barry noticed that they were near another one of his favourite pubs. He extricated himself from the struggle, got out of the car and slammed the door behind him. As he walked away he shouted 'Leave me alone or I'll call the cops'. Christine's anger was still welling up inside her and she recalled her threats earlier in the day. She started up the car and drove after him. Just as she was about to run him down, she pulled away and cruised Colchester to calm her nerves. She drove round and round and round, knowing that inevitably Barry would soon be staggering out of one of the pubs on his way back home. Her PMS had heightened her tension and pain and desperately she fought its effects. Finally she saw Barry and pulled over and picked him up.

Immediately they began arguing again; he hit her and then hit her again. The fight seemed to be getting them nowhere until Barry said 'I never want to see you again'. With that he climbed out of the car again and stalked off. This time Christine could not control herself. She pushed down the accelerator and raced towards the disappearing figure of Barry.

As the car hit him Christine seemed to snap out of her trance and when she got out of the car she saw Barry pinned between the car and a lamp post, with his right leg almost severed. He pleaded 'Get it off me, get it off me'. When Christine realised what she had done she became hysterical, but for Barry it was too late. He languished in hospital for two weeks before dying and on 10 November 1981 Christine English found herself before Justice Perchas at Norwich Crown Court. She pleaded guilty to manslaughter on the grounds of diminished responsibility.

The judge, in giving Christine a conditional discharge, recognised that PMS, coupled with the circumstances of the death, were sufficient mitigating circumstances to let her walk free.

* * * * *

It would appear that age does not calm overwhelming feelings of jealousy or stop women from reacting against their feelings of rejection. **Pamela Megginson**, a grandmother of two, at the age of 61, killed her 79-year-old lover. Apparently the man, Alec Hubbers, was a well-known womaniser, but he and Megginson had been lovers for some time. They were making love in their luxury holiday home in the south of France in 1982 when Hubbers informed Megginson that he was ending their relationship and replacing her with a younger woman. Megginson was so enraged that she started to attack him with a champagne bottle and ended up battering him to death. Apparently she was afraid that losing him would reduce her income greatly and thus change the lifestyle she had become accustomed to. She was sentenced to life imprisonment at the Old Bailey for the murder of her self-made millionaire lover.

* * * * *

Jealousy of another woman can provide sufficient motive for murder. What then if the other woman is a relative? Worse, what then if she is your sister? Better still, your twin sister. This was the situation that **Gillian Philpott** found herself in after having married Graham. Her new husband was considerably older; he was 45, divorced and had three children. They had lived together for five years, he was Gillian's boss at the bank and they lived in a respectable area in Orpington in Kent. Gillian was a 21-year-old clerk in the bank, and was described as attractive, immaculately dressed and a very friendly and approachable person.

While life looked rosy for Gillian and Graham, their peace was to be interrupted a few days before the wedding by the arrival of Gillian's twin sister, Janet. They were not quite identical twins; if anything Janet was the slightly more sophisticated of the two. She seemed more worldly and Graham was immediately attracted to her. Janet had arrived to attend the wedding in the aftermath of ending a rather turbulent love affair.

When Gillian suggested to Graham that her sister should accompany them on their honeymoon in Bali, she was delighted when he agreed. On the honeymoon they ate together, went on excursions and walked barefoot along the beaches. Graham found himself continually comparing the two sisters; there seemed much about Janet that he preferred.

When the honeymoon ended and they returned to England, Graham became obsessed with Janet. Sometime after their return Janet asked whether she could stay with Gillian and Graham. When Graham, later, had the opportunity to take both of the girls out to a party, no sooner had Gillian wandered off to talk to someone, than Graham took the chance of dancing with Janet. For Graham this dance confirmed everything that he had tried to suppress, but it was obvious that Janet felt rather uncomfortable about her brother-in-law's attentions. Later Graham taped a message to Janet which said:

> It was the first time I really had an opportunity of dancing with you the way I really wanted to. God, I can feel it now. I think it is probably the best way I have ever danced. I was moving to the way your body was moving and I was certainly responding the way you were. If anyone was watching my eyes they must have known I was so in love with you.

Gillian had noticed and by December 1989, although she had never seen her husband in a compromising situation with her sister, she was sure that they were having an affair. When Gillian asked Janet outright, she denied it and told her sister that she thought Graham probably just had a crush on her. Gradually Gillian began to believe that her sister was lying to her. When Janet and Graham went out Christmas shopping together Gillian decided to search her sister's bedroom. She found a Christmas card which read 'To my darling, I wish you every happiness at Christmas. I am so fortunate to spend my life with you always.' Gillian was determined to confront them as soon as they came home.

The conversation did not go as Gillian had planned. Gillian announced 'She has got to go' and Graham responded 'Then you will have to go as well'. 'Please love me. Not her' Gillian pleaded. At this stage Janet ran upstairs to pack her belongings. Gillian continued 'Have all the affairs you want, if I don't satisfy you. But you'll never find another woman who would do all the things I did for you. I'll do anything you want to make our marriage work. You must believe me. I love you so much'. Graham simply replied 'I want a divorce from you.'

Janet fled the house but could not escape Graham's continued obsessive attention. He sent her cards and messages, while at home there was a frosty silence from Gillian. They hardly talked but tried to maintain a façade of normality to the outside world. On 30 December they went to neighbours for a party together and Graham had told a friend there 'We are thinking of going to Bali for a second honeymoon'. By the end of the evening both Gillian and Graham were hopelessly drunk and they staggered into their house at 2.30am the following morning. It was time for another argument. Graham repeated that he wanted a divorce. Gillian pleaded to share a bed with him but Graham told her that he didn't want her. Desperately Gillian told her husband that she was even prepared to allow Graham to sleep with Janet under the same roof, as long as they remained married. The argument abruptly turned to money and Graham told Gillian that he intended to keep the house and that she could go wherever she wanted, but that she could take nothing with her.

Almost instinctively Gillian began twisting a dressing gown cord around her fist. Graham began to sway in his drunkenness and anger and stumbled forward, grabbing Gillian by the neck to steady himself. In an instant she wrapped the cord around his neck and pulled it tighter and tighter until his eyes began to protrude. With one last wrench of the cord he slumped to the floor. Drawing great strength from somewhere, Gillian dragged Graham's body to the landing and tied a longer piece of cord around his neck. She secured the other end to the banister, then she gradually eased Graham's body to an upright position, before tipping him over the banister. With cool presence of mind Gillian wrote a joint suicide note which read:

> We couldn't live separately. We wanted to die together. Please keep us together –
> I beg of you. We love one another so much.

With that Gillian collected a bottle of whisky and a bottle of aspirin and slumped onto the bed. She tipped the whole bottle of pills into her mouth and took a swig of whisky. Unfortunately it did not have the desired effect and within a few minutes she had vomited her suicide mixture. She was still determined to kill herself.

By the early morning of 31 December 1990 Gillian had driven her car to Beachy Head and was roaring across the grass near the cliff edge. The car pitched over and the last thing Gillian felt was her head hitting the steering wheel. Incredibly, when two policemen climbed down to inspect the car, they discovered that Gillian had only sustained superficial injuries. The car had only plunged down 20 feet and had landed on a ledge.

Gillian Philpott was found guilty of the manslaughter of Graham Philpott at the Old Bailey in January 1991. Despite Gillian's attempts to make his death appear to be part of a suicide pact, forensic evidence clearly pointed to murder. Gillian was sentenced to just two years imprisonment. Despite Graham's obsession with Janet, she maintained throughout that she had never slept with her sister's husband.

* * * * *

On 10 May 1991 **Yvonne Sleightholme** was jailed for life at Leeds Crown Court by Justice Waite. He concluded 'When your fiancé broke off the engagement and married another woman you wrought on the newly married couple a terrible revenge. You planned in cold fury and executed with ruthless precision the killing of your rival'.

Yvonne had met William Smith on New Year's Eve 1979. He ran Broat's Farm in North Yorkshire. After an 18-month courtship which had culminated in Yvonne moving into the farm, William began to realise that he did not love Yvonne but had become reliant upon her. Reluctantly he told her that as far as he was concerned their relationship was over. But Yvonne was not prepared to give up William so easily.

Several weeks after their separation, Yvonne told William that she had contracted leukaemia and that she considered that it was his fault. William was forced by guilt to rekindle their courtship but within weeks of getting back together with Yvonne all signs of the leukaemia had disappeared and Yvonne was planning their marriage. She had set the date for six months in the future to give her time to organise the event. Unfortunately on one of his many visits to the tailors, to have his morning suit fitted, William bumped into an old friend called Jayne Wilford. They had had a relationship in the past and when she had heard of his impending marriage, Jayne had deliberately sought him out to try to persuade him not to marry Yvonne.

Yvonne continued to plan while William had increasing doubts. Then Yvonne fell pregnant, but tragically she lost the baby through a miscarriage. By now William had rekindled a sexual relationship with Jayne, but he still felt guilt when he told Yvonne that he had fallen for another woman. Reluctantly the devastated Yvonne left the farm once again and within a few months Jayne moved in with William. If either Jayne or William thought that Yvonne would give up, then they were both mistaken.

After Jayne and William were married in May 1988, they began to receive a series of threatening phone calls and they thought they could recognise the voice. Soon after someone set fire to their barn and then they received a wreath with a message saying 'Jayne. I'll always remember you'. William informed the police and seemed satisfied that Yvonne had had nothing to do with any of the incidents. Indeed, shortly after this Yvonne had found a new boyfriend, an ambulance driver called Anthony Berry. He was not William, however, and Yvonne was apparently determined to make Jayne pay for taking her man.

On 13 December, a Tuesday, Yvonne knew that William would leave the farm early to play football. She drove to Broat's Farm, parked and waited for William to leave. She saw him drive away, waited 10 minutes and then walked across the yard and as she reached the farmhouse door, she pulled a rifle out from underneath her anorak. She pressed the doorbell and Jayne hurried to open the door. Calmly Yvonne levelled the gun at Jayne and gestured to her to come into the yard. She then put a bullet in her rival's head. Crouching to pull off Jayne's wedding ring, Yvonne then ripped open Jayne's nursing tunic. She pulled Jayne's dress down and undid her bra and then bruised her upper body in several places. Yvonne then virtually stripped Jayne's body and removed her underwear in order to make it look as if Jayne had been sexually attacked.

Almost 24 hours later, in Anthony's arms, Yvonne admitted what she had done the day before. Nevertheless the police were perplexed. It seemed to them that Jayne's killer had raped her and must have been a man, but locals believed that the killer had to be Yvonne. Certainly when the police interviewed Yvonne she appeared shocked and cried when told of Jayne's death. The police finally began to look more deeply into Yvonne's relationship with William, which prompted them to carry out forensic tests on her car. Here they found bloodstains which matched Jayne's blood group and they also discovered that Yvonne had not spent the night of 13 December in a cottage on the Scottish Borders as she had claimed. Jayne's wedding ring was never recovered but shortly before her burial William purchased an identical ring from the same jewellers and paid a last, sad visit to his wife's body to place the replica on Jayne's finger.

CHAPTER SEVEN

A BITTER PILL

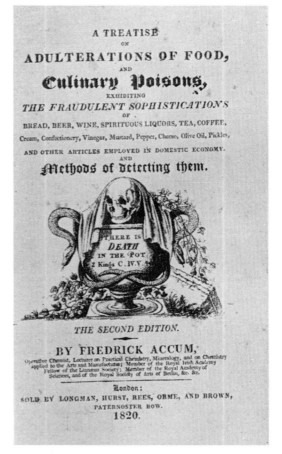

The title page of Accum's first edition.

Research into murders carried out by women has always suggested that poison is the preferred method. Certainly the vast numbers of women that have resorted to poisoning their husbands, lovers or other people seem to bear this out. It has also been suggested that the reason behind this popular form of killing is the fact that poisoning does not require any physical strength on the part of the woman. It does, however, require great psychological strength to watch a former loved one suffer this agonising death.

* * * * *

MARY CHANNEL was the daughter of a well-respected family who lived near Dorchester in Dorset. She was considered by many to be something of a beauty, very imaginative, polite, graceful and witty. She attracted the attention of many potential suitors, one of whom was Mr Channel, a grocer in Dorchester. By all accounts his only attractive feature was his wealth. He was described as a very ungainly man and somewhat ugly. Mary was not in the remotest bit interested in Mr Channel, but her father considered him to be a good match. Under severe pressure from her parents she eventually agreed to marry Channel but it soon became very clear that she wished to rid herself of her new husband at the earliest possible opportunity.

She sent her maid to a chemist to buy white mercury, claiming that this was to deal

130

with rats and mice. As soon as she had the poison she made some rice milk and added the mercury to it. She served it to her husband for his breakfast but he seems to have thought that it tasted rather strange and firstly offered it to his wife's brother to try. But Mary interceded and stopped it. Her husband then asked her maid to try it but just before she could lift it to her lips Mary took the cup away from her.

Within a day or two her husband's body had begun to swell and a doctor was convinced that he had been poisoned. Suspicion immediately fell on Mary and after her husband died she was committed for murder at the Dorchester Assizes.

Given the evidence and public opinion against her, she was sentenced to be burned at the stake. The sentence was carried out in April 1703 when Mary was just 18 years old.

* * * * *

Elizabeth Mason worked as a maid for her godmother. It was her intention to ensure that she inherited the estate of Jane Scoles after she had died. Elizabeth, it seems, was keen to bring this event forward as much as possible, and so she purchased some arsenic from a local chemist and sprinkled it into some coffee that she served to Jane. Elizabeth obviously put a considerable amount of the poison into the coffee because Jane was dead within hours. It was Easter 1712 but Elizabeth's job was not yet done.

Jane had a close friend called Mrs Cholwell whom she suspected would be the beneficiary of her godmother's estate. Somehow Elizabeth contrived to introduce arsenic into Mrs Cholwell's body as well, but the same chemist who had sold Elizabeth the yellow arsenic only days before managed to save the life of Mrs Cholwell. It did not take a great leap of intelligence to link the sale of the yellow arsenic to the death of Jane and the illness of Mrs Cholwell.

Consequently Elizabeth was arrested and tried on 6 June 1712. She made a full confession and was executed at Tyburn on 18 June.

* * * * *

The case of **Amy Hutchinson**, who was executed at Ely on 7 November 1750 for the murder of her husband, is particularly remembered for her advice to other women that might find themselves in a similar situation to her own. She left the following in the hands of a clergyman shortly before she was hanged:

All the good I can do now, after my repentance and abhorrence of my abominable crime, and prayers to God, is;

First; to warn all young women to acquaint their friends when any addresses are made to them; and, above all, if any base or immodest man dare to insult you, with anything shocking to chaste ears

Secondly; that they should never leave the person that they are engaged to in a pet, nor wed another to whom they are indifferent, in spite; for if they come together without affection, the smallest matter will separate them

Thirdly; that being married, all persons should mutually love, forgive and forebear, and afford no room for busy meddlers to raise and ferment jealousy between two who should be one.

Amy was just 16 when she fell in love and it seems that the man took full advantage of her affection. Clearly, from what little we do know about Amy, she allowed the man into her bed, but he let her down and moved to London, promising that when he returned he would marry her. Amy was distraught but her father was delighted as he had never approved of the young man. Obviously in an emotional state Amy very quickly accepted a marriage proposal from John Hutchinson, a man she had never really liked. She married him the day after she had agreed to become his wife.

Tragically Amy's original lover returned from London to see her on the arm of John, emerging from the church. This must have had a marked impact on Amy because only a few days into their marriage she admitted to her husband that she had slept with the other man. Hutchinson was beside himself with anger and jealousy and often beat Amy. He also turned to drink.

Very quickly Amy resumed her liaison with the other man and resolved to poison her husband. There was ample opportunity to slip the arsenic into John Hutchinson's ale, which she did. Having administered the dose she went to meet her lover and told him about what she had done and he advised her to buy more poison in case the dose that she had given John was not sufficient to kill him. In the event it was and he died the following day. His body was buried on the next Sunday.

It seems that Amy and her lover were very indiscreet and it did not take long before gossips had conveyed their suspicions to the coroner, resulting in the exhumation of John Hutchinson's body. A post-mortem was carried out and it was established that the cause of death had been poisoning by arsenic. This view was supported by the coroner's jury and consequently Amy was arrested and imprisoned in Ely. The evidence was overwhelming and she was hanged on 7 November 1750.

* * * * *

Mary Blandy, convicted of poisoning her father with arsenic. Seen here wearing chains.

The charge against **Mary Blandy** stated that she:

... knowingly, wilfully and feloniously, and of your malice aforethought, mix, and mingle certain deadly poison to wit, white arsenic, in certain tea, which had been at diverse times, during the time above specified, prepared for the use of the said Francis Blandy, to be drank by him...

Mary Blandy pleaded not guilty on 29 February 1752 at the Oxford Assizes to the charge that she had murdered her father, Francis Blandy, who had been so passionately fond of her.

Francis Blandy, an attorney at law, had, by all accounts, been a doting father and six years earlier had selfishly considered that it was time his daughter found a husband. He had bestowed a £10,000 dowry on Mary.

Unfortunately for Francis, Mary had met and fallen in love with one Captain William Henry Cranstoun, who, it would seem, had heard of the amount of the dowry and 'fallen in love' with Mary. Despite the fact that Cranstoun was a married man with children, he proposed to Mary and she accepted. When Francis found out he was horrified and realised what a bad match Cranstoun was for his daughter. He forbad her to see him again.

Apparently Cranstoun attempted to have his marriage annulled and persuaded his wife to give him a letter stating that the ceremony had never actually taken place. He claimed to her that his career in the army would be more successful if he could prove that he had no family ties; apparently the wife believed this claim and wrote him the required statement.

Secretly Mary and Cranstoun continued to communicate through letters and during the course of these writings they decided that the only way they could be together was to get rid of Francis Blandy.

In order to set the scene in the household, Mary began to tell her servants, friends and neighbours that she had heard music in the house and had seen apparitions. She wanted people to believe that she could see into the future and start to think that maybe the death of her father was imminent. While this scene-setting was going on in the house in Oxford, Cranstoun was making enquiries about types of poison and trying to think of a good way of sending it to Mary through the post. Presumably they felt it was too dangerous for Mary to be witnessed buying the poison in her local area, and finally it was decided that Cranstoun would send it disguised as Scottish pebbles and powder to clean them.

Mary began adding the arsenic to her father's tea. Francis Blandy began to complain of feeling unwell. He said he had developed pains in his bowels, was retching and feeling sick, and his teeth had started dropping out whole from their sockets. In June 1751 Francis Blandy left some of his tea and Ann Emmet, a charwoman at the house, drank some. She became violently ill and to show her concern for the woman's well-being Mary sent her some sack whey and thin mutton broth – exactly what a doctor would have prescribed for the condition.

Soon afterwards, Susan Gunnell, another employee, stole some of the tea and after drinking it she, too, became ill. This frightened Mary who wrote and asked the Cranstoun's advice. He suggested that she mix it with 'a more thickish liquid' and Mary began adding it to her father's water gruel. She did, however, take the precaution of warning Susan Gunnell not to take any as she had been so ill. She even spoke to Betty Binfield, another household servant, and asked her to make sure that Susan Gunnell ate no gruel.

On the 18 July Cranstoun wrote to Mary:

> I am sorry there are such occasions to clean your pebbles; you must make use of the powder to them, by putting it in anything of substance, wherein it will not swim a-top of the water, of which I wrote to you of in one of my last. I am afraid it will be too weak to take off their rust or at least it will take too long a time.

*Captain William
Henry Cranstoun.
He helped Mary
Blandy to poison
her father.*

Mary followed his advice and doubled the dose she was administering to her father. Francis grew worse and Mary told the servants that he had complained of a 'fireball in his stomach'.

On Saturday 3 August Susan Gunnell made her master a pan of water gruel and placed it in the pantry for use throughout the next few days. On the Monday Mary added some poison to the gruel, but afraid that she had been witnessed doing so, she told the servants 'I have been into the pantry and after stirring Papa's water gruel, I have eaten the oatmeal at the bottom'.

Francis Blandy had scarcely swallowed the gruel when he was taken violently ill and this continued through until the following day, the man being wracked by griping pains, purging and vomiting. Mary ordered another bowl to be prepared for him on the Tuesday and she took it upstairs to his room and fed him with it herself. He had drunk about half of it when he became seized from head to foot with the most violent pricking pains and continual retching and vomiting.

On the Wednesday Mary attempted to feed her father more of the gruel but he refused, saying that it tasted strange. Mary offered to make him more gruel but again Francis refused and asked that Susan Gunnell make it. When Susan went to throw away the old gruel, as she tipped the pan she saw white powder in the bottom of it. She took the pan to a neighbour, Mrs Mounteney, who immediately went to the local apothecary. The chemist, also suspicious of the nature of the white powder, took the pan to the local physician who found it to be white arsenic.

Susan Gunnell told Francis Blandy what had been happening. Apparently Mary's father, still showing his doting nature, cried out 'Poor love-sick girl. What will not a woman do for the man she loves? But who do you think gave her the powder?' Susan Gunnell suggested to her master that it could have been Captain Cranstoun, to which Francis Blandy replied 'I always thought there was mischief in those cursed Scotch pebbles'. Susan Gunnell had also, apparently, extracted some papers that Mary had been attempting to burn in the fire grate. They were smeared with what was later proved to be white arsenic and were in Captain Cranstoun's handwriting.

Francis Blandy died the following Wednesday afternoon and Mary Blandy was arrested, tried at Oxford Assizes and sentenced to death. On Monday 6 April 1752, the day of her execution, she was said to be serene and composed. Her execution was watched by 5,000 people and Mary made a statement saying that she was unaware that the powder was noxious or poisonous and she had no intention of hurting, much less destroying, her father by giving him the powder. Apparently, at the time of her trial, it was said of Mary Blandy:

> A crime so shocking in its own nature and so aggravated in all its circumstances, as will justly render her infamous to the latest posterity and make our children's

children, when they read the horrid tale of this day, blush to think that such an inhuman creature ever had an existence.

Throughout her trial Mary had claimed that Cranstoun had given her the powders which he had described as being a love philtre, designed to make her father like him. It is significant that Cranstoun made himself scarce and no sooner had Mary been arrested for the murder of her father, than he ran off to France. He died six months later. It is also significant that although Mary's father had offered a dowry of £10,000, the true value of his estate on his death amounted to just £4,000.

* * * * *

A straightforward arsenic poisoning of a husband in 1752 would not have attracted the attention of the public had it not been for the fact that the accused were self-confessed lesbians. This was a shocking and appalling admission to make in those times and not likely to engender any sympathy from a court. **Ann Whale** had been born in Horsham, Sussex. Her father died when she was young and she did not seem to have had a good relationship with her mother. Indeed, as a teenager she had run away from home and had fallen in with some very undesirable characters. Her mother managed to persuade her to return home and a truce of sorts was concluded.

Her mother set about finding her a husband that could control her wicked ways and presently found the man she was looking for in the form of James Whale. Ann was a good enough catch for James as she was about to inherit £80 from a deceased relative. They married and moved to Steepwood, but eventually settled in lodgings in Horsham with **Sarah Pledge**.

Sarah lived alone and from the outset was obviously attracted to James and tried unsuccessfully to seduce him. James told Sarah that not only was he not interested but she should also stay away from their part of the house. Sarah's quest for companionship and love was not to be denied and she turned her attentions towards Ann, who, it seems, was much more receptive. They became lovers, but their minds soon turned towards disposing of James so that they could live more openly together.

At first they tried roasted spiders in his beer, but this proved ineffective. So Sarah paid a visit to a chemist in Horsham and purchased some arsenic. Ann prepared a very special supper for her husband that night.

James died in agony the next day, but tongues were already wagging and after his body was examined by a local surgeon the case was referred to the coroner. Arsenic poisoning was the clear cause of death and the jury returned a verdict of wilful murder, sealing the fate of the two lovers.

They were imprisoned in Horsham jail and later made confessions which corroborated the facts of their relationship and their plot to murder James Whale. They were consequently sentenced to be hanged on 14 August 1752, but their reactions to the sentence were entirely different. Ann accepted her fate and seemed genuinely regretful that she had been party to the murder. Sarah, on the other hand, swore that she would fight the hangman if he came anywhere near her. Their methods of execution were to be different according to the law. Whereas Sarah Pledge was hanged, Ann, at just 21 years old, was first strangled and then burned.

* * * * *

A very similar heterosexual case occurred in the following year. **Ann Williams** had fallen in love with her own butler and administered white mercury to her husband through his food. The dose was sufficient to kill him the following day but not before he had been seen by his doctor, to whom he confided his belief that his wife had poisoned him. He had also told the doctor that he suspected that Ann was committing adultery with one of the servants. No sooner had Ann Williams's husband died than she was arrested for his murder and she was burned at the stake in Gloucester.

* * * * *

The 18th century had not been kind to the Scottish Ogilvie family. Lord Ogilvie had been imprisoned in Edinburgh Castle after the defeat of Bonnie Prince Charlie at Culloden. In 1748 their eldest son had committed suicide. The family now relied on the fortunes of Thomas and Patrick. Thomas was nearly 40 when he met 19-year-old **Katharine Nairn**, the daughter of Sir Thomas Nairn. The younger son, Patrick, was a lieutenant in the 89th Regiment of Foot and had just been invalided home from the East Indies. The third remaining son, Alexander, was already written off after having married a commoner in Edinburgh after his medical studies had ended in failure.

Thomas Ogilvie married the beautiful Katharine on 30 January 1765 and they moved into the family home of Eastmiln in Forfar. All remained calm until March. A new arrival at the house was Ann Clarke, to whom Katharine confided her dislike of her new husband. By 19 May it was clear that Katharine had begun a relationship with Thomas's brother, Patrick. By the 23rd, despite indignantly denying any interest in Thomas's wife, the brothers had a blazing row which led to Thomas dismissing Patrick from the house. He went to live about three miles away. It seems clear, however, that they continued to see one another and Ann was later to claim that Thomas was prepared to leave the family home so that Patrick could be with Katharine as, as far as he was concerned, their marriage was over.

Katharine and Patrick had continued to meet secretly. She had begged Patrick to come back but he refused, although he did promise to perform another service for her. He undertook to obtain some poison and on 31 May he bought a glass phial of laudanum of between half an ounce and an ounce from a friend, Dr Carnegie, when they met for a meal at an inn in Brechin. Three days later he met with his brother-in-law, Andrew Stuart, and arranged for the man to deliver the poison to Katharine, telling him that they were medicines for his sister-in-law.

On Wednesday 5 June Andrew Stuart delivered the 'medicines' to Eastmiln and met with Ann Clarke to whom he privately handed the package. He explained that he had been asked to bring the parcel of medicines for Katharine but Ann explained to him that she was afraid for Thomas Ogilvie's life. Ann also voiced her fears to Thomas and Patrick's mother.

That night the family members, Thomas, Katharine, Andrew and Ann ate together at a pub in the Kirkton of Glenisla and on their return home Ann warned Thomas of her suspicions against Katharine. It seems that he did not take any significant notice of her but promised that he would not take food or drink from Katharine's hands. Thomas and Katharine retired early and at the insistence of Ann, Andrew and Thomas's mother considered searching for the packet which had arrived during the day. In the event they decided against it and on the following morning Thomas felt unwell and did not rise in time for breakfast. Katharine prepared him a bowl of tea from the teapot and she mixed the tea with the poisons en route to the bedroom. Thomas drank the tea, rose, dressed and went out on visits in a normal state of health.

Within the hour he became ill with retching and vomiting and was taken home and put to bed. Initially he was tended by Katharine, who tried to exclude everyone from bothering her husband. Apart from the vomiting and purging Thomas complained of heartburn, pain in his legs and a terrible thirst. Ann gave him water and beer and later a glass of wine but he couldn't keep any of it down. He was convinced that his wife had poisoned him and when he saw one of the servants offering a drink of water from the same bowl that he had drunk the tea from that morning, he shouted 'Damn that bowl! For I have got my death in it already.' Anyone who did manage to get into the room he told that he had been poisoned. At length he died at around midnight, just four months after he had been married.

Rather belatedly Dr Meik arrived and later remarked that Katharine appeared to be very upset about her husband's death. He could draw no conclusions as to what had killed Thomas.

Despite Ann's suspicions, the following morning there was no clear proof of what had happened and even when she noticed some residue at the bottom of the tea bowl and mixed it with broth to give to one of the dogs, nothing happened to the animal.

Thomas's funeral was organised for Tuesday 11 June, but there were many matters to be settled before then. When Alexander Ogilvie arrived on the morning of the funeral he refused to allow his brother's body to be buried and demanded that Dr Meik and Dr Ramsay carry out a post-mortem. No one seemed to object and the sheriff attended the post-mortem. As a result of the finding Katharine and Patrick were arrested on Friday 14 June and sent to Forfar jail.

Alexander was already assuming that he was the new laird, with one brother dead and the other doomed. Katharine and Patrick were taken to Edinburgh on 21 June and committed for trial. There was huge public interest in the murder and at one stage it seemed that the two of them might be lynched by a mob.

The trial commenced at the High Court of Justiciary in Edinburgh on 5 August 1765 before Lord Justice-Clerk Sir Gilbert Elliot and five other lords. Katharine and Patrick Ogilvie were brought before the court on the charge of incest and murder. The circumstantial evidence was overwhelming and the inevitable outcome was that both were found guilty of conspiring to murder Thomas Ogilvie.

Patrick was sentenced to be executed in the Grassmarket on 13 November 1765, having delayed his original date of 25 September after a failed appeal.

As for Katharine, as a pregnant woman, her sentence was delayed until 10 March 1766. Katharine gave birth to a daughter on 27 February, and when the court met again on 10 March to consider her death sentence, a doctor and two nurses proclaimed her unfit to attend. The decision was delayed for another week, but at 7pm on Saturday 15 March she managed to escape. Her disappearance was not discovered until the Sunday afternoon. She had dressed herself as a man, quite probably in a uniform of the 89th Regiment of Foot, and had calmly walked through the prison and to freedom. On 17 Monday 100 guineas was offered for her capture and a further 100 was added on 22 March. But the bird had flown.

She had been accompanied by a servant and had reached Haddington by midnight on the Saturday of her escape. By Wednesday, still dressed as an officer, she was in Dover but had failed to get on board a ship to France. She returned to London and then made for Gravesend, where she paid eight guineas to a captain to take her to Calais. She even promised to pay him a guinea a day to wait for her in Calais for four days and then bring her back to England. Of course she had not returned to the boat but she had given herself another four days before the captain would report her missing.

It is believed that Katharine left France and settled in America, where she married a Dutchman. Alternative stories say that she stayed in France and later returned to England before she died. Her daughter, tragically, died at the age of two months.

As for Alexander Ogilvie, he was arrested for bigamy on 1 March 1766 and given two months to settle his affairs in Scotland before being banished for seven years. In the event, he either accidentally died or committed suicide when he fell out of a window.

* * * * *

Mary Bateman was born Mary Harker in Aisenby, Yorkshire, in 1768. It seems that she carried out her first crime at the tender age of five, when she stole a pair of shoes. By the age of 12 she had had a string of jobs in the Thirsk area; each time she stole from her employers. Her behaviour did not change when at 24 she married a wheelwright called John Bateman. Despite all of the things that she was to do to him over the next few years, he was to be constantly by her side.

On one occasion she told John that his father was ill and that he should immediately go to Thirsk as the old man was dying. When John arrived he saw his father, who was the town crier, wandering around, perfectly healthy, ringing his bell. While John was away Mary sold everything that John had owned. A few weeks later she sold all John's clothes and John thought that the only way out was to enlist in the army.

In 1796 Mary hit on another fraudulent idea after a large factory in the area had burned down. She toured the area telling everyone that one of her children had been burned very badly in the fire and she was given clothes, blankets and a variety of other items which she then promptly sold. Her next scam was to dress up as a nurse and visit the local hospital. She was able to con them out of all of their linen, which she then sold at a pawnbrokers.

Whilst she was doing all this she began to build up another business as a provider of charms and love potions. It was a clever scam as she claimed to be the agent of Mrs Blythe and Mrs Moore who had the ability to receive messages from the spirit world. By simply acting as a go-between, Mary could avoid any accusations of witchcraft and, when the messages from the two wise women did not work, they could be blamed instead of Mary. She had no shortage of customers and managed to convince one woman that her husband had been kidnapped and that unless she gave Mary gold coins to melt down as part of a spell, the kidnappers would certainly kill the woman's husband. Some days later the husband returned home safe and sound, completely oblivious to the fact that he had been 'kidnapped'.

On another occasion Mary extracted gold, leather, blotting paper and brass screws from a woman as payment to prevent her husband's hanging. Mary disappeared and the husband was executed. Her price to stop a husband from having an affair with another woman was around three half-crowns. One such woman believed her husband was having an affair while he was abroad, employed as a soldier. When the man came home he had a tough time convincing his wife that he had never been unfaithful. Another woman lost nearly everything as Mary came up with progressively more expensive ways of maintaining the woman's husband's affections for her. Before she turned to more deadly trades Mary's last major triumph was to claim that one of her chickens had laid an egg which bore the inscription 'Christ is coming'. She charged hundreds of people a penny each to see the egg.

William and Rebecca Perigo, who lived near Leeds, came to see Mary when Rebecca claimed that a neighbour had cursed her and caused her to have severe chest pains. By now Mary's reputation had grown and she was known locally as the 'Yorkshire Witch'. Between 1806 and May 1808 Mary systematically reduced the well-heeled couple to poverty. It began with a payment of four guineas, which Mary claimed that she had sewn into a pillow case which Rebecca should place her head upon at night. Mary had, in fact, substituted the four notes for worthless pieces of paper. Over the next few months the Perigos parted with geese, shirts, cloth, shawls, waistcoats, butter, tea, sugar, eggs and spirits until they were reduced to missing out on food themselves in order to pay for Mary's increasingly complex charms to protect them. Mary had been clever throughout and had given Rebecca a mild poison to keep her ill enough that they would continue to use her.

Rather belatedly, William began to be sceptical about Mary's healing abilities and, in any case, the Perigos had nothing left to offer Mary. Mary Bateman then produced the trump card in the form of a letter supposedly written by Mrs Blythe, which claimed that they would both fall seriously ill in May 1808 and, more chillingly, would appear to be dead but would, in fact, be alive. In order to counteract this premonition Mary gave Rebecca a mixture of arsenic and mercuric chloride, which she told the couple to put in a pie which should last them six days. They were to begin eating the pie on 15 May.

After the first portion of the pie, both William and Rebecca fell seriously ill. William refused to eat any more but Rebecca was fully under Mary's spell and continued eating it until she died on 24 May. Mary had cleverly told the Perigos that if a doctor was called in, then this would wipe out the benefits of the potion and charms. But William called in a doctor nevertheless and when they fed some of the pie to a cat, it died within minutes.

The next day Mary was arrested and charged with the murder of Rebecca Perigo. Mary's first reaction was to feign illness herself and claim that William had poisoned her and killed his own wife. In the event, the authorities discovered various poisons in Mary's home and over a period of time managed to track down servants that had worked for her who confirmed that Mary had given poisons to various people over the years.

Mary finally found herself in court at York before Judge Sir Simon le Blane and was found guilty of murder on 17 March 1809. Mary's last attempted con was to claim that she was pregnant, so the court called in 12 married women who had had children to examine her for signs of pregnancy. They came to the very quick conclusion that she was not pregnant at all and therefore Mary was hanged at 5am on 20 March by John Curry in front of a huge crowd. Significantly no one cheered or showed signs of pleasure that the wicked woman had finally met her end. Mary's reputation was so great as a witch that they feared that she would come back to get them from beyond the grave. Mary's body was sent to the Leeds Infirmary and her skin was later tanned and pieces of it sold as anti-witchcraft charms.

* * * * *

As far as **Jane Cox**'s guilt is concerned for the murder of 16-month-old John Trenaman, it is an open and shut case. What is significant is that she may have only administered the arsenic as a result of being paid to do so by the child's natural father, who was acquitted.

On 25 June 1811 Cox claimed that she was asked by Arthur Tucker, a farmer at Hatherleigh in Devon, to poison with arsenic his illegitimate child. Jane put arsenic into the child's hand and presently the infant licked the powder and died in agony about two hours later. It seems that the authorities had no difficulty in identifying Jane as the person who had provided the poison and in her written confession she claimed that Tucker had persuaded her to do it. She claimed that he had provided the arsenic and that he had given her £1 to carry out the poisoning.

At the trial in Exeter Tucker absolutely denied any wrongdoing and as a result of the testimony of several witnesses, who were able to throw light on his character, he was acquitted. Cox was not so lucky and she was executed on Monday 12 August 1811 in front of a large crowd. Before her execution she spoke to the crowd at length, complaining that Tucker had been the cause of the murder and that he should be with her facing the hangman.

* * * * *

However unfair it may have been that Jane Cox went to the gallows alone, 1815 saw the hanging of **Eliza Fenning** who

> …feloniously and unlawfully did administer to, and cause to be administered to, Orlibar Turner, Robert Gregson Turner and Charlotte Turner, his wife certain deadly poison – to wit, arsenic – with intent to kill and murder the said persons.

To the very end she protested her innocence and it is now strongly believed that Robert Turner, who had been suffering from mental illness, should have been taken seriously. He said before the poisonings 'If I am at liberty, I shall do some mischief; I shall destroy myself and my wife'.

Eliza was 22 in January 1815 when she became the cook for Olibar Turner at his home at 68 Chancery Lane, London. The poisoning was said to have taken place on 21 March when it was alleged that Eliza had mixed arsenic into the dough to make dumplings for the family. When Olibar's wife arrived at the house later that day she discovered that her husband, son, daughter-in-law and Eliza were all ill and vomiting. A doctor, Mr John Marshall, was called in that evening, arriving at about 8.45pm. He noted that all of the victims had the same symptoms. His investigations the following morning discovered arsenic in a dish. The packet of arsenic that had been kept in one of the kitchen drawers, to kill rats and mice, was gone, and nobody could explain how the arsenic had ended up in the pan in which the dumplings had been cooked.

In summing up the evidence the judge told the jury:

> Gentlemen, you have now heard the evidence given on this trial, and the case lies in a very narrow compass. There are but two questions for your consideration, and these are, whether the poison was administered, in all, to four persons, and by what hand such poison was given. That these persons were poisoned appears certain from the evidence of Mrs Charlotte Turner, Orlibar Turner, Roger Gadsden, the apprentice, and Robert Turner; for each of these persons ate of the dumplings, and were all more or less affected – that is they were everyone poisoned. That the poison was in the dough of which these dumplings were composed has been fully proved, I think, by the testimony of the surgeon who examined the remains of the dough left in the dish in which the dumplings had been mixed and divided; he deposes that the powder which had subsided at the bottom of the dish was arsenic. That the arsenic was not in the flour I think appears plain, from the circumstance that the crust of a pie had been made that very morning with some of the same flour of which the dumplings were made and the persons who dined off the pie felt no inconvenience whatever; that it was not in the yeast nor in the milk has also been proved; neither could it be in the sauce, for two of the persons who were ill never touched a particle of the sauce, and yet were violently affected with retching and sickness. From all these circumstances it must follow that the poisonous ingredient was in the dough alone; for besides that the persons who partook of the dumplings at dinner were more or less affected by what they had eaten, it was observed by one of the witnesses that the dough retained the same shape it had when first put into the dish to rise, and that it appeared dark, and was heavy, and in fact never did rise. The other question for your consideration is, by what hand the poison was administered; and although we have nothing before us but circumstantial evidence, yet it often happens that circumstances are more conclusive than most positive testimony. The prisoner, when taxed with poisoning the dumplings, threw the blame first on the milk, next on the yeast, and then on the sauce; but it has been proved, most satisfactorily, that none of these contained it, and it was in the dumplings alone, which no person but the prisoner had made. Gentlemen, if poison had been given to a dog, one would suppose that common humanity would have prompted us to assist it in its agonies: here is the case of a master and mistress being both poisoned, and no assistance was offered. Gentlemen, I have now stated all the facts as they have arisen, and leave the case in your hands, being fully persuaded that, whatever your verdict may be, you will conscientiously discharge your duty both to your God and to your country.

It took the jury just a few minutes to pass the verdict of 'guilty' on Eliza, and her execution was set for 26 June. Before sentence could be carried out she addressed the assembled crowd 'Before the just and almighty God, and by the faith of the Holy Sacrament I have taken, I am innocent of the offence with which I am charged. My innocence will be manifested in the course of the day. I hope God will forgive me.'

The execution was carried out at 8.30am and the funeral was set to take place on 31 June. Eliza's father had had to pay 4s 6d to retrieve his daughter's body. The funeral procession left Eliza's father's house near Red Lion Square at 3.30pm and was watched by tens of thousands of people. When the funeral cortège reached the churchyard of St George the Martyr around 10,000 people were present. There had been an enormous public outcry about the verdict and execution and appeals had been made to the Lord Chancellor, the Home Secretary and the Prince Regent, all to no avail.

* * * * *

Madeleine Smith was the daughter of a wealthy Glasgow architect and at the very centre of the city's vibrant social life. Emile L'Angelier was a Channel Islander of French descent and was employed as a clerk for a company based in Bothwell Street. He was determined to improve his station in life and through a friend managed to be introduced to the beautiful and very eligible Madeleine.

It seems from the outset that their relationship was a very passionate one and if they were not sleeping with one another by the spring of 1856, they had at least pledged themselves to one another by then. Certainly by 1857 they were exchanging passionate letters, but the young Channel Islander would never be acceptable to Madeleine's parents.

They had been cultivating the prospect of her marrying William Minnock, who moved in the right circles in Glasgow and was considered very much a gentleman. On 28 January 1857 Madeleine rather prematurely accepted Minnock's offer of marriage, but there was still the problem of Emile.

Madeleine Smith and Emile L'Angelier.

Madeleine began by asking him, as a gentleman, to not only deny their relationship but to return all of the letters that she had sent him over the months. On various occasions he either refused or simply ignored her pleas. At some point it must have dawned on Emile that despite his attachment to Madeleine, the relationship was, in effect, over. But he was not prepared to let Madeleine just walk out of his life.

It seems clear now that he intended to ruin Madeleine and lay a trail of evidence to her door that would lead the authorities to believe that she had conspired to kill him. Whether he actually intended to kill himself is unclear. Certainly a number of witnesses would later come out of his past to prove that over the years he had often taken dangerous poisons which he believed improved his physical well-being. Circumstantially, at least, Madeleine was foolish enough to continue some contact with him while he was plotting to bring her life crashing down around her.

When Emile's body was discovered, on Monday 22 March 1857, a post-mortem revealed 82 grains of arsenic in his stomach. When the police acquired Madeleine's love letters that she had been so desperate to retrieve, the authorities thought that they had their murderer and arrested her on 31 March. Throughout she denied having anything to do with the murder of Emile but she had been in possession of arsenic, which had been purchased at various chemists in Glasgow and elsewhere in Scotland.

Her relationship with Emile had been a complex one and this only served to throw more suspicion on her. The newspapers were full of frank and shocking tales of a well-connected and respectable woman engaging in pre-marital sex. It was widely believed that if she lacked the morals to reserve herself for her husband, then she could have considered murder as a means of covering up a scandal.

There was considerable debate in court about the opportunities that Madeleine had had to administer the poison. Although Emile's diary was not considered admissible evidence in court, the implication from the entries suggested that every time he had accepted food or drink from Madeleine, he had fallen ill. Madeleine was fortunate in having an extremely skilled and eloquent defence counsel who was able, step by step, to undermine the circumstantial evidence that linked her to the poisoning.

However, when the jury considered their verdict their deliberations left neither the prosecution nor the defence completely satisfied. A peculiarity of the Scottish legal system was that the jury could return a verdict of 'not proven'. The verdict neither convicted Madeleine of the poisoning, nor cleared her name.

Madeleine fled Scotland. Although a free woman, her reputation and notoriety had ruined her. After spending a period of time in London, where she married George Wardle, she eventually moved to New York, married again and died at the age of 93 on 12 April 1928.

* * * * *

Catherine Wilson was born in 1842 and by 1862 had established herself as a nurse. Her speciality was looking after the long-term ill and at some point it must have occurred to Wilson that there was an opportunity here to make herself a very rich woman. In constant contact with her patients, she was able to gradually befriend them and convince them to change their wills, leaving her as the major or only beneficiary. Once in possession of a suitable legal document, she would then use a variety of poisons to dispose of the patient and thus collect her inheritance.

It is not exactly clear how many patients she murdered in this way, but what is significant is that when the police finally searched her home they found a huge variety and a massive volume of different poisons. It is also believed that at some point she lived with a man called Dixon, who was probably well aware of her activities. Wilson could not afford to have any loose ends and, concerned that Dixon might blurt out something while he was drunk, she chose to poison him as well.

Wilson's downfall came in 1862 after she had secured a will in her favour from Mrs Sarah Carnell. She was looking after the woman in her own home and administered a drink to soothe the woman's fever. Sarah took a mouthful of the drink and immediately it burned the inside of her mouth. She spat it out and the liquid burned a whole in the rug beside the bed. She screamed for her husband and Wilson fled the scene. The police were called to the house and examined the liquid that had been given to Sarah. It was found to contain a considerable amount of sulphuric acid and a warrant was signed for Catherine Wilson's arrest.

The police caught up with her a couple of days later but at her trial for attempted murder her defence counsel successfully argued that the liquid had been supplied by a chemist. They argued that the chemist had obviously given Catherine the wrong medicine. She was released but immediately re-arrested because the police had arranged the exhumation of no fewer than seven bodies. They had carried out post-mortems on all of the bodies and discovered that each and every one of them had died from poisons administered by Catherine Wilson.

Her re-trial at the Old Bailey resulted in a guilty verdict for the murders. She was hanged outside the very court in which she had been tried on 20 October 1862, before a massive crowd of 20,000.

* * * * *

Arsenic was the chosen poison of **Priscilla Biggadyke**, the last woman to be hanged at Lincoln Castle. She was executed on 28 December 1868. Her husband Richard had a successful well-sinking business. His skills were so sought after that he worked extremely long hours and would often make a start in the early hours of the morning.

Priscilla added to the already considerable income of the household by taking in lodgers, one of whom was John Proctor. At some point Richard must have suspected that no sooner had he left his home and bed early in the morning, than it would be occupied by John Proctor. No doubt when challenged Priscilla denied the allegations but it became clear to her that it was time for Richard to go.

When Richard returned home from a hard day's work on 30 September 1868, Priscilla had already prepared his meal, which he ate before settling down in front of the fire and dozing off. He hardly slept that night and by the early hours he was in extreme pain and passed away the following morning. When a doctor was called to sign a death certificate he declined. He had known Richard for a number of years and knew him to be healthy and rarely ill. Consequently, he arranged a post-mortem and the analysis of Richard's stomach contents revealed a large quantity of arsenic.

The police were immediately called and Priscilla tearfully told them that she had seen John Proctor adding something to her husband's tea.

Proctor utterly denied any wrong doing and it seems clear that the police were convinced that Priscilla had administered the poison herself. She was found guilty at her trial and sentenced to hang. It seems that on the day of her execution her self-assuredness and bravado abandoned her and she fainted as soon as she saw the hangman. She had to be held up while the noose was being placed around her neck.

* * * * *

Florence Bravo was at the centre of a case that was to become known as the 'Balham Mystery'. She had married Captain Ricardo in 1864 but it had been a disastrous marriage, marred by her husband's drinking. Florence had achieved a separation in 1870 and her husband had died abroad the following year. She then began a long-term relationship with a man nearly 40 years older than her. He was a respectable hydro-therapist called Dr Gully, who had a successful practice at Malvern. Florence's relationship with Gully was intense and would eventually ruin them both. Despite the fact that Gully was already married, Florence miscarried two of his children in 1872 and

Florence Bravo.

Charles Bravo.

1875. Gully's wife was an invalid and had been a long-term patient in a home.

Later in 1875 Florence met the barrister, Charles Bravo. He had a long-term mistress, but he and Florence soon became lovers. Florence rather cruelly dispensed with Dr Gully and before they married on 7 December 1875, Charles agreed to leave his mistress. There was also considerable unpleasantness prior to the marriage regarding property. Florence was an independent woman as a result of money she still received from her first husband's estate. Charles was determined that once they married everything should be his. Poor Dr Gully was brought in to help negotiate.

Right from the beginning the Bravo marriage was dogged by arguments about money. Charles considered Florence to be a spendthrift while he himself could charitably be called mean. They moved into Florence's home at the Priory in Balham, where Charles also inherited Florence's close friend and confidante **Jane Cox**. Jane would too become a bone of contention, particularly after Charles had worked out that she was costing the household over £400 a year. Florence miscarried again in February 1876; this time the father was probably Charles. His wife's poor health from then on went some way to rebuilding some of the bridges between the couple, but it seems clear that Charles was continually concerned that Dr Gully was still very much in his wife's mind.

Florence miscarried again on 6 April and her communication with Gully seems to have begun again when, through Jane, she asked him to provide her with homeopathic remedies and painkillers. As it was, the Easter break of 1876 was to be the last holiday that Charles would enjoy. Cracks were already beginning to appear again as Charles was particularly concerned that Dr Gully was living nearby.

Charles, Jane and Florence ate together for the last time on 18 April, with Charles consuming his usual two bottles or so of burgundy. He had had a scare earlier in the day when his horse had bolted and he retired at about 9.30pm. The two women had retired earlier, having drunk a considerable amount of alcohol themselves. No sooner had the household settled down than Charles emerged from his bedroom screaming for his wife, who was asleep in her own room. Jane and one of the maids were first to respond and found that Charles had been vomiting and was in a terrible state.

When Florence was finally awoken she immediately called for a doctor while Jane administered what aid she could to Charles. A bewildering number of doctors attended Charles that night and in the early hours of the morning. At first Charles told them that he had taken poison but did not elaborate. Initial analysis of some of the vomit that had been taken away proved little, but the doctors, by the afternoon of the following day, were beginning to believe that Charles's illness was the result of arsenic poisoning. Charles struggled on throughout the day and finally passed away at 5.30 the following morning.

The strangest part of this story is that there would be two coroner's inquests and yet no one would ever be brought to trial for the murder of Charles Bravo. The evidence swayed this way and that during the inquests, at one point clearly indicating that either Florence, or Jane, or the pair of them, had murdered Charles Bravo, and at another indicating that Charles had taken the poison himself.

The newspapers were full of the story and although the first inquest had been held in the relative secrecy of the Priory itself, the second had been thrown open to the public and the press at the nearby Bedford Hotel. Gossip was rife about infidelity, murder and conspiracy. Dr Gully was dragged into the rumours and the papers were full of the impropriety of his relationship with Florence. He was even accused of giving Florence drugs to help her miscarry. However, it turned out that arsenic was not the cause of death; it was antimony, and this opened a whole new line of debate.

Antimony was used with horses and both Florence's stables and those of Dr Gully contained the drug. In the event, the jury still seemed unclear and simply returned a verdict that someone had murdered Charles Bravo, but that there was insufficient evidence to bring charges against anyone.

For weeks the newspapers proposed their own theories but life was not to be kind to anyone involved in the Bravo case. Dr Gully's reputation was in tatters and he died seven years later. Florence re-wrote her will in February 1877 and died an alcoholic in September 1878. As for Jane Cox, all that we know is that she eventually moved to Jamaica and was last seen, rather chillingly, sitting next to the bed of an ailing relative.

*   *   *   *   *

Louisa Taylor was born in 1846 and it seems that throughout her entire adult life she was hopelessly attracted to men much older than herself. Her husband had died in March 1882; he had been a retired dock worker and was more than twice her age. Before her husband had died she had met William Tregellis, who by 1882 was 85 years old. He lived with his wife, Mary Anne, three years younger than himself, in Plumstead. His wife was not well and in August 1882 William asked Louisa whether she would be prepared to move in with them to help him look after his wife as she was bed-ridden.

The arrangement seemed perfectly amicable for all concerned. Louisa lived in the cottage with them rent-free and much of the day-to-day responsibility for looking after his wife had been taken off William's shoulders. It did not take long for Louisa to start stealing from the house, but the old couple put the disappearances down to their failing memories.

In around September 1882, following a conversation with William regarding his future should his wife die before him, Louisa propositioned the old man and suggested that they run off together. William does not seem to have particularly taken with the idea but Louisa had seen, perhaps, a glint in the old man's eye that told her that if his wife were out of the way then he would reconsider her offer.

For some time a Dr Smith had been administering medicines to Mary Anne and on each occasion Louisa had asked him to bring some lead acetate with him. She told the doctor that she used the chemical for a skin complaint and gradually, over the weeks, Louisa had amassed quite a lot of the material. Meanwhile, Dr Smith had noted that Mary Anne's condition was deteriorating and that she could barely keep any food down.

Matters came to a head on 6 October when William called in the police. He had just gone to collect his pension and was accosted by Louisa, who told him that his wife wanted the money so that she could keep it under her pillow. He gave her the money but a short time after that the Tregellis' landlady had seen Louisa leaving the house with the money that William had just collected. Unfortunately, this all coincided with another visit by Dr Smith. He arrived just as the police answered William's summons.

Facts were quickly put together and a police doctor was called in to examine Mary Anne. When he opened the old woman's mouth he could see a dark blue line all around her gums, which suggested lead poisoning. Dr Smith confirmed that he had been supplying Louisa with lead acetate and Mary Anne told both of the doctors that Louisa had mixed her medicine for her and that whenever she had vomited, which was often, the matter was black.

When Louisa returned to the Tregellis' home she was promptly arrested for theft. Unfortunately for her Mary Anne died on 23 October and the post-mortem revealed what the doctors had suspected; there was a large amount of lead acetate in her stomach. The police promptly added the charge of murder to the one they had already made.

Louise Jane Taylor was found guilty of the murder of Mary Anne Tregellis and was hanged in Maidstone Prison on 2 January 1883.

* * * * *

Margaret Higgins, aged 41, and her 55-year-old sister, **Catherine Flanagan**, had a slightly different spin on Catherine Wilson's murderous career. They were arsenic poisoners and their method of working was to take out insurance policies on their victims before they murdered them. Their career came to an end towards the end of September 1883 when Margaret's husband, Thomas Higgins, died.

The women had taken out no fewer than five separate insurance policies, which they then planned to collect. Rather stupidly they had pulled the same trick when they had murdered Mary Jennings, a lodger in their home, earlier that year. Two deaths in the same household gave rise to enough suspicion to prompt the police to order the exhumation and post-mortem of both bodies. It was obvious that the cause of death in both cases had been arsenic poisoning.

The pair were brought before Liverpool Assizes on 16 February 1884. The police had spent a considerable amount of time and energy prior to the trial trying to track down the names and last resting places of several other people that they now believed had been murdered by the two sisters. They were convicted of the two specimen murders of Mary Jennings and Thomas Higgins and sentenced to hang on 5 March 1884. It is believed that Catherine Flanagan made a full confession of all of her murders before her date with the hangman, Samuel Heath.

* * * * *

Queen Victoria's surgeon, Sir James Paget, was once quoted as saying 'Now the case is over, she should tell us in the interests of science how she did it'. Such was the confusion and interest in the murder drama that brought **Adelaide Bartlett** into court for the murder of Edwin, her seemingly doting husband. Adelaide had a fascinating history. She

was born in France in 1856 and it was strongly rumoured that although her marriage certificate claimed otherwise, she was the daughter of a well-connected English aristocrat that had accompanied Queen Victoria on a tour of France in 1855. By 1875 she was in England, where she met Edwin, whom she would eventually marry.

He was a 29-year-old partner in a grocery and provision business and their relationship from the outset was strange, to say the least. Edwin did not propose that his marriage with Adelaide should be a sexual one and instead of a honeymoon Adelaide was packed off to a finishing school and then a convent in Brussels. She hardly saw Edwin until 1878. She moved into rooms above one of Edwin's shops, along with his brother, Frederick. It was strongly suggested at the time and much later that Adelaide slept with Edwin's brother whenever her husband was not around. Following the death of the Bartletts' mother, they invited their father to live with them, which was a big mistake. He and Adelaide hated one another.

By 1881 Edwin began to have designs on his wife's body and it was said that the only time they ever had intercourse occurred one Sunday afternoon and resulted in Adelaide falling pregnant. At the crucial time when Adelaide was about to deliver the child, Edwin adamantly refused to allow another man, even if he was a doctor, to touch his wife. By the time he conceded it was too late and the child was stillborn.

Edwin Bartlett was a bizarre man. He was a hypochondriac, he regularly took drugs which we now know to be poisons to improve his health and, most bizarrely, as a young man he had had all of his teeth sawn off at the roots so that he could have dentures. This was a decision that was to prove to be a big mistake.

In 1883 the Bartletts, without the cantankerous father, were in new accommodation above another of Edwin's shops in East Dulwich. It was a better period for the couple, but they moved again several times in 1885, picking up on the way a Wesleyan preacher by the name of George Dyson. Edwin was entranced by the man's education and encouraged him to visit the house as often as he could. Eventually he convinced Dyson to improve Adelaide's own education with one-to-one tuition.

This was a poor decision on Edwin's behalf. He spend a considerable amount of time away from home and it was not long before George and Adelaide were making love behind the pinned curtains of their front windows. Edwin, whether aware of what was going on or not, continued to encourage Dyson until finally on 8 December 1885, Edwin fell seriously ill. He was being sick, he had diarrhoea and began haemorrhaging from the bowels.

When a doctor was called he was appalled at the state of Edwin's mouth. Not only was there evidence that Edwin had taken mercury, but all of the roots remaining in his gums had begun to rot. It is also possible that Edwin had syphilis and this may account for the fact that a number of condoms were discovered in his pocket after he had died.

Over the next few days Edwin's condition first worsened, then improved and then worsened again. A second medical opinion was sought but events were beginning to overtake the medical experts.

On 27 December, on behalf of Adelaide, Dyson bought some chloroform. According to Adelaide, much to her horror, Edwin had begun to show definite signs that he wished to rekindle his sexual relationship with his wife. As far as Adelaide was concerned, Edwin had all but promised her to George Dyson in the event of his death and she therefore considered sleeping with Edwin to be a bizarre form of adultery against George.

On the day before Edwin died he ate well and throughout the New Year celebrations Adelaide dutifully sat beside her husband's bed. Only 15 minutes into the New Year Adelaide was screaming for the doctor. Her husband was dead. The doctor could give no reason for the sudden death and by now Edwin's father had reappeared and was denouncing his daughter-in-law as a poisoner.

Edwin's post-mortem was carried out on 2 January and a large quantity of chloroform was found in his stomach. But how had it got there? Chloroform is a particularly unpleasant fluid that burns skin and would certainly have blistered the throat had it been drunk. The Home Office analysts could not explain it but Adelaide, when she appeared at the coroner's inquest, discovered to her horror that George Dyson was prepared to pin all the blame on her. He admitted to buying the chloroform and this prompted Adelaide's arrest.

The trial opened at the Old Bailey on 13 April and Adelaide was defended by one of the most expensive advocates of the period. It was suggested that her mysterious father had paid the bill. Her defence counsel had done his homework and although George Dyson had been considered the star prosecution witness, his reputation and actions were ripped to shreds in court. Various medical witnesses were examined and none could explain how the chloroform had got into Edwin Bartlett's stomach. The defence painted a picture of Adelaide as a woman who sacrificed herself through love and affection for her husband. A woman who had called in doctors; a woman who had nursed her husband; how could she be a murderess? How was it possible for her to administer the chloroform when not even the most highly trained doctors in the country could explain how it had been done? Clarke's final summing up was listened to by a crowded court. It was an eloquent speech which cast Adelaide as a woman so pure that she would not even sleep with her own husband for fear of betraying the man that Edwin had chosen to succeed him. Before a hushed court the jury found Adelaide 'not guilty'. There was an eruption of applause as she was led to freedom.

Many people still believed that Adelaide had perpetrated a pre-meditated murder on a hypochondriac and, frankly, weird husband, but none could prove it. It was later suggested that she hypnotised him to make him drink the chloroform, but this never explained why there was no chloroform in any other part of Edwin's body. A final solution was offered more than 100 years after the events, when it was discovered that chloroform, when poured into a glass of brandy, hung, suspended, within the alcohol. It could then have been swiftly drunk without the chloroform ever touching tissue until it hit the stomach.

It is difficult to trace Adelaide's movements after her acquittal. Despite the verdict she was ruined and was beset by journalists who dogged her for the truth. It seems likely that she either returned to her place of birth in France or emigrated to America.

* * * * *

As if the Florence Bravo and Adelaide Bartlett cases were not enough, along with the scandal surrounding Madeleine Smith, the case of **Florence Maybrick** rocked the Victorian establishment. Once again a woman was to be painted as a notorious poisoner. Her case revealed much about Victorian prejudices and the state of the English legal system. The Criminal Court of Appeal was established largely as an indirect result of Florence's conviction.

Setting aside the fact that the victim, James Maybrick, is considered by many to be a viable Jack the Ripper suspect, Florence Maybrick, as an American, had as colourful a life as Adelaide Bartlett.

She was born in Alabama in 1862 and, after moving around America and Europe with her mother, she met James on board a ship in the Atlantic in March 1881. They married on 27 July the same year but James, while appearing to be a successful Liverpool cotton broker, had a great many skeletons in his closet. He was a habitual drug user and he had a mistress who had borne him several children. In Maybrick's defence, he had contracted malaria some time before and was taking arsenic and strychnine to control its ill-effects. But by the time they settled in Liverpool in 1887 Maybrick's business was beginning to suffer as a result of his drug addiction.

His use of arsenic reached fever pitch in 1888 and to console herself Florence had an affair with another cotton broker called Alfred Brierley. They were still seeing one another in the middle of 1889. James Maybrick began to suffer from the ill-effects of his drug-taking in around April, and a series of incidents around that time later helped to condemn Florence.

She had bought a number of fly papers that contained arsenic, which she soaked in a sink so that she could use the fluid to deal with skin blemishes on her face. There was considerable gossip in the household, which linked the arsenic in the fly papers with James Maybrick's worsening condition. The principal accuser was Alice Yapp, the household nurse, and at her insistence doctors took away various bodily fluids from James for examination. None of them showed any signs of containing arsenic.

On the night of 9 May Florence was seen to be tampering with a bottle of meat juice that had been prescribed to James and on the following morning it was taken away and revealed to contain half a grain of arsenic. By now James's brothers, Edwin and Michael, were on the scene and convinced that Florence was poisoning their brother. They searched the house and collected up a series of items, all of which were later proved to have been exposed to arsenic.

On 11 May 1889 James lapsed into a coma and died. There was a post-mortem which led to Florence's arrest. The coroner's inquest finally took place on 28 May, and recommended that Florence should be brought before the Liverpool Assizes in July. Tragically for Florence events were to conspire not to give her the fairest of hearings.

The judge was in the latter stages of a severe mental illness which affected his judgement, and although Florence was defended by Sir Charles Russell, he, too, was well past his prime. Despite hearing evidence that James Maybrick had often taken arsenic and other drugs, going back even to his time in America, the jury was finally convinced, largely by circumstantial evidence, of Florence's guilt. Russell had, however, been able to undermine the testimony of numerous witnesses. Although the jury accepted that Maybrick was a chronic arsenic-eater, it took them just 35 minutes to find Florence guilty of wilful murder. The judge sentenced her to death, but tens of thousands of people demanded her reprieve. The judge was pulled over the coals by the Home Secretary and the Chancellor. All the time Florence could see the scaffold being erected outside her cell. Finally the Home Secretary reviewed her sentence and commuted it to life imprisonment. Florence spent 15 years in prison and was released in 1904. Until his death in 1900, her defence counsel had tried to have the sentence overturned.

Florence was never to see her children again. James's brother Michael, throughout her

prison term, would not allow them to see her, and even after she was released they were disinclined to see their mother. Florence died at the age of 79 on 23 October 1941. She was living the life of a recluse in Connecticut and had never accepted that her sentence was just.

* * * * *

One of Florence Maybrick's fellow prisoners was **Edith Carew**. Her case, had it been heard in England, would have attracted as much attention, but Edith was found guilty in a foreign land, and barely escaped the hangman's noose.

Edith was the daughter of the Mayor of Glastonbury and had married Walter Carew, who had an import/export business in Japan. They moved to Yokohama in 1889 where Walter and Edith enjoyed a pleasant ex-patriot lifestyle. However, her decision to marry Walter had been a horrible mistake. He was a womaniser and had numerous affairs during their marriage. One significant woman in Walter's life was Annie Luke, who may well have been the writer of several strange letters to Walter and the mysterious 'woman in black'.

When Walter fell ill in October 1896 he consulted his doctor, who thought he was suffering from a bilious attack. Dr Wheeler, however, asked for a second opinion after another episode a few days later. Walter was admitted to hospital and died just two hours after his admission. The story now took a strange course.

An unsigned letter was pushed under Dr Wheeler's door which read 'Three bottles of arsenic in one week!' Below it was written the name of a local chemist. When Wheeler visited the chemist, called Maruya, he discovered that Edith Carew had, in fact, bought three bottles of arsenic. He went to see her and Edith told him that her husband had asked her to buy it in order to cure a long-standing illness.

There was, of course, an inquest, where it was revealed that Annie Luke was still very much in Walter's life. In fact, on one occasion, only two weeks before he had died, she had turned up at the Carew's house dressed in black with a veil over her face. She had simply left a calling card with the initials AL written on it. The letters were more perplexing. One read:

> I must see you. I cannot meet her again. She makes me mad when I think of what I might have done for you. I cannot give you any address. I am living wherever I can find shelter; but you can find me and help me if you will, as I know you will for the sake of old times.

Edith's legal representative had also received a strange letter, written in the same hand:

> Dead men tell no tales; no, nor dead women either, for I am going to join him. Do you know what it means, waiting for eight long weary years? I have watched and waited. Waited until I knew he would grow tired of that silly little fool, and then I came to him. What is the result? We, between us, electrify Japan. I have never pretended to be a good woman but, for the sake of a few lines, I do not see why I should let a silly, innocent woman be condemned for what she knows nothing about.

Henry Dickinson belonged to the British club of which Walter was the secretary. He had encountered a woman dressed in black with the same veil that Edith had seen, looking for Walter. He could neither confirm nor refute the suggestion that it was Annie Luke.

The outcome of the inquest was that there was 'No direct evidence to show by whom it had been administered', but the cause of death was arsenic poisoning. Edith Carew was arrested a week after the inquest but before the trial could begin there was to be another sensation.

Mary Jacob worked for the Carews as a nurse and governess to their two children. Her relationship with Edith was difficult, and she suspected that Edith had been intercepting letters that had been addressed to her. In her search for her own correspondence she had found love letters discarded in the bottom of a waste-paper basket. They had been written to Edith by none other than Henry Dickinson. As far as the prosecution was concerned this gave an additional motive for Edith to have murdered her husband. Indeed, during the trial Henry Dickinson admitted that he was infatuated with Edith and that on more than one occasion they had discussed the possibility of her divorcing Walter. He adamantly denied that he had ever slept with her.

There was considerable debate about who had written the two letters. The prosecution maintained that Edith had written them herself and the defence contended that they had been written by Mary Jacob. Mary Jacob was arrested for a short period of time, but since nothing could be linked to her directly she was released. Edith even offered a £500 reward for information leading to the discovery of Annie Luke, but nothing was forthcoming.

Edith was found guilty of murdering her husband and was sentenced to death. But her execution was commuted to life imprisonment and she was sent back to England to serve her sentence. She died on 27 June 1968 in Wales, never revealing whether she had, in fact, poisoned her husband over 70 years before.

* * * * *

Ethel Lillie Major was born in Lincolnshire in 1891. She was brought up with her three brothers on the estate of Sir Henry Hawley but scandal entered her life in 1914 when she fell pregnant and gave birth to an illegitimate daughter called Auriel. Her family rallied round and the child was brought up as Ethel's sister.

Arthur Major entered Ethel's life in 1918. He had been invalided home from World War One and the couple married on 1 June 1918. She gave birth to her son Lawrence the following year and the family moved to Kirkby-on-Bain, near Horncastle, in 1929. Ethel made no attempt to make any friends in her new home and there was an undercurrent between the couple about the true identity of Auriel. Arthur wanted to know the truth and finally Ethel admitted it, but would never tell him who the father of her first child was. This seemed to destroy the marriage and from then on Ethel never slept at her new home, only spending the daytime and evening with her husband, and sleeping at her parents' house at night.

By the beginning of 1934 Ethel seemed to have got it into her head that Arthur was having an affair with a neighbour called Rose Kettleborough. She even went to the extent of forging love letters between the pair of them to wave in front of Arthur's face. By the spring Arthur was beginning to worry about his wife and even commented to one of his work mates at the gravel pit where he was employed that he was sure that Ethel was trying to poison him. He and his fellow worker watched as birds eating a sandwich he had discarded fell down dead.

Whatever his fears, he seemed to be still eating food prepared for him by Ethel, but matters came to a head on 23 May when he had to come home from work because he felt so ill. Dr Smith arrived and found Arthur in convulsions and unable to talk to him. As far as the doctor was concerned, Arthur was having an epileptic fit and he gave him a sedative. He had heard from Ethel that Arthur had been having fits on and off for a year or two. Dr Smith was stunned when Ethel went to his surgery the following day and told him that Arthur had died in the night.

Two days after Arthur's death, and with Ethel in the middle of organising his funeral, the local police received an anonymous letter. It was signed 'Fairplay'. It read:

> Sir, have you heard of a wife poisoning her husband? Look no further into the death of Mr Major of Kirkby-on-Bain. Why did he complain of his food tasting nasty and throw it to a neighbour's dog, which has since died? Ask the undertaker if he looked natural after death. Why did he stiffen so quickly? Why was he so jerky when dying? I myself have heard her threaten to poison him years ago. In the name of the law, I beg you to analyse the contents of his stomach.

Ethel Lillie Major, who poisoned her husband.

Clearly the police did not consider this to be a crank communication as they had the funeral postponed and Arthur's body examined by the Home Office pathologist, Dr Roche Lynch, at St Mary's Hospital, Paddington. They even had the body of the neighbour's dog exhumed. Both corpses showed signs that the cause of death had been strychnine poisoning.

It was apparent that the strychnine had been contained in corned beef in some of Arthur's sandwiches but Ethel denied either ever having bought corned beef or making sandwiches for her husband from it. At a crucial point in the interview she told Chief Inspector Young 'I do not know my husband died from strychnine poisoning.' Young replied 'I never mentioned strychnine, how did you know that?' to which Ethel replied 'Oh, I'm sorry I must have made a mistake'. Despite this admission the police had not found any strychnine in the house but Young was certain that Ethel Major had got the poison from somewhere. He contacted Ethel's father and asked him whether he had any strychnine; he confirmed that he had and that it was used to kill rats and mice, but that it was perfectly safe and no one could have obtained access to it as it was kept in a locked box. He went on to say that he was the only person who had the key. Then, sadly for Ethel, he remembered that there had once been another key, which had disappeared about 10 years earlier. Young returned to Arthur and Ethel's house and found an old key. It did not fit any of the locks in the house and when he took it back to Mr Brown's house it fitted perfectly in the lock of the poison box.

Ethel Major was brought to trial at Lincoln Assizes. The trial lasted from 29 October to 1 November 1934. The jury found her guilty but asked the judge to show mercy in his sentencing. Clearly the judge, Justice Charles, did not agree, as he sentenced Ethel to be hanged on 19 December 1934 in Hull Prison.

* * * * *

As a nurse **Dorothea Waddingham** was well placed to poison her patients with morphine. She was born in 1899 and had never actually trained to be a nurse. She had been employed as a ward maid in a workhouse infirmary. She had been married before to an older man, Thomas Willoughby Leech, who had died of throat cancer. Although he had been considerably older than her, she had produced five children as a result of the marriage. Following her husband's death she set up a nursing home in Devon Drive, Nottingham, reverted to her maiden name and advertised for patients. She was ably assisted by her lover, 39-year-old Ronald Joseph Sullivan.

Two patients arrived in January 1935. One was 89-year-old Mrs Baguley. The old woman was senile and bedridden and with her came her daughter, Ada Louisa, who was in her fifties and was suffering from disseminated sclerosis, a form of paralysis. Waddingham was to be paid £3 a week to look after the two women.

Looking after the Baguleys was hard work. Ada was a large woman and presented a considerable challenge to bathe and care for. The Baguleys must have been very happy with their new situation, as on 6 May 1935 Ada rewrote her will, leaving their not inconsiderable £1,600 fortune to Waddingham and Sullivan. The deal was that the nurse and her assistant would look after the two women until their deaths, at which time they would receive the £1,600, but in the meantime there would be no more weekly charges. Little did the Baguleys know that they were signing their own death warrants.

Mrs Baguley was the first to go, just six days after the will had been changed. Her cause of death was given as old age. Four months later on 10 September Ada also died and her cause of death was given as a cerebral haemorrhage. Waddingham sent a letter to Dr Cyril Banks who was then the Nottingham Medical Health Officer. It purported to have been written by Ada on 29 August and it requested that her body should be cremated and that her relatives 'shall not know of my death'. The source of the letter was given as 'The Nursing Home, 32 Devon Drive'. Banks knew of no registered nursing home at that address and was very uncomfortable with the letter. He ordered a post-mortem of Ada's body and it was discovered that she had not died from a cerebral haemorrhage, but from three grains of morphine in her body, more than sufficient for an overdose. Again the post-mortem was carried out by Dr Roche Lynch.

Banks informed the police and arranged for the exhumation of Mrs Baguley's body. Again a morphine overdose was found to be the cause of death. The police arrested Waddingham and Sullivan and charged them with murder.

The trial began at Nottingham on 4 February 1936. Sullivan was lucky; the evidence in his case was only circumstantial and he was acquitted. His lover Dorothea faced judgement alone. She began by claiming that the nursing home's doctor, Dr Manfield, had prescribed five doses of two morphine tablets to Ada to combat her stomach pains, which she believed may have been cancer. This flew in the face of the fact that the contents of Ada's stomach, despite her alleged stomach problems, contained two portions of her evening meal. When Dr Manfield was called to answer Dorothea's allegations, he told the court that he had prescribed morphine for a Mrs Kemp, but she had died soon after the Baguleys had become patients at the nursing home.

Waddingham was found guilty of murder but the jury entered a strong plea for mercy. The judge, nevertheless, sentenced her to hang and this was confirmed by the Home Secretary after Waddingham's appeal was turned down. The sentence was carried out at Winson Green Prison in Birmingham on 16 April 1936.

* * * * *

Charlotte Bryant was born Charlotte McHugh in 1903. She was an illiterate Irish girl and her future husband, Frederick, six years older than her, was a soldier in the British army. They met against the backdrop of the Irish troubles in the 1920s but by 1923 she

Charlotte Bryant.

had moved to England to marry him. In 1925 they moved into a tied cottage at Over Compton, near Yeovil in Somerset. Frederick was a farm labourer and over the next few years four children were added to the tiny little cottage. Charlotte was not a great mother, nor much of a home maker. She preferred going out for boozy sessions in the evenings in the local pubs, where she gained a reputation as an amateur prostitute. On several occasions she even brought her customers home.

At some point in late 1933 she met a gypsy peddler called Leonard Parsons. He had been constantly in and out of the area, selling horses. Although Charlotte did not know it, he had a common-law wife, Priscilla Loveridge, with whom he had four children. It seems that Charlotte brought him home as a client on one occasion but she was able to persuade Fred to allow Parsons to be an irregular lodger at the house. Fred was perfectly happy to allow Parsons to share his wife as well as his home and on occasions when Parsons needed to move around for his work, Charlotte sometimes followed him.

Charlotte's relationship with Parsons did not seem to prevent her from sleeping with several other men in the area and, probably as a result of her reputation, Fred was sacked in early 1934. Charlotte was variously known as 'Black Bess', 'Compton Bess' or 'Killarney Kate'. Since the cottage was tied, the family were forced to move to Coombe near Sherbourne in Dorset and from then on cracks began to appear, not in Fred and Charlotte's relationship, but in her relationship with Parsons.

The Bryant cottage.

The kitchen at the Bryant cottage.

She had asked Parsons on a number of occasions 'Would you marry me if I were a widow?' His reply is not recorded but it seems that by May 1935 Charlotte was taking steps to make herself a widow. Fred had a series of illnesses in May which a local doctor suggested was gastro-enteritis. Whatever Charlotte had given him was not enough to kill the robust 39-year-old Fred. So Parsons left that autumn.

By now Charlotte had given birth to another child and it was widely believed that the father was Parsons and not her husband. No sooner had Parsons left the isolated cottage in Coombe than he was followed by Charlotte. There is no indication that she ever caught up with him, but at Weston-super-Mare she found Priscilla and Parsons' four children. Priscilla did not have a good word to say about Parsons and told Charlotte in no uncertain terms that he was a womaniser and a home-breaker.

Charlotte returned to Coombe and the events over the next few days were to prove that she had not taken Priscilla's advice seriously – she was determined to become a widow. Frederick fell ill again on 11 December and hung on until 22 December, when his body finally gave out. The final dose was delivered to him in a cup of Oxo. Fred's body was given a post-mortem and four grains of arsenic were discovered in his stomach.

Charlotte was damned by her friend Lucy Ostler, who recounted to the police the Oxo drink incident and the fact that Charlotte had been trying to destroy a tin of weed-killer. The police found the remains of the tin on a rubbish dump and matched it to a sale made by a local chemist. Charlotte had signed the poison register with an X.

She was arrested on 10 February 1936 and her trial opened in Dorchester on 27 May 1936. The evidence was damning and Justice MacNaghten sentenced her to hang just three days later. Despite an appeal and a telegram to the king, the execution was only

Bryant's husband had traces of arsenic in his stomach.

delayed by six weeks. It is said that Charlotte's jet black hair turned to white in fear of what was to come. The sentence was duly carried out by Thomas Pierrepoint at Exeter Prison on Wednesday 15 July 1936.

* * * * *

Alfred Merrifield was **Louisa Merrifield**'s third husband. Prior to their marriage in February 1953 she had had 20 domestic jobs in three years and had also served a prison term for ration book fraud. They became housekeepers to Sarah Ann Ricketts on 12 March. Sarah was nearly 80 years old, Alfred was a sprightly 74 and Louisa was 46. Regrettably Sarah would not see her eightieth birthday.

Sarah owned a new bungalow in the seaside resort of Blackpool and the Merrifields seemed to have found the ideal position. Sarah often complained in the few short weeks that remained of her life that most of the housekeeping money was spent on rum and that she was not being fed properly. Even before her death Louisa was telling people that Sarah was dead and had left her the bungalow, worth £3,000. Sarah died in agony on 14 April, some time during the evening, but a doctor was not called until the following morning.

Louisa was desperate to have Sarah's body cremated at the earliest opportunity but the authorities were suspicious and carried out a post-mortem on the corpse. The cause of death was phosphorous poisoning and both of the Merrifields were arrested.

Their trial began in July and when the jury returned their verdict they were certain that Louisa was guilty but they could not decide on whether Alfred had known anything about what was going on. Consequently, shortly after Louisa was hanged at Strangeways on 18 September 1953, Alfred was able to inherit half of Sarah's estate and live on for another six years.

* * * * *

Susan Barber married Michael in 1970 and by 1980 they were living with their three children in Osborne Road, Westcliffe-on-Sea, Essex. On Saturday 31 March 1981 Michael left the house at 4am to go on a fishing trip with friends. In the event the trip was cancelled due to bad weather, but when he returned home he found his 15-year-old friend, Richard Collins, lying in bed with Susan. They had been having an affair for some time but this was the first that Michael knew of it. Michael hit them both and chased Richard out of the house.

On 4 June Michael began suffering from headaches and on the following day he felt nauseous and had stomach pains. On the Saturday a doctor prescribed him some antibiotics but his condition worsened and on the following Monday he was admitted to Southend Hospital.

On 17 June he was transferred to Hammersmith Hospital and blood and urine samples were taken as doctors believed he was suffering from paraquat poisoning. The results proved negative but nevertheless Michael died on 27 June and a post-mortem was carried out. Significantly Professor David Evans, the pathologist, retained some of Michael's organs before his body was cremated on 3 July.

Susan Barber, left, who used the name 'nympho' as her call sign and enjoyed many private sex parties.

Straight after the cremation Richard moved in with Susan and she collected her husband's death benefit and a £900 annual allowance for the children. With some of her money she bought a CB radio and, using the call sign 'nympho', she began to make regular arrangements with a number of local men to come back to her house for sex.

Meanwhile Professor Evans was doggedly investigating Michael's unexplained death. It had been believed that he was an early HIV sufferer but new tests showed that paraquat was in some of the organs. There was a case conference in January 1982 and it was quickly discovered that the samples that had originally been sent to the National Poisons Reference Centre had never arrived, and that someone, in error, had returned the negative results. New samples were sent to ICI, who had made the paraquat, and positive results were returned.

When the police arrested Susan and Richard the young man was quick to blame Susan. They were no longer lovers and he had been replaced by a long string of different men who had attended Susan's private sex parties. Their trial opened at Chelmsford on 1 November 1982. Susan was charged with murder, conspiracy to murder and administering poison. Richard was charged with conspiracy.

Although Susan admitted poisoning Michael's food, she claimed that she had not intended to kill him. She confirmed that she had put the paraquat in gravy which only Michael ate. The jury found them both guilty. Richard was sentenced to two years and Susan to life imprisonment. In July 1983 Susan married one of her CB lovers in prison.

* * * * *

Murder by poisoning has not gone out of fashion. The lack of more recent examples has much more to do with the very tight controls over poisons since the 1920s. Gradually it has become increasingly difficult to obtain deadly chemicals as a much more stringent monitoring system is now in place, making it difficult to obtain poisons without leaving a damning paper trail. It is also significant that attitudes to what we now know to be poisons were entirely different in the past. Substances such as arsenic were used to improve health and phosphorous was considered to be an aphrodisiac. The method of slowly poisoning a victim, so that their condition gradually deteriorates over a period of weeks or months, is a particularly striking, and creepy, image. Some very determined women resorted to this form of murder.

CHAPTER EIGHT

HEINOUS HORRORS

The cases of four women stand out from all the others covered in this book. They stand out not because they attracted considerable publicity at the time, and cause general shock and disgust, but because each, in its own way, is completely inexplicable. Many women have killed for money, jealousy, hatred and as a side effect of other crimes. These four women, all mass murderers, repulsed the nation with their complete indifference to the suffering they caused. Only one committed her crimes at a time when society could exact the ultimate punishment; the other three, convicted of monstrous and incomprehensible deeds, will probably never be released from prison. The general public almost universally supported the sentences meted out to the four women; so deeply shocked were they by the depravity of the crimes.

VICTORIAN LONDON had been absorbed by the cases of Adelaide Bartlett and Florence Bravo and would later be stunned by such crimes as the Whitechapel murders. But in 1873 a 40-year-old ex-nurse from a small mining village in West Auckland would shatter the image of murderous women.

Mary Ann Cotton was born Mary Ann Robson in October 1832 in County Durham. Many considered her to be an attractive woman who was never short of admirers. At the age of 20 she married a 26-year-old miner called William Mowbray, and in the first four years of their marriage Mary bore three children, all of whom tragically died. In 1860 she had another son and in 1864 a daughter; both died of gastric fever. After her husband spent a short time at sea he returned in January 1865 with a foot injury, and soon he had severe stomach problems which proved to be fatal. When William died Mary Ann collected £35 in insurance and the childless widow moved on to Sunderland.

She began working at the Sunderland Infirmary, which was used to house patients with contagious diseases. It was there that she met, fell in love with and married George Ward, on 28 August 1865. Within four months George fell seriously ill and the doctors believed that he had a liver complaint. His death certificate for 21 October 1866 gave the cause of death as fever.

Again the poor widow moved on, staying in Sunderland and becoming housekeeper for James Robinson. He was a widower with four children and was employed as a shipwright. The first of his children to die, his 10-month-old son, was buried on 23 December 1866. He was later joined in his grave by his six-year-old brother and his eight-year-old sister. Each time the cause of death was gastric fever and it seems that Mary was particularly busy during this time, as when she went to stay with her mother in March 1867, it took just nine days for the old woman to die.

Despite all the tragedies, James Robinson married a pregnant Mary Ann on 11 August 1867. She gave birth to a daughter on 29 November 1867, but the child died of gastric fever aged just four months.

James Robinson was lucky. No doubt Mary Ann had planned a similar fate for him, but when he realised that she had been stealing mortgage money from him, they had a blazing row and Mary Ann fled the home. She was soon conspiring other outrages and took a job as a housekeeper for a ship's captain. She obviously made a good impression on the man because she was left in charge of his house when he went off on a voyage. No sooner had the ship sailed than Mary sold off the entire contents of the household and disappeared.

She then moved to Walbottle in Northumberland, where she worked for a short time for a doctor. The doctor sacked Mary Ann when he realised that she had been stealing money from him. Every cloud had a silver lining, however, because while at Walbottle she met Frederick Cotton, another widower. She had been introduced to him by her friend Margaret Cotton. Mary Ann was still dragging around her sole remaining daughter, but when she and Frederick Cotton fell in love, it was time for the girl to disappear. She died of typhus on 28 January 1871. There was also time to do away with Frederick's sister, Margaret, who died on 25 March. She married Frederick in September, covering the bigamous marriage by claiming to be Mary Ann Mowbray, the name of her dead husband. She took out a life insurance policy on Frederick's two sons and in January 1872 she gave birth to a son fathered by Frederick. After an argument with one of the neighbours, Mary Ann poisoned all of the family's pigs.

The Cotton family now consisted of Frederick, Mary Ann, their child and Frederick's two sons. They moved to West Auckland. Frederick died first, heavily insured, at the age of 39.

Mary immediately took a new lover called Joseph Nattrass, but she was actually pregnant with the child of another man, named Quick-Manning, who was a local excise officer. In short order Nattrass died of gastric fever; Mary Ann and Frederick's child and Frederick's eldest son all died between 10 March and 1 April 1872. Quick-Manning's child also died in the March, leaving only Frederick's youngest son Charles.

So far every person who had died at Mary's hands had been insured and when Charles joined them in July 1872 wagging tongues sealed Mary Ann's fate.

A doctor was persuaded to carry out a post-mortem on young Charles's body and this confirmed that the boy had not died of gastric fever but had been poisoned with arsenic. Other recently dead victims were also exhumed; all had been killed by arsenic. Mary was finally charged with murder and brought before the Durham Assizes in March 1873. She claimed that the only possible explanation for the arsenic was that it must have come from the wallpaper in their house.

The prosecution had a big surprise for her when they revealed to the court that they had evidence that Mary Ann had actually bought arsenic, claiming to the chemist that she was going to use it to kill bed bugs. She was found guilty and sentenced to hang, but she was carrying Quick-Manning's child. This did not save her from her date with the hangman. She gave birth on 19 March 1873 and was executed by 73-year-old William Calcraft at Durham Prison on 24 March 1873.

It is believed that Mary Ann Cotton, over a 20-year period, had killed at least 21 people. It later emerged that her preferred method of delivering the arsenic was in cups of tea.

* * * * *

Another poisoner, **Mary Elizabeth Wilson**, found her career finally cut short in 1957. Wilson was notorious not for the number of murders that she committed, but for the fact that she systematically disposed of four unwanted men in just three years. She became known as the 'Widow of Windy Nook'.

Mary Wilson married John Knowles in 1914, a marriage that would last for 41 years. Gradually, over the years, John and Mary's relationship deteriorated to the point that they ceased to sleep with one another and only ever communicated on general household matters. At some point in the early 1950s the Wilsons took in a lodger, a chimney sweep by the name of John George Russell. Very soon after Russell began to share Mary's bed but, by all accounts, providing her husband was physically cared for, this did not present a problem for him. Everything changed in July 1955 when Mary's husband, always known for his strength and fitness, died after a fortnight's illness.

Mary discussed with her neighbours the prospect of moving on and buying another house. It is believed that Mary hoped that Russell would marry her but it seems that he must have turned her down because at Christmas he too fell ill and died in early January 1956.

In June 1956 Mary welcomed a new lodger, the retired estate agent, Oliver James Leonard, aged 76. It was a whirlwind romance and they married in Jarrow on 21 September. Just 13 days after their wedding Mary's neighbour, Ellen, answered the door to a frantic Mary. She told her that her husband was ill and when Ellen went next door, Oliver was writhing around on the bedroom floor. The two women put him into bed and Mary made a pot of tea which Ellen took up to him, but he knocked the cup out of her hand. He died the next day and the doctor was content that the cause of death was heart failure.

Mary Elizabeth Wilson, the Widow of Windy Nook.

A year passed and Mary married once again and moved in to the home of Ernest George Lawrence Wilson. He was a 75-year-old retired engineer. Ernest was to last a fortnight. At first the doctor attended him for a stomach complaint and then, a few days later, when he returned to see how his patient was getting on, he found him dead. The cause of death

was given as cardiac muscular failure. Mary's behaviour around this time had been very odd.

At her wedding reception she had said, regarding the large amount of food that was still sitting on the tables at the end of the event, 'Well, we can always keep it for the funeral'. On the night before the doctor found that Ernest was dead, Mary had called on a friend, Grace Liddle, and asked if she could spend the night with her, as her husband was unwell and was being looked after by the doctor. Shortly before the doctor actually arrived the following morning, Grace had gone back to Mary's house with her, and saw Ernest already laid out in the table in the front room. Even at Ernest's funeral Mary had joked with the undertaker about obtaining a discount from him because she had put so much business his way.

Although Mary had not earned a great deal from these murders, with her first husband and Russell leaving her around £46, Oliver Leonard £50, and Ernest £100 plus his life insurance, the police were beginning to take an interest. They ordered that all four corpses should be exhumed. Each showed signs of having been poisoned with a rat poison called Rodine, which was liberally laced with phosphorous.

In the event, no charges were made against Mary for the killing of her first husband and John Russell as their bodies were too decomposed. Open verdicts were returned on their deaths. But Mary found herself standing trial at Leeds Assizes in March 1958 for the murder of her other two husbands.

In court it emerged that the doctor that had signed Oliver's death certificate had not actually seen the body and the doctor that had signed Ernest's only gave it a cursory examination. It was proposed by the prosecution that the poison had been given either in jam or cough mixture. While the defence pointed out that no Rodine had been found in Mary's possession, the prosecution simply replied that this must, therefore, rule out suicide or accidental poisoning. The defence also tried to suggest that Ernest and Oliver had been taking phosphorous purely to rekindle their sex drive, but it was pointed out that three bottles of the aphrodisiac would have to be taken before it became lethal.

Mary did not give evidence at her own trial and she was found guilty of the murders of Ernest and Oliver. The judge sentenced her to death but it was commuted to life imprisonment by the Home Secretary. She died aged 70 in Holloway Prison on 5 December 1962.

* * * * *

Had the sadistic child killers Ian Brady and **Myra Hindley** been captured only a few years before, they would undoubtedly have faced the death penalty. Capital punishment had only just been abolished when they found themselves convicted of crimes that were truly incomprehensible. Despite the passing of time, the Moors Murders still rank as the most cold-blooded and calculated in British criminal history.

The two had begun their lives in entirely different circumstances. Brady was born on 2 January 1938. He was the illegitimate son of a Scottish waitress and had been brought up in Glasgow. At a very early age he had shown marked psychopathic tendencies and was known to torture and kill cats and birds. By the age of 20 he had a string of convictions behind him for burglary and theft and had spent some time in Borstal. At the end of this period he moved to Gorton in Manchester to live with his mother, who had married Patrick Brady. So it was that Ian Duncan Stewart became Ian Brady.

February 1959 found him working as a clerk in Millwards, a chemical and soap company, after having studied accountancy, and it was here that he was to meet his partner, Myra Hindley. Hindley was born on 23 July 1942 and was a shy loner as a child. She had a dominant mother but went to live with her grandmother shortly after her youngest sister, Maureen, was born. Her closest friend was Michael Higgins, who tragically drowned in a disused reservoir in 1957. This death was to have a profound impact on her life.

At the age of 19, in 1961, Hindley took a job at Millwards as a typist. It was not long before she became attracted to the young Brady, who sat quietly during his lunch break, reading Nazi literature. One day Hindley accepted Brady's invitation to accompany him to the cinema; it was New Year's Eve and the two were to spend the first of many nights together.

From then on they were inseparable and seemingly obsessed with Hitler and all aspects of the Nazi regime. Hindley even died her hair blonde and Brady called her Myra Hess. To make extra money and for kicks they took nude photographs of one another and tried to sell them. They also planned a bank robbery, with Hindley attending a gun club to learn shooting and taking driving lessons so that she could be the getaway driver. Still as inseparable as ever, Brady moved in to Hindley's grandmother's house in Wardle Brook Avenue, Hattersley, to be with Myra in September 1964.

Although none were to know it, Brady and Hindley had already explored far beyond their Nazi-flavoured sadomasochistic practices, and with Hindley behind the steering

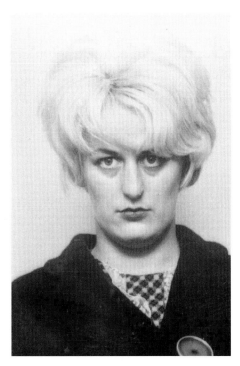

Myra Hindley, who together with Ian Brady murdered several children.

wheel of their rented car, they had paid frequent secret visits to the countryside. So far everything that they had done remained a secret between them, but Brady wanted to involve others. He found the perfect potential recruit in David Smith, the 17-year-old husband of Hindley's sister, Maureen. Smith had married Maureen shortly after discovering that his girlfriend was pregnant. Neither knew that Brady and Hindley had also married on 15 August 1964.

It seems that Hindley and Brady chose to act together for only another year, but Brady would often boast to Smith that he had murdered and that he was planning armed robberies. His boasting turned to action on 6 October 1965 and was to prove to be the undoing of the pair. Shortly before midnight Hindley disturbed Maureen and David and asked David to take her home, which he agreed to do. David waited outside Wardle Brooke Avenue while Hindley went inside to find Brady. She flicked on the landing light twice as a signal for David to follow her into the house. In the living room sat Brady and a 17-year-old called Edward Evans. Brady had picked the boy up earlier in the evening and as Hindley and David entered the room, Brady began smashing his skull in with an axe. Smith looked on stunned and after inflicting enormous damage to Evans's head, Brady simply said 'That was the messiest yet. It normally only takes one blow.' Brady then made sure that Evans was dead by strangling him with electrical wire.

For some reason, probably fear, Smith helped Hindley and Brady clean up the living room and wrap Evans's body in a polythene sheet. The corpse was then carried upstairs. Smith's worst fears were reinforced when Hindley told him that she had been sitting in a car on Saddleworth Moor with a body in the boot, while Brady had dug a grave. She laughed as she told him that the police had asked her whether she needed any help. Somehow Smith managed to extricate himself from the situation and fled home to his wife. After recounting what he had seen and heard, armed with a bread knife and a large screwdriver for protection, he went to the local police station.

The police were stunned by what they heard and immediately raided the house in Wardle Brook Avenue. Despite Hindley's protestations the police gained entry to the house and found Evans's body in the bedroom. They also found two left luggage tickets for lockers at Manchester Central Station hidden in the spine of a book. In the lockers they were to find photographs of naked children, coshes, wigs and tape recordings. Brady was arrested and the police were desperate to discover where the three or four other murder victims that Brady had boasted of had been buried.

It did not take the police very long to identify one of the photographs as being that of Lesley Ann Downey, who had disappeared on Boxing Day 1964. The tape recordings contained the sounds of the little girl begging and pleading for her life. In the car parked outside Wardle Brooke Avenue were detailed instructions of where to bury Evans's body on Saddleworth Moor.

Superintendent Talbot and his men painstakingly searched the house and eventually, in an exercise book, they found a list of names, which included one that stood out. It simply said 'John Kilbride' and it struck a chord in Talbot's mind. He rang the police in Ashton-under-Lyne and confirmed that the 12-year-old had disappeared in November 1963. Together with Joe Mounsey, an officer from Ashton-under-Lyne, Talbot pored over the stacks of photographs and albums that they had recovered from the house. They were particularly interested in those of Brady and Hindley on Saddleworth Moor. Initial interviews with Brady and Hindley had met with blank-faced denials and both suspects had simply said that they had made up the stories of the murders and the burials simply to impress David Smith. There was nothing for it but for the police to systematically try to identify the exact sites where the photographs of Brady and Hindley had been taken. It was not to be an easy task, physically or psychologically, for the searchers.

On 16 October 1965 the police found their first hard evidence. Buried in a shallow grave was the body of 10-year-old Lesley Ann Downey. One of the photographs particularly interested Mounsey. It showed Hindley crouching on the ground with a puppy. As far as he was concerned Hindley was not looking into the camera or at the puppy but staring at the ground beside her. He had the photograph enlarged and set off with a photographer onto the moors to try and locate the exact spot. He had one clue, as in the photograph's background was a distinctive group of rocks. Eventually they found the place and there they discovered the body of John Kilbride.

The police were not convinced that this was the end of the investigation, but they were content to commit Brady and Hindley to trial at Chester Assizes in 1966. Throughout the trial they denied murdering either Lesley Ann Downey or John Kilbride. As far as Lesley Ann was concerned, they claimed that they had given her 10 shillings to pose naked for photographs and that she had left them unharmed. Hindley's protestations that she had not been present when Lesley Ann was murdered were utterly destroyed when the court was played tape recordings of the last minutes of the young girl's life. It was clear to the jury that one of the voices on the tape was Hindley's. Brady was found guilty of three murders and Hindley of two and they were both sentenced to life imprisonment.

Still there was concern that they had not been brought to justice for all of their crimes and it was not until 1987 that Hindley confessed that the pair had murdered Pauline Reade on 12 July 1963 and Keith Bennett on 16 June 1964. Ian Brady confirmed the confession Hindley had made.

Sixteen-year-old Pauline had disappeared on her way to a dance, and 12-year-old Keith disappeared from Manchester. Hindley took the police back onto Saddleworth Moor in 1987 and was able to identify the burial spot of Pauline, but she could not identify the shallow grave of Keith Bennett.

Even now, over 25 years since the murders took place, and despite the work of reformers and campaigners on their behalf, Brady and Hindley remain in prison with little prospect of parole. Since 1999 Brady has been on hunger strike in Ashworth Hospital, Merseyside, but this has not prevented him from co-authoring a book on serial killers which, incidentally, makes no mention of the Saddleworth Moor killings.

* * * * *

There can be few people that will fail to recognise the address 25 Cromwell Street, Gloucester. It was an ordinary three-storey house in Gloucester and the home of Fred and **Rosemary West**. Fortunately the place no longer exists but for the police who arrived there in February 1994, it will remain a nightmare.

The story goes back to 1941 when Fred West was born in Herefordshire, one of six children. He had a close relationship with his mother and considered his father to be something of a role model. When Fred left school at the age of 15 he first took a job working on a farm. At around this time, following in the footsteps of his father, it seems that Fred took an interest in incest. It was later claimed that one of Fred's sisters fell pregnant as a result. He claimed, much later, that his father's creed was, as far as his daughters were concerned 'I made you so I am entitled to have you'.

At 17 Fred was involved in a motorcycle accident, leaving him with a metal plate in his head and one leg permanently shorter than the other. Again, as he would later claim, this was another turning point in his life, since the injuries had affected his ability to control himself. Soon after, Fred was seriously injured when he was thrown off a fire escape by a girl who objected to him shoving his hand up her skirt. By 1961 Fred had had his first brush with the police, having been caught in possession of the proceeds of a burglary he had committed on a jewellery shop.

Now 20, Fred showed the first public signs of his increasingly perverse sexual appetites. He had slept with a 13-year-old girl and had said at the time 'Well doesn't everyone do it?' Somehow he managed to avoid a jail sentence and returned to his parents' home in 1962. It was there that he rekindled a relationship which had begun shortly after his motorcycle accident. He was still very much in love with the thief, burglar and prostitute Catherine Bernadette Costello, known as Rena. Initially their rediscovered relationship was complicated by the fact that Rena was carrying the child of an Asian bus driver. This did not seem to put Fred off and in November 1962 they married, with his parents believing that Rena was pregnant with Fred's child. When Charmaine West was born Rena told Fred's mother that their natural child had died during childbirth and that they had adopted Charmaine.

Fred's sexual appetite was growing and even Rena could not satisfy him. His job as an ice-cream van driver gave him ample opportunity to have sex with many women. By 1964 he had fathered another daughter, Anna Maria. After a tragic road accident in which Fred, at the wheel of the ice-cream van, knocked over and killed a young boy, he and Rena decided to move back to Gloucester. They brought with them the two children and a newly found friend, Anna McFall. Fred took a job in a slaughterhouse and became progressively more obsessed with sex. Rena fled back to Glasgow. When she returned to see her daughters in July 1966 she found Anna McFall had taken her place in Fred's bed. Also during this short period there were no fewer than eight sexual assaults in the Gloucester area. Later it was pointed out that Fred fitted the description of the attacker.

By early 1967 McFall was pregnant with Fred's child. Despite her attempts to get Fred to divorce Rena, Fred had other ideas. At some point in July 1967 he murdered Anna McFall and their unborn child. There was to be a characteristic ritual performed on the corpse. When the body was finally found the fingers and toes had been cut off. Without a qualm Rena moved back in with Fred and he sent her out to earn extra money from prostitution. Sexually he had turned at least part of his attention to Rena's daughter, Charmaine. Although never directly attributed to Fred, 15-year-old Mary Bastholm disappeared from a bus stop in January 1968; she was never seen again. The links between her and Fred were circumstantial; Fred later abducted women from bus stops, Mary had served him tea in a café, a witness claimed to have seen Mary in Fred's car and Mary may have been a friend of Anna McFall.

In February 1968 Fred committed a series of thefts following the death of his mother. Fatefully he began a new job on 29 November 1968 as a delivery man for a bakery. It was here that he met 15-year-old Rosemary Letts.

Rose had been born in November 1953 in Devon. Her mother, Daisy, was a manic depressive and her father, Bill, was a schizophrenic. Bill demanded complete obedience from his wife and children and took every opportunity to beat them. If the children were noisy they were beaten with wood or his belt; if they got up too late they would have buckets of cold water thrown over them. Rose's mother found it impossible to cope with her violent husband and four children and in 1953, shortly before she gave birth to Rose, she had been given electro-convulsive therapy. This treatment may have severely affected the unborn Rose as it seems that although she was an attractive girl, she had strange repetitive habits, such as rocking her head and sitting in a trance-like state. The family called her 'Dozy Rosie' and her weight increased disproportionately to her years. She became her father's favourite, often being the only one in the family that would avoid beatings.

At school, constantly teased about her weight, she would lash out and seriously injure anyone who tormented her. By the time she was an early teenager, Rose had developed the habit of walking around the house naked after she had had a bath and molesting her younger brothers. Local boys did not seem particularly interested in Rose, but she wanted to attract the attention of older men. On at least one occasion in 1968 she put herself in a position where her desire for an older man led to her being raped. Her mother, meanwhile, left Rose's father in early 1969 and moved in with her daughter Glenys and her husband. She took Rose with her and without her father's close attention Rose was able to sleep with many men in the local area. Glenys's husband, Jim Tyler, later claimed that Rose had tried to seduce him.

Whether it be truth or fiction regarding an incestuous relationship with her father, Rose unaccountably moved back in with him in the middle of 1969. When she met Fred her father was outraged when he discovered that the two were sleeping together. Fred spent a short period in prison for non-payment of fines and Rose settled temporarily back with her father, but shortly before Fred was released, Rose's father discovered that she was carrying Fred's child. She immediately moved in to Fred's trailer and set up home with him and his two daughters. She gave birth to Heather in 1970; Fred was in and out of prison the whole time and from the very beginning Rose resented looking after Rena's children.

Sometime in the summer of 1971 Rose murdered Charmaine. Since Fred was in jail at the time the body must have been hidden until Fred was released. When it was found over 20 years later, the fingers, toes and kneecaps had been removed. Charmaine's body was buried under the kitchen floor of a house they occupied in Midland Road.

Rose's father was keen to see his daughter and granddaughter back with him in his own home, but on a number of occasions Rose told him, regarding Fred, 'You don't know him there's nothing he wouldn't do, even murder'. Fred was eager to earn more money and experience ever more bizarre sexual acts. He convinced Rose to take up prostitution and was particularly keen for her to attract local West Indian men. He would watch her having sex with them through a peep-hole. Fred took photographs of Rose and sent them to contact magazines to attract people to have sex with Rose and himself and anyone else that they cared to bring along.

There was one cloud on the horizon. In August 1971 Rena reappeared, looking for Charmaine. Fred lured her to his house, got her drunk and then strangled her. Again the signature mutilation took place.

Towards the end of 1971 Fred and Rose hit on another plan to find sexual partners. They took to cruising around the Gloucester area looking for young girls. As Fred confided in neighbour, Elizabeth Agius, Rose's presence in the car allayed their fears of being picked up by a stranger. Elizabeth baby-sat for them on several occasions, believing what Fred had told her to be a joke. Elizabeth may have been drugged and raped by Fred at some stage, but she was not murdered.

In January 1972 Fred and Rose married at Gloucester Registry Office and in June Rose gave birth to Mae West. They decided to move from Midland Road and rent 25 Cromwell Street. Fred was in work, Rose made money from prostitution and they also proposed to have lodgers to help contribute towards the rent. One of the first things the couple did was to convert the cellar into a torture chamber so that Rose would have a place of work to take her clients. They christened the torture chamber by Fred raping his eight-year-old daughter Anna Marie. This was not to be the only time.

In late 1972 on one of their cruising expeditions, Fred and Rose picked up the attractive 17-year-old Caroline Owens. Both of them wanted to seduce her so they abducted her and raped her in the cellar. She was then told that she would have to stay with them and if not, 'I'll keep you in the cellar and let my black friends have you, and when we're finished we'll kill you and bury you under the paving stones of Gloucester'. Somehow Caroline managed to escape and informed the police and the Wests found themselves in a magistrate's court in January 1973. Rose was pregnant again and Fred was able to convince the magistrates that Caroline had been a willing partner in sex. The couple were simply fined.

Other visitors and tenants were not as lucky as Caroline Owens. The Wests persuaded Lynda Gough to move into the house with them to look after the children. She did not live long and suffered the same fate as Anna McFall and Rena, this time being buried under the garage. The West's son, Stephen, was born in August and in November they abducted 15-year-old Carol Ann Cooper. She was incarcerated in the cellar for as long as it amused the Wests and then was finally strangled or suffocated and buried, following the same ritual.

Throughout the year Fred had been working on improving the house. He had enlarged the cellar and pulled down the garage to build an extension. There was to be one more murder in 1973. On 27 December a university student, Lucy Partington, left a friend's house at 10pm and was abducted by Fred and Rose. She was raped and tortured for a week, just as Carol Ann had been, and then buried at the Cromwell Street address. Unlike many of the other murders, the date of the burial can be more accurately assessed because Fred had to go to the accident and emergency department of the hospital on 3 January 1974 with a serious cut that required stitches, probably got while burying the body.

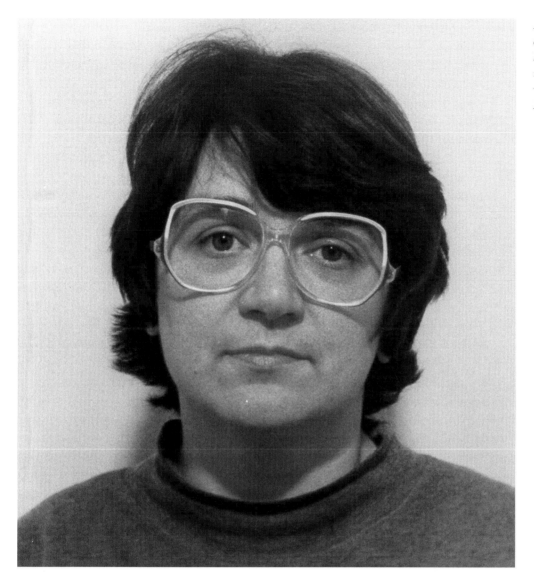

Rosemary West, currently serving 10 life sentences for murders committed with her husband Fred.

Three other girls were abducted, raped and tortured and finally killed between April 1974 and April 1975. The first was probably Therese Siegenthaler, aged 21, followed by Shirley Hubbard, aged 15, and Juanita Mott, aged 18. When these bodies were found much later their causes of death pointed to ever more extreme and violent deaths.

Fred continued to burgle houses and fence stolen goods, which on more than one occasion brought him to the attention of the local police. The court was later to hear evidence from a girl who was only ever referred to as Miss A. She had been brought to the house at some point in 1976 and had seen with her own eyes two naked girls that were being held prisoner in the cellar. Miss A was sexually assaulted by Rose and raped by Fred. Fred also seemed keen to involve other men in his activities and often enjoyed watching them have sex with Anna Marie.

In 1977 18-year-old Shirley Robinson arrived on the scene. She was a bi-sexual former prostitute and fell pregnant with Fred's child while Rose was carrying the child of one of her black clients. It seems that Shirley tried to convince Fred to do away with Rose and install her as his wife. After Rose gave birth to Tara in December 1977, Shirley had just seven months to live, being murdered and buried with her unborn child in the back garden.

November 1978 saw two more pregnancies in the household. Rose delivered Fred's child, Louise, and Anna Marie fell pregnant with her father's child. It was an ectopic pregnancy and was terminated.

Towards the end of 1979 the Wests murdered another teenager called Alison Chambers, but by now their children were becoming aware of what was going on in the house. Anna Marie moved out that year and Fred began to take a sexual interest in Heather and Mae.

June 1980 saw Rose giving birth to Barry, Fred's second natural son and in April 1982 she gave birth to Rosemary Junior, the daughter of another of her black clients. She followed this in July 1983 with another mixed-race daughter called Lucy Anna. Throughout there were still more abductions and murders but none were buried at 25 Cromwell Street.

Three years passed before Heather, in 1986, confided to a girlfriend that she had been raped by her father and feared for her life. Heather disappeared at the age of 16 in 1987. Fred's son, Stephen, helped to dig the grave in the back garden.

The Wests decided that the best way to make money would be to set up their own brothel and they attracted several women, including Katherine Halliday, to work as a prostitute under their direction. She lived with them for some time but she was clearly alarmed by the bondage aspects and fled.

The police net was beginning to close around the Wests. One of the young girls that had been raped but not murdered by the Wests told the police. The case was assigned to Detective Constable Hazel Savage; she knew of Fred West and remembered the time when Rena had asked for her help, claiming that Fred was a sexual pervert. The police raided Cromwell Street on 6 August 1992; they were looking for evidence of child abuse and found a mountain of pornography. Fred was arrested for the rape of a minor and Rose for assisting him.

Detective Savage interviewed Anna Marie and learned of the sexual abuse that she had suffered. She also told of her worries about the disappearance of Charmaine, Rena and Heather. All the younger children were taken into care and Rose, now alone in the house on bail, attempted to commit suicide but was saved by her son Stephen. Fred, although clearly concerned that his terrible secrets were about to be uncovered, escaped justice when two witnesses decided not to testify. Fred was released and the charges dropped.

But for the tenacity of Detective Savage, who was certain that Fred and Rose knew much more about the disappearances than they were prepared to divulge, the Wests might never have been stopped. The West children were silent and would not cooperate; over the years the terror of their father had taught them of the stupidity of getting in his way.

Detective Superintendent John Bennett finally managed to get a search warrant for the house in Cromwell Street and executed it on 24 February 1994. He proposed to excavate the whole site in the search for the missing females. When the police arrived in the afternoon Rose rang her husband's mobile and calmly informed him 'They're going to dig up the garden, looking for Heather'. He did not seem overly perturbed at this prospect and when he dropped in to the police station on his way home from work, he told the police that neither he nor his wife knew where Heather was and said 'Lots of girls disappear, take a different name and go into prostitution'. He also added to assist them that Heather had a drug problem and that she was a lesbian.

The police had no evidence on which to hold or charge the Wests, and despite the fact that Fred had confessed to killing Heather after they had found some human bones, he was temporarily released. Rose had told the police that her husband had sent her out of the house the day that Heather had disappeared. Therefore, improbably, both Fred and Rose stood by as the police systematically dug up their garden. The police first found one decapitated and dismembered young woman and then another. Fred was charged with three murders; Heather, Shirley Robinson and an unknown third woman. He claimed full responsibility and sought to protect his wife. He then admitted that there were other bodies buried in the cellar. Strangely, he told the police that he had murdered them all but he had not raped them and that they had come to him to have sex. In the end no fewer than nine different sets of bones were found in the cellar.

The police faced a nightmare in trying to match the missing persons with the remains. Fred claimed that he could not remember some of the women's names, nor when he had murdered them. He helped the police find the bodies of Anna McFall, Charmaine and Rena but refused to help in discovering where he had buried Mary Bastholm.

By now Rose was desperately trying to distance herself from her doomed husband. She even refused to let him touch her at the hearing. It was not, however, to save her and she was to face trial alone. Fred West was formally charged with 12 murders on 13 December 1994 and, on remand at Winson Green Prison in Birmingham at noon on New Year's Day 1995, he committed suicide by hanging himself in his cell.

As far as Rose was concerned there was a great deal of circumstantial evidence to link her to a number of the murders. Her trial began on 3 October 1995 and it was the task of Brian Leveson QC to marshall the witnesses to provide evidence of Rose's numerous sexual assaults on other women. The court heard from Miss A, Anna Marie, Caroline Owens and a number of other women who had survived their encounters with the Wests. Rose's defence counsel, Richard Ferguson QC, attempted to convince the court that although his client was guilty of sexual assault, she was never present when her husband murdered the women, nor did she have any knowledge of where he had buried them.

There were three turning points in the trial, the first of which was the evidence of Janet Leach, who had been Fred West's witness during his police interviews. Fred had told her that Rose had murdered Charmaine and Shirley Robinson herself, and, knowing that he would not escape the other charges against him, had agreed with Rose to claim that he had murdered them himself. The defence attempted to use taped evidence given by Fred West during interview as proof that Rose was not present when the murders had taken place. The prosecution easily proved that Fred was lying on a number of issues and that his evidence could not be trusted. Fatally, the third key issue was Ferguson's decision to allow Rose to give evidence herself. In the witness box she frequently became angry at the prosecution's cross-examination and she left the court with the distinct impression that she was a habitual liar and that she had made her own children suffer throughout their lives.

Rose West was found guilty on 10 counts of murder and sentenced to 10 life sentences. Rose West is as unlikely to be released from prison as Myra Hindley.

CHAPTER NINE

FELONIOUS FEMALES

Over the centuries many women with criminal tendencies have been quick to take advantage of society's natural inclination to trust them more than their male counterparts. Several women were brilliant and habitual criminals; perfectly capable of cashing in on this advantage which still left them open to the same levels of punishment at the hands of the law courts.

PROBABLY one of the most notorious and successful female criminals was born in Aldersgate Street in the Barbican area of London in 1589. She is variously described as being a master thief and a woman who habitually dressed as a man. Despite her tender, affectionate and considerate upbringing, **Mary Frith**, from her very early years, seemed to be something of a tomboy. Her shoemaker father and doting mother tried everything to wean their daughter into stitching, sewing and other sedentary female pastimes. They could not cure her of her unruly behaviour and whenever she had the chance she fought and played with boys. Even her uncle, who was a church minister, tried to change her manner.

As a last resort the family arranged for Mary to take a voyage to America and bundled her on board a merchant ship lying off Gravesend in Kent. Mary's self-taught, masculine education led her to be able to jump overboard and swim back to the shore; from then on she avoided her pious uncle. Churches and convents were no place for her; she felt at home in the disreputable places in London, such as Bloomsbury, Covent Garden, Cheapside and Cornhill. Her parents were mortified to see her dressed as a man, unwilling to undertake women's work, adamant that she should not accept domesticity and completely averse to marriage or motherhood. It is said that dressed as a woman Mary was considered to be rather ugly, but that as a man she was accepted, and enjoyed the pleasures and freedom which that gender gave her. Unwilling to accept a routine job, and keen to enjoy the freedom of drinking and carousing wherever and whenever she pleased, she needed to find a source of income. It was no big step for her to fall into criminal ways. Mary Frith was no more; **Moll Cutpurse**, the master thief, had been born.

There were rich pickings to be had in the city of London if a thief was well-trained and determined. These land pirates made their living from picking pockets and cutting purses in the bustling markets and fairs. Moll was not always entirely successful and in a short period of time she had been branded on her hand four times by the courts after she had been apprehended for these robberies. Some, if not all, of her early crimes seemed to have some kind of political motivation too, as invariably she chose victims who were opposed to King Charles I. This did not, however, prevent her from being punished whenever she was caught.

Eventually her reputation required her to consider alternative employment and Moll Cutpurse took to highway robbery. On one notable occasion Moll had the audacity to hold up none other than General Fairfax on Hounslow Heath. She levelled pistols at the general and stole approximately £250, shooting him through the arm when he tried to grapple with her. After the robbery she took off across the heath and was pursued by two of Fairfax's servants. Calmly Moll stopped her horse, turned and shot the horses out from underneath the two men.

Unfortunately there were a number of Parliamentarians quartered in Hounslow and they gave chase after being alerted by Fairfax's men. They tracked Moll as far as Turnham Green, where her horse foundered and she was dragged in chains to Newgate Prison. Inevitably, given the weight of evidence against her, she was condemned to death. But she bought her pardon from Fairfax for a staggering £2,000.

This marked an end to Moll's highway robbing days, but not an end to her criminal career. She moved into a house in Fleet Street, near the Globe Tavern, and initially set it up as a drinking den. It was here that she took to smoking a pipe, still dressed in the clothes of a man. Moll set herself up as something between a broker and a fencing operation. She would buy stolen rings, jewels and watches and those that had lost them would know that they simply had to pay Moll slightly more than she had paid the thief in order to recover their possessions.

On one such occasion a man had his watch pick-pocketed. The way it was done serves to illustrate how cunning some of the thieves must have been, and attests to the fact that Moll must have been even more skilled in being able to deal with them. The man had been spotted by two pick-pockets and followed towards Smithfield. The two thieves overtook him and manufactured a brawl to divert his attention. While he was watching the scuffle a third man appeared and took the watch. Moll told the robbery victim that it might take a day or two to recover his watch and foolishly he told her that it was so valuable to him that he would have not have swapped it for twice its value. When the man returned to Moll she had obtained the watch and promptly sold it back to him for 20 guineas.

Moll also got involved with a new set of criminals known as 'heavers'. They would enter a shop and not steal any goods but take the trader's invaluable records of transactions. The traders would be lost by not knowing what they had bought and sold and Moll was only too happy to retrieve their records for them for a suitable financial consideration.

Sometime around this period a competitor in crime denounced Moll for indecently wearing men's clothes. While this was not necessarily a crime, she accepted the court's decision to make her stand in a white sheet at St Paul's Cross during a Sunday morning sermon. In the event, Moll took full advantage of the situation, and while a crowd gawped at her penance, her associates systematically robbed them. In no way did this event affect Moll's choice of clothing or lifestyle, and she soon added another criminal activity to her armoury of talents.

She had acquired some spectacles which she claimed were magical. Customers flocked to see her, as, when she wore them, she claimed to be able to give them vital information about where their stolen possessions were, and, on other occasions, who they might marry.

Reeling home drunk one night, after a long session in the Devil Tavern, Moll tripped over a black pig in the final stages of giving birth to a clutch of piglets. She drove the animal home and soon after the pig gave birth to 11 piglets. Moll kept the mother until the piglets were fat enough to eat and then turned the sow out. Like a homing pigeon, it returned to its master in Islington. The man was distraught that she had not brought the piglets home and, after feeding it, let the sow wander away in the hope that she would lead him to the piglets. The pig went straight to Moll's door, as the man had hoped, and the owner asked Moll whether she had seen the sow's piglets. Moll let the man look around her house, secure in the knowledge that any mess the piglets had made was now gone and that she and her friends had enjoyed several good meals between them.

Moll continued to diversify and became a very good counterfeiter. She was even able to copy Oliver Cromwell's signature, and with it managed to fraudulently take money from the Exchequer and Customs and Excise.

By the time Moll was 70 years old, years of drink and hard living had begun to take their toll. She contracted dropsy, which bloated her body with water. Reluctantly she wrote out her will, leaving £30 to her three maids and the rest of her estate to a relative who lived in Reddriff, with the useful advice to stay at home and get drunk on the proceeds. She made it clear that when she was buried she wished to be interred upside-down, so that she could be as preposterous in death as she had been in life. Moll died in 1663 and was buried according to her wishes in St Bridget's churchyard. Unfortunately her marble tombstone was lost forever during the Great Fire of London but it was claimed that Milton himself had written the inscription:

Here lies, under this same marble,
Dust, for Time's last sieve to garble;
Dust, to perplex a Sadducee,
Whether it rise a He or She,
Or two in one, a single pair,
Nature's sport, and now her care.
For how she'll clothe it at last day,
Unless she sighs it all away;
Or where she'll place it, none can tell:
Some middle place 'twixt Heaven and Hell
And well 'tis Purgatory's found,
Else she must hide her under ground.
These reliques do deserve the doom,
Of that cheat Mahomet's fine tomb
For no communion she had,
Nor sorted with the good or bad;
That when the world shall be calcin'd,
And the mixd' mass of human kind
Shall sep'rate by that melting fire,
She'll stand alone, and none come nigh her.
Reader, here she lies till then,
When, truly, you'll see her again.

* * * * *

Shortly after Moll Cutpurse's death, three other Molls found themselves in much less agreeable circumstances at Tyburn. **Moll Jones** was born in the year of the Great Fire of London in Chancery Lane. She was a skilled maker of hoods and scarves and worked at the New Exchange on the Strand. It was here that she met and married her husband, who was an apprentice. He was an extravagant man, but unable to maintain the lifestyle he craved. Initially Moll worked day and night, legally, to provide for his needs. She wanted him to look like a gentleman, but her meagre income was insufficient. In order to support her husband she embarked on a career of crime, beginning in St James's Park, where she happened upon a milliner by the name of Mr Price, who also kept a shop at the New Exchange. Moll engaged him in conversation about a Mrs Zouch who had been one of Price's servants before she had murdered her own illegitimate child. Price was rather hard of hearing and fumbled in his pocket to pull out his ear trumpet. While Moll spoke into the tin object her hands reached into his breeches and pulled out a purse containing 15 guineas. One of Moll's next victims was Jacob Delafay, a Jewish chocolate maker, who lived in York Buildings on the Strand. For this crime Moll was convicted and branded on the hand at Newgate.

For the next three or four years she turned her criminal attentions to shoplifting. She was caught stealing half a dozen pairs of silk stockings from the hosier, Mr Wansel, in Exeter Exchange. She had been spotted carrying out the deed by the landlord of the Rose and Crown in the Strand. Unfortunately for Moll he was also a constable and having seen the deed done he took Moll straight to Justice Brydal, who committed her to Newgate for another branding.

Her final crime was to steal some satin from a shop on Ludgate Hill. At the time she had chosen to impersonate the late Duchess of Norfolk. The shop owner saw through the ruse and once again Moll found herself in Newgate. This time, after her appearance at the Old Bailey, she was condemned to be hanged at Tyburn on 18 December 1691.

* * * * *

Moll Raby, who was also known as Mary Raby, Moll Rogers, Moll Jackson and Moll Brown, was born at St Martin's-in-the-Field in 1670. Like Moll Cutpurse, she had thrown herself into London's criminal scene as a counterfeiter, pickpocket, burglar and thief.

It seems that she was a very audacious woman and on one occasion masqueraded as an heiress and took a house in Great Russell Street. She ran up bills with every tradesman in the area and in order to ensure that she had spending money, forged a document which she asked a porter to present at a bank in Lombard Street. For the time it was an incredible amount of money, £150, and Moll had requested that the porter collect the cash in gold. In order to get the maid out of the way Moll asked her to accompany the porter to make sure that he did not run off with the money. When they arrived and presented the bill to the bank in Lombard Street, the two were arrested, but they protested their innocence and claimed that they had only been sent on an errand by their mistress. They were taken back to the house in Great Russell Street, only to find that Moll had absconded with £80 cash, £160 worth of silver plate and any other object in the house that she thought that she could sell. Moll perpetrated this kind of offence on a number of occasions and was captured at least three times and branded for it.

She then married a butcher called Humphry Jackson. Rather than settling down she trained her husband to help her become a successful street robber. Moll would go into a pub and pick up a man and take him down a dark alley. Humphry would lurk in the shadows until Moll, in a clinch with the victim, had succeeded in removing valuables from his clothing. On a given signal Humphry would appear, indignant to find another man with his wife, and knock the victim to the ground. Unfortunately their career was not to last very long as Humphry suddenly died and Moll was reduced to relying on her old ways to provide for herself.

On one occasion Moll was passing Downing Street and saw that one of the doors was half open. She crept in and hid underneath a bed. Moll remained hidden while servants busied themselves preparing a meal and table for the household. She watched as five or six people sat down and ate their meal. On this occasion circumstances had obviously spooked Moll so that she wrapped herself up in a sheet and sneaked out of the house at the first opportunity.

On 3 March 1703 she burgled the house of Lady Cavendish in Soho Square. For whatever reason, two other criminals, Arthur Chambers and Joseph Hatfield, informed the authorities that Moll was responsible for the robbery. They even gave testimony against her in court. With a long string of convictions against her, the court sentenced Moll to be hanged at Tyburn on 3 November 1703.

* * * * *

The third Moll operating in London at around the same time was a habitual thief by the name of **Moll Hawkins**. She was around 26 years old and had been born in St Giles in the Fields. For some years she had worked as a button maker in Maiden Lane, near Covent Garden. Clearly this occupation did not give her sufficient income, but it did give her a good idea of how to make some easy money. She would arrive at a respectable household early in the morning and present herself as a milliner or seamstress's apprentice. She would ensure that she had already ascertained the sleeping habits of the mistress of the house and that the servant who opened the door to her would be happy to admit the apprentice. Having gained access to the house, Moll assumed that the servant would then go upstairs to rouse the mistress. The moment the servant disappeared Moll would stuff as much as she could into the empty bandbox that she was carrying and then slip out of the door before the mistress or servant emerged. On one such occasion she robbed the home of Lady Arabella Howard who lived on Soho Square. Moll used exactly the same technique, claiming to have brought the mistress of the house gloves and fans. This time Moll got away with £50-worth of silver plate that had been invitingly left on a sideboard in the parlour.

Moll's downfall occurred on 3 March 1703 after having been convicted of shoplifting from a Mrs Hobday in Paternoster Row. Moll had claimed that she was pregnant and the authorities had delayed their final decision on her execution for nine months. Unfortunately for Moll she could not produce a child to save herself and she was hanged at Tyburn on 22 December 1703.

* * * * *

Various women over the years were involved in the treasonable offence of coining. This involved either creating or changing the appearance of coins to represent a higher value currency. The unfortunate but habitual coiner **Barbara Spencer** was probably one of the first women to be executed for this offence at Tyburn. She met her end on 5 July 1721. It is not clear when she was born, but her place of birth was St Giles without Cripplegate. It seems that she was a rather tempestuous girl in her youth and after various tribulations her mother apprenticed her to a mantle maker. Her final break with her mother occurred when Barbara wished to see an execution being carried out at Tyburn. They argued about the decency of the young woman attending this spectacle. After her mother struck her, Barbara went to Tyburn and moved into a house near St Giles Pound, never to return home. In this different environment she fell in with a gang of coiners and she helped them to counterfeit money. Fairly shortly after this the gang was caught and Barbara found herself both fined and imprisoned. Shortly after her release she became a coiner herself and when she was arrested and convicted for the second offence, she faced the far more serious charge of treason. The punishment was especially brutal in order to dissuade others from following in her footsteps. The sentence was that she was to be strangled and then burned. So incensed was the general public by her crimes that even when she knelt to say her final prayers before the sentence was carried out, she was pelted with stones and mud.

* * * * *

Barbara was not the only woman to be executed for high treason during the 18th century. In 1779 **Isabella London** met the same fate, as did **Phoebe Harris** in 1786, **Christiane Murphy** in 1789 and **Anne Warner** in 1798. Nine years before Barbara's execution, another woman, **Jane Housden**, found herself awaiting trial for coining in Newgate. If found guilty Jane would certainly have been executed as Barbara was to be. She had already been found guilty on a previous occasion of coining, but had been pardoned. Events were to conspire to save her from this fate of being strangled and burned, but not from death. Her lover, William Johnson, visited her on the day of her trial, but the turnkey would not allow him to see her. Johnson promptly pulled out a pistol and shot him dead. Jane was then charged as an accessory to the murder of the prison official and both she and Johnson met their end with the hangman.

* * * * *

Mary Young, who was born in Northern Ireland, was arguably one of the most skilled and successful pickpockets of her era. From a very early age Mary was attracted to the big cities; she had no desire to live in a rural corner of the country. At the age of 15 she was wooed by a servant to a gentleman who lived in the same neighbourhood. She swore that she would marry him, provided he took her to London. They began their life together with crime, for before they boarded a ship bound for Liverpool, Mary's boyfriend stole 80 guineas and a gold watch from his employer. They lived together as man and wife for a short while in Liverpool, largely due to the fact that Mary had fallen ill, and they awaited her return to health before they made the journey on to London. Regrettably they had tarried too long in Liverpool, because on the day before they were due to leave for London Mary's partner was recognised by a man who had been sent from Ireland to find him and was promptly arrested. Mary sent her intended his clothes and some money then calmly boarded the coach for London alone.

While her lover faced trial for theft in Ireland, for which he was condemned to death but escaped with transportation, Mary established herself with a newly found Irish friend, Anne Murphy, in lodgings in Long Acre. Anne was already part of a gang of organised thieves and they would work together wherever there was a crowd, systematically going through men's pockets and cutting off women's purses. They generally worked around theatres, markets and major shopping areas. Mary accompanied them on her first night and was amazed that in a very short space of time they had collected £80 in cash and a gold watch. Although Mary had just observed how they had stolen these items, the gang seemed keen to include her in their future plans and accordingly gave her 10 guineas. Over the next few weeks she was tutored for at least two hours a day in the art of pick-pocketing and purse-cutting. Within a very short period of time Mary became the gang's star performer and was given the name **Jenny Diver** in recognition of her manual dexterity in being able to extract almost any item from a victim.

To illustrate her skill there is one particular story that recounts the theft of a ring. Jenny and some of her associates awaited their opportunity outside a church in Old

Jewry. Jenny spotted a man with an expensive diamond ring on his finger. As she approached the man in the crowd she held out her hand and instinctively the man grasped it to help her squeeze through to reach the steps. In a flash she had slipped off the ring from the man's finger without him even realising it. He did not notice his loss until he came out of the service, but by then Jenny was long gone.

Jenny was not content to restrict her activity to opportunist thefts and bought a pair of false arms and hands. With the aid of an accomplice Jenny sat in her sedan chair with the fake arms inside the clothing, her real hands concealed beneath the coat. Her accomplice would wheel her into a church, having carefully selected the correct position for the sedan chair, and during the service Jenny would be able to pickpocket at will whoever was sitting to her right or left. On one such occasion she sat between two elderly women and during prayer she stole both their watches. On this occasion she was so flushed with her success that she returned to the same church that evening in a different dress and took a man's gold watch.

It seems that the gang were entirely under her control and were content to pool all of their proceeds and share it equally with Jenny, regardless of whether she had contributed or not. By all accounts she was a good actress too, as on one occasion she knew that there would be a sizeable crowd in St James's Park to watch the king visit the House of Lords. Dressed as a lady and accompanied by one of her gang dressed as a footman, she dramatically collapsed among the crowd. Immediately she was surrounded by concerned individuals and while she writhed around on the ground in pain the footman and another female member of the gang helped themselves to two diamond girdle buckles, a gold watch, a gold snuff box and two purses with 40 guineas in them.

On another occasion Jenny and her trusty 'footman', actually a man with whom Jenny lived, perpetrated a crime in Burr Street, Wapping. Having chosen a suitable house, the footman knocked on the door and explained to the servant that his mistress had been taken ill in the street and begged that she should be admitted to allow her to recover. After Jenny had been lifted into the house, the owner and his servant ran upstairs to find smelling salts and other medicines to aid her. While the mistress of the house applied the smelling salts Jenny picked her pocket. The footman, meanwhile, who had been told to go into the kitchen, stole six silver tablespoons, a pepper box and a salt cellar. Having achieved their aims, the footman was sent out to order a cab and Jenny and her accomplice made their thankful farewells and left.

Jenny seemed to be skilful in almost every aspect of theft and on another occasion, again with her footman, she picked a gentleman's pocket and was delighted to be the possessor of a £200 bank note. Her notoriety and successes meant that the authorities were beginning to close in on her and the gang. Temporarily she left London and continued her career in other towns and cities up and down the country. But the lure of the capital was too much and shortly after Jenny returned to London she was arrested for picking a man's pocket. She was sent to Newgate and spent four months there before she was due to be transported. Even in the prison she traded in stolen goods and by the time she boarded the boat to America she had virtually a wagon-load of goods to make her life in Virginia far more comfortable.

By all accounts Jenny lived a good life in America but still yearned to return to London. She persuaded a gullible young man that she had fallen in love with him; in reality he was her ticket back to England, as he had already arranged passage on a ship bound for London. He remained unaware of her true purpose until the ship reached Gravesend. Here Jenny robbed him and disappeared. She travelled around the country, still skilled in her own old ways, and finally returned to London in the hope that she could find her old gang. Unable to discover their whereabouts she began operating on her own and was frequently seen around the Royal Exchange, London Bridge and theatre land.

It seems that by now some of her abilities were beginning to wane as she was arrested after picking a man's pocket on London Bridge. She was brought before a magistrate but did not reveal her true identity and it was under the name of Jane Webb that she was found guilty of theft and sentenced to be transported once more. Within a year she was back and up to her old tricks.

In an attempt to steal 13s 1d from the pocket of a woman in Walbrook, Jenny was again arrested and committed to Newgate for trial. This time, unlike the two previous occasions, the value of what she had stolen was in excess of one shilling. Transportation could not be an option if she was found guilty under the law of the time. After a trial at the Old Bailey the jury found her guilty and she was hanged at Tyburn on 18 March 1740. Her body was buried in St Pancras churchyard.

* * * * *

If some women who were facing the hangman went quietly, and were resigned to the fact that they were going to die, not so **Hannah Dagoe**. This Irish-born basket woman who worked at Covent Garden market emptied out and sold the entire contents of the home of an acquaintance Eleanor Hussey. She was brought to trial at the Old Bailey on a charge of robbery and burglary and found guilty and sentenced to death at Tyburn. While she was incarcerated at Newgate glimpses of her true personality were seen. By all accounts she was a strong, masculine woman, who literally terrorised male and female prisoners alike. She even stabbed, though not fatally, one of the men who gave evidence against her. It also seems that Hannah was not content to go to the gallows meekly. As she approached the gallows she stood erect, ignoring the Roman Catholic priest who was giving her last rites. As the cart was brought underneath the gallows Hannah somehow managed to get her arms and hands loose from the ropes that bound her. She struck the executioner so hard that it nearly knocked him down. Standing in the cart she threw off her hat and cloak and cast them into the crowd and dared the executioner to approach her. After a significant struggle the rope was finally placed around her neck but Hannah was not finished. She pulled out her handkerchief and wrapped it around her face and leapt out of the cart herself before the executioner was ready. She died immediately on the scaffold once they managed to get her there on 4 May 1763.

* * * * *

Elizabeth Harriet Greeve was an audacious swindler and imposter. At various times she purported to be the cousin of Lord North, the second cousin of the Duke of Grafton, a relation of Lady Fitzroy or the close friend of Lord Guildford. Elizabeth first appeared before the Bow Street court on 3 November 1773. On this occasion she claimed to be the Honourable Elizabeth Harriet Greeve. The offence was that she had promised to secure employment for various men for a cash consideration using her aristocratic contacts. She had taken £36 from William Kidwell on the promise of a job as a clerk in the Victualling Office. William Kent from Berkshire paid £280 to secure a job as a coast waiter. He had given up his job in Berkshire and actually come to London with his wife and children, only to discover that he had been duped. One of Elizabeth's victims was even less fortunate and died of a heart attack when he discovered that he had been defrauded. Consequently, his widow, Elizabeth Cooper, explained that Elizabeth had conned her husband out of £62. Elizabeth was so good at her fraudulent activities that she had even taken in her own clerk and friend, Francis Crook. She was sentenced to be transported and it emerged that she had already appeared before a court and had been given the same sentence, but had crept back into the country in under two years. Unfortunately it is not known whether Elizabeth ever returned to England to rekindle her career.

* * * * *

The unfortunate case of **Sarah Lloyd** aroused great public interest and disgust in April 1800. She was working in a substantial house and was duped by a man who proclaimed his love for her. She managed to secure the man a post in the house and he repaid her by robbing the master and setting the house on fire. Sarah was brought before the court on a charge of larceny and condemned to death. This outraged many critics of the legal system at the time and although opinion was divided as to whether she was involved or not, the vast majority believed that she should have been acquitted of any charges. She was described as being respectable, modest and although unhappy, resigned to the fact that she was going to die for her mistake. Alternative opinion denounced Sarah as being the organiser of the robbery and fire and went on to suggest that the secondary purpose of the arson was to kill her employer. Many people signed a petition begging for mercy for Sarah but the government sent word that the execution should be carried out as swiftly as possible. Even at her execution, on 23 April 1800, a rainy and windy morning, Sarah remained dignified and composed. The newspapers were outraged that their efforts and the petition had been ignored and that an innocent woman had been hanged.

* * * * *

Husband and wife team, Thomas and **Elizabeth Leach**, found themselves before the judges at the Old Bailey in July 1811. They were part of a growing trend for counterfeiting bank notes. The industry had sprung up about three years before and the fraud was very clever. Although the bank notes looked very similar to the genuine article, the forgers had been very innovative in that they had substituted 'governor and company of the Bank of England' with 'governor and company of the Bank of Fleet'. In other cases pound notes read pence and genuine lower denomination notes had been altered. The trade in these forged notes was generally entrusted to women and the notes themselves were called either Fleet Notes or Flash Screens. One such woman who tried to pass a 2d note as a £2 note was apprehended in the act in St John's Street, Clerkenwell. **Agnes Adams** was given six months hard labour.

The Leaches, on the other hand, were charged with defrauding the Bank of England itself. The key was whether the court could prove that they had manufactured the notes and intended to pass them off as the genuine article. Eager to save his own skin, Thomas Leach pleaded guilty to possession of the forged bank note and was given the sentence of 14 years transportation. Unfortunately Elizabeth, his wife, in pleading not guilty to all of the charges on the indictment, faced a full trial. When she was searched it had been discovered that she had various genuine bank notes, but in her work basket was a bundle of forged notes. Her defence counsel desperately tried to convince the court that she was only carrying the notes on her husband's behalf. But the jury was not sympathetic to this argument and returned a verdict of guilty. She was condemned to death.

* * * * *

An opportunist theft on Saturday 8 June 1811 at the King's Head public house, Earl Street, Blackfriars, led to three women being brought before the judges at the Old Bailey on 21 September 1811. **Elizabeth King**, **Elizabeth Blott** and **Philadelphia Walton** started drinking in the pub at about 8pm and sat in one of the bars. The landlord, Mr Coombe, frequently left the bar to tend other customers. The women had explained to him that they were waiting to see a Mr Lloyd. At some point Blott and Walton went out to find the man, leaving King in the bar alone. Presently Lloyd and the other two women joined King in the bar and they drank for a short while and then left. When the landlord was ready for his bed at around midnight, he discovered that a silk bag, which had been deposited in a canvas bag on the back of a chair in the bar, had been stolen. It was his property and inside had been 36 gold guineas. Coombe immediately attracted the attention of a Bow Street officer and Elizabeth King was quickly apprehended. She confessed immediately and told the officer that she had exchanged the guineas for bank notes and that she had spent six of them. She had then given the notes to another publican called Mr Slyford in Brooke's Market. Slyford had been unaware that the money was stolen and in court, although the three women stood charged with robbery, the case against Walton and Blott was dropped and Elizabeth King was found guilty and sentenced to death.

* * * * *

If **Betty Jones** and Karl Gustav Hulten fancied themselves as a Welsh-American equivalent of Bonny and Clyde, they were wrong, but at least partly they came to the same sticky end. Betty Jones was born in South Wales on 5 July 1926. In 1941 she married Corporal Stanley Jones who was 10 years older than her. The marriage was doomed from the start. Stanley hit her on her wedding day and she left him.

By January 1943, with her husband stationed abroad, Betty had moved to London and after various poorly paid jobs, such as waitressing and working in bars, she changed her name to Georgina Grayson and became a stripper. She made a reasonable living for almost a year but then lost her job in the spring of 1944 and was reduced to subsisting on whatever money she could extract from Stanley.

Tuesday 3 October 1944 found Betty sat in a café in Hammersmith Broadway with a friend called Len Bexley. He introduced her to a man calling himself Ricky who claimed to be an American army lieutenant. He was nothing of the kind and although he was an American, he was, in fact, a private in a paratroop regiment and had been absent without leave for six weeks. The couple seemed to hit it off immediately, which prompted the American to ask Betty out that very night. They arranged to meet outside a cinema at 11.30pm but after waiting a while Betty was sure that her date had stood her up. She started to head home to King Street when the American pulled up beside her in a two-and-a-half ton truck. He came clean with her and told her that he was not Second Lieutenant Richard Allen of the 501st Parachute Regiment, but was in fact Karl Gustav Hulten. He told her that the truck was stolen and that he was armed.

They drove to Reading and saw a girl riding a bicycle along the road. Hulten stopped the truck ahead of the cyclist and as she approached he got out of the cab and pushed her off her bike and stole her purse. The couple then drove back to London with a few shillings and some clothing coupons that they had found in the purse. They went out again the following evening and Hulten slept in Betty's room that night.

On Thursday 5 October they went out for a meal at 5.30pm and then on to the cinema at 8.45pm. After that they cruised around in the truck and at Betty's insistence they decided to hold up a taxi driver. They chose a likely candidate and followed the cab to Cricklewood where they forced the driver to stop and threatened him with the gun. There was still a passenger in the back seat and this seems to have spooked the couple as they drove off again towards Marble Arch. On the Edgware Road they picked up a girl and offered to drive her to Reading. They stopped at Runnymede Park and Hulten hit the girl with an iron bar and then started to strangle her. They dumped the girl's body and stole five shillings from her.

At 11pm the following evening they again tried to rob a taxi driver on the Hammersmith Road. They hailed George Heath's cab and asked him to take them to Chiswick roundabout. No sooner had they stopped at the destination than Hulten shot the man and Betty stole the driver's wallet, watch, cigarette case and loose change. When they dumped George's body in Staines he was not dead but bled to death in the ditch. Betty had disposed of George's personal effects and these had already been found and given to the police.

It did not take the police long to identify Heath's body and to circulate the registration number of his car to police stations all around London.

After pawning George's possessions Betty and Hulten went to the White City dog track and on the evening of Sunday 8 October, after driving around for some time, they abandoned George's car near an air-raid shelter. The police found the car the following morning and lay in wait to see if anybody returned to the car. At 9pm, foolishly, Hulten did and was immediately jumped on by Inspector Read and other officers. They even found the gun that had killed George in Hulten's trouser pocket.

Later at Hammersmith Police Station Hulten still claimed that he was Lieutenant Richard Allen, but when an American CID officer, Lieutenant Robert Earl de Mott, interviewed him at 3am in the morning, Hulten's real identity was soon uncovered.

Hulten claimed to know nothing about the murder but admitted that he had stolen the abandoned car in Newbury.

American servicemen could not be tried by British courts so consequently Hulten found himself at the American CID headquarters on Piccadilly. He told them that he had spent the Friday night with Betty Jones which prompted Betty's arrest by the British police. She quickly confessed and implicated Hulten in the murder. The Americans washed their hands of Hulten and allowed British justice to take its course.

On 16 January 1945 Betty and Hulten appeared before Justice Charles at the Old Bailey. After a six-day trial they were both condemned to death for murder. Their appeals were turned down in the February and while Hulten was hanged at Pentonville on 8 March 1945, just two days before Betty's sentence was commuted to imprisonment. She served just nine years, being released under license in 1954.

* * * * *

It seems that women did not have to be habitual criminals in order to meet a tragic end at the hands of British justice. Many of the women were consummate players in the art of crime; others were less fortunate opportunists, driven to commit desperate acts in order to survive. As the centuries progressed the number of capital crimes diminished and although many women were executed in complete equality with their male counterparts, each time there was shock and outrage that a woman could find herself in that position. The establishment made no distinction between male and female and no concessions other than pregnancy. We may not feel that shoplifters, fraudsters and burglars represent particularly shocking examples of criminality, but at the time their acts were considered outrageous and unforgivable, just as much as their executions dismayed the public.

CHAPTER TEN

CRADLE ROCKERS

Society has always found it difficult to accept that a woman, a mother, or even a grandmother could ever contemplate harming a child. Throughout criminal history there have been women who have killed their own children, or, more frequently, other people's children, for a variety of reasons. Some were clearly mentally ill when the crime was carried out, but in many cases the acts occurred as a result of a careful and pre-meditated plan or as the culmination of a period of intense suffering from the point of view of the victim. It is perhaps unfair to include some of the desperate women mentioned in this chapter in the same breath as multiple murderesses such as Amelia Dyer or Elizabeth Brownrigg. Nevertheless, all of these killers were women, recognised by society as protectors of children, who caused shock and hatred when their cases became public knowledge.

THE STORY of 'Half-hanged Maggie' dates back to an execution that took place in Edinburgh in 1728. **Margaret Dixon** was born in Musselburgh in 1670 and in her teens she married a local fisherman. They had a good but hard life, Margaret selling her husband's catches on the streets of Edinburgh. Over the years they had several children.

At some point her husband was press-ganged into the Navy and during his absence from home Margaret had an affair with another man. Unfortunately Margaret fell pregnant and since it was known that her husband was out of the country, there could be no simple explanation that she could give to explain her pregnancy. During these times women who had been seen to be adulterous would be told to sit in a particular seat in church and be publicly chastised by the minister. Like many other Scottish women finding themselves in this position, Margaret probably killed the child soon after it was born, although she always claimed that it had been stillborn.

Be that as it may, her neighbours reported her as a child murderer and she was arrested and imprisoned in Edinburgh. Witnesses swore that she had been pregnant and that since the child was clearly not alive, Margaret was assumed to have murdered it. Consequently a jury found her guilty and she was sentenced to hang.

When she was led to the gallows she still protested her innocence and after the hanging had been carried out her body was cut down and given to her friends and family for burial. As the family set out with Margaret's body on the cart, they stopped off at Peffer Mill for a drink as it was a hot day. They sat around the coffin and toasted Margaret and then they saw the lid of the coffin move. Someone was brave enough to take the coffin lid off and Margaret sat upright and terrified everyone.

Margaret was taken into the pub, bled and tucked up in bed. She was well enough the following morning to walk home herself. As far as the law was concerned she had already been duly hanged as the court had demanded and no one attempted to slip the noose around her neck again.

Margaret's death and rebirth caused considerable confusion. For one thing her marriage was dissolved by her execution and therefore as soon as her husband arrived back in Scotland they had to remarry. As for the sheriff who had officiated at the execution, he found himself having to answer a prosecution lodged by the King's Counsel in the High Court. He was jailed for not carrying out his duties properly.

'Half-hanged Maggie' protested her innocence to her dying day and passed away from natural causes in 1753.

* * * * *

A much more unsavoury pair were **Elizabeth** and **Mary Branch**, mother and daughter, who lived in Somerset. Elizabeth had married a wealthy farmer and was notorious for her violent treatment of servants. When Mr Branch died Elizabeth and Mary were left with a fortune by contemporary standards and if their abuse of servants had been vicious before, their torture and abuse after his death reached new levels of depravity.

Their principal target was Jane Butterworth, who was an orphan and not especially bright. On numerous occasions Elizabeth and Mary beat her to within an inch of her life. On one occasion their attack simply went too far. Jane had been sent out to buy some yeast but had taken far longer than Elizabeth or Mary thought acceptable. They dragged her into the farmhouse, stripped her and beat her with broomsticks. Not content with this they then poured salt into her wounds. When the milkmaid Ann Somers came in Jane was lying naked, dead, in a pool of blood and the cruel employers were sat warming themselves in front of the fire.

Although they may not have shown it at the time, Elizabeth and Mary were concerned that Ann had seen the body and at some point during the night they dragged the corpse into a field and buried it. As soon as their backs were turned Ann ran to the local Justice of the Peace who ordered Mary and Elizabeth's arrest.

They came to trial at the assizes in Taunton in March 1730 and were charged with the wilful murder of Jane Butterworth. The court heard testimony from Ann and several other servants of the women's cruelty. As it was not clear which of the women had actually delivered the fatal blow, the jury found them both guilty of murder.

By now the local population was baying for their blood and it seemed clear to the court that unless the execution was carried out in secrecy, then the two women would probably be lynched before they could arrive at Ivelchester, where the execution was to take place. Accordingly, at 3 or 4am on 3 May 1730 the mother and daughter were conveyed to the execution spot accompanied only by the jailer and a few other people.

The locals were not to be denied, however, and someone had cut down the gibbet which delayed the execution until 6am, by which time a large crowd had gathered.

Shortly before the execution Elizabeth admitted to killing Jane and begged for her daughter's forgiveness. They were both hanged together and while they were still swinging at the end of the rope, several local clergymen delivered lectures to the audience about the evils of beating servants. It seems that the crowd endured the droning lectures in order to ensure that Elizabeth and Mary were definitely on their way to Hell.

* * * * *

There can be no doubt that one of the most appalling sadistic psychopaths to have stalked the British Isles was **Elizabeth Brownrigg**. Brownrigg was born in about 1720 and was married to James at an early age, with whom she went on to bear 16 children. For some seven years she and her plumber husband lived in Greenwich, but it was

Elizabeth Brownrigg.

during their stay at Flower-de-Luce Court in Fleet Street that Elizabeth developed her sadistic practices.

Having given birth to 16 children it was considered by the local St Dunstan's parish that Brownrigg would be an ideal person to look after the poor of the neighbourhood. Both the women who found dubious refuge in the Brownrigg household and the parish notables were to regret this decision. Brownrigg took in various women and children to act as apprentices. One of the first was Mary Mitchell, who came to the Brownriggs in 1765. She was soon joined by Mary Jones, an orphan from the Foundling Hospital. The parish also sent her a number of poor, pregnant women in the knowledge that they would be well looked after due to Brownrigg's midwifery skills.

Initially everything seemed to be perfectly above board, but somehow Brownrigg began to replace her civility with cruelty. To begin with her savagery was directed at Mary Jones. Brownrigg would make the girl lie across two chairs in the kitchen while she whipped her, after which she would throw a bucket of water on her or nearly drown her in the water. After several attacks like this Mary was determined to escape and managed to get out of a room in which she had been locked. Mary managed to find her way back to the Foundling Hospital where she was examined by a doctor. The hospital governors were shocked and had their solicitor, Mr Plumbtree, write a threatening letter to James Brownrigg. No further action was taken.

Elizabeth Brownrigg now turned her attention to Mary Mitchell. She, too, tried to escape after several assaults but was dragged back into the house by Brownrigg's son. Meanwhile, Mary Clifford had been sent to the household and it seems that she suffered some of the worst treatment meted out by the Brownriggs. On numerous occasions she was stripped and beaten with a cane, a horse whip or a broom. At night she was thrown into the coal hole with only a sack and some straw for a bed. She was barely fed and only then with bread and water. Desperate, Mary Clifford broke into a cupboard to try to find

Artist's impression of Brownrigg whipping one of the many orphans sent by the Foundling Hospital.

food but could find none. She also was desperate for water and when Elizabeth Brownrigg found what she had done Mary was stripped once more, tied up and beaten with a whip. In order to prevent her from doing it again Elizabeth Brownrigg fastened a chain around Mary's neck and attached it to the yard door. There she was left during the day until she was thrown back into the coal hole at night with her hands tied behind her back.

It seems that Brownrigg's husband was often party to these assaults and hooks were fixed to the beams of the kitchen so that the naked women could be suspended to enable his wife to whip them thoroughly. When Mary Clifford managed to complain about her treatment to a French woman that was lodging in the house, Elizabeth Brownrigg dragged her away and cut her tongue in two places with a pair of scissors.

On 12 July 1767 the 14-year-old Mary Clifford's stepmother Mrs Deacon arrived to try to see her stepdaughter, but she was refused entry to the house. On the following day Mary was severely whipped and thrown into a tub of cold water. By now the parish authorities were beginning to show some concern about the treatment of the apprentices sent to the Brownrigg's house.

When they arrived and demanded to see Mary Clifford they were instead presented with Mary Mitchell. She was in such a poor state that the girl was rushed immediately to hospital. The parish officials then forced their way into the house to search for Mary and found her bound in a small cupboard. She, too, was sent to St Bartholomew's Hospital. They arrested James Brownrigg on the spot but Elizabeth and her son, John, managed to escape, taking with them a gold watch and some money.

They disguised themselves and took lodgings in Wandsworth at the home of Mr Dunbar. Meanwhile, James Brownrigg had been committed to trial for cruelty. The unfortunate Mary Clifford died in hospital and at the coroner's inquest the charges against the three Brownriggs were changed to wilful murder.

Elizabeth and John Brownrigg lay low until 15 August when Mr Dunbar realised that his two lodgers were being sought by the police for murder. He turned them in and they were arrested. At their trial at the Old Bailey, which lasted 11 hours, Elizabeth Brownrigg was found guilty of murder and was sentenced to death. James and John were acquitted of the murder and each given six months in jail.

After Elizabeth Brownrigg's sentence had been passed she confessed all her crimes to a clergyman. On 14 September 1767, after a tearful farewell to her husband and son, Elizabeth Brownrigg was taken in an open cart to Tyburn. A vast crowd followed her

Brownrigg in her cell.

progress through the streets of London and after her death her body was taken to Surgeon's Hall, where it was dissected. Her skeleton was hung in the hall.

It is also significant to recount that although Elizabeth Brownrigg had given birth to 16 children, only three of them reached maturity. Although she was never charged for any crimes against her own children, it was widely believed that she had been responsible for their deaths. Feelings were running so high at her execution that the hangman dispensed with many of the customary preparations and carried out the sentence on Elizabeth Brownrigg the moment she stepped foot on the scaffold. Apparently the authorities had been very concerned that the angry mob would lynch her before the hangman could do his work.

* * * * *

In July 1768 a stunned court listened to the barbarities of **Sarah** and **Sarah Morgan Metyard**, mother and daughter. They were milliners in Bruton Street, Hanover Square, London, and had five apprentice girls working for them from various parish workhouses.

Anne Naylor and her sister were two of these unfortunate girls. Anne herself appears not to have been physically strong and was therefore unable to do as much work as the other girls. It was, perhaps, for this reason that the Metyards made her the object of their vicious attacks. Anne in particular had been beaten and starved and on one occasion she had attempted to escape and been dragged back inside and locked in one of the upper rooms of the house. For some time she had remained there, only being fed on bread and water. After suffering in this way for a considerable period Anne again took an opportunity to try to escape and she ran into the street and asked a passing milkman to protect her. Seconds later Sarah Morgan Metyard ran up behind her, grabbed her by the throat and dragged her back into the house. For this she was beaten with a broom and locked into a room on the second storey.

This time the Metyards were not taking any chances and they tied her up so that she could neither lie nor sit down. They left her up there for three days, barely giving her any food at all. The other girls were shown Anne and told that this would be their fate if they did not work hard. By the fourth day, as a result of the beatings and lack of food, drink and comfort, Anne died.

When one of the other girls reported that Anne had collapsed, the younger Metyard simply took off her shoe and beat Anne's corpse around the head. They told the other apprentices that Anne had had a fit but that she was to be kept upstairs in order to prevent her from escaping. For several days they carried on the pretence that the girl was still alive, until finally they put the body in a box and locked it away in a garret. After this they told the other apprentices that Anne had run away but Anne's sister was suspicious because Anne would not have left without taking her clothes. The body remained in the garret for two months until decomposition demanded that the Metyards dispose of the body.

On the evening of 25 December 1764 they cut the body up and tied the remains into cloth bundles. They intended to burn it but were concerned that the smell would draw unwelcome interest. Consequently they took the bundles to Chick Lane and tried to

throw them into the common sewer. In the event, they could not throw them over the wall so they left the pieces in the mud and water in the grate near the sewer.

At midnight the body parts were discovered by a night watchman and the coroner, Mr Umferville, examined them the following day and assumed that they were parts of a corpse which had been illegally exhumed from a churchyard and cut up by a surgeon.

For four years no link was made to the Metyards, but Sarah Morgan found herself suffering many of the ordeals that the apprentices had endured at the hands of her mother.

It is actually unclear exactly how the Metyards came to the attentions of the authorities. One account mentions a tea dealer called Mr Rooker who had employed the younger Metyard as a servant. He may have heard the two women talking about their crimes and reported the conversation to John Fielding, the blind brother of the writer Joseph Fielding. John was a Bow Street magistrate and it may have been him that organised their arrest.

Alternatively, Sarah Morgan may have been in fear of her own life and reported her mother in order to protect herself. If this was the case and she had hoped to have protected herself by disposing of her mother, then she was wrong. They were both found guilty at the Old Bailey and sentenced to hang on 19 July 1768.

On the day of the execution the mother was in an almost uncontrollable fit and had to be carried to Tyburn. She was in such a disturbed mental state that she was probably unaware of the day's proceedings. Their bodies were left hanging at Tyburn and attracted considerable crowds. They were sent for dissection at Surgeon's Hall.

* * * * *

Rebecca Howard was one of thousands of unfortunate women who found themselves carrying an illegitimate child in the 18th century. Not only was there severe stigma attached to births out of wedlock, but there was also very little support for women who found themselves in this situation.

She was tried in August 1797 for the wilful murder of her illegitimate child, and although this was not shocking in itself, it was her statement before sentence was carried out on 27 August at noon that is particularly telling and significant.

With great presence of mind, she asked the hangman to pause for a moment while she addressed the assembled crowd. She warned all young women to avoid temptation and to be on their guard against deceitful men who would abandon them to their fate. She said that had it not been for such a deceitful man she would not have found herself there that day and although she fully accepted her sentence, she wanted all to know that she had been treated with respect despite her crime. Her last words were 'Lord have mercy on me, God bless you all.'

* * * * *

Women whose treatment of children fell short of murder were, comparatively speaking, dealt with in a more lenient manner. **Sarah Marlborough** was James's second wife and he had two children from a previous marriage. From the moment Sarah had begun to take responsibility for the little girl and boy, she had beaten them unmercifully. Her barbarity was particularly aimed at the daughter, Mary, and many neighbours heard screams from the house.

On 9 October 1809 neighbours heard crying from the front cellar where the Marlboroughs kept a pig. They could stand it no longer and several neighbours forced their way into the house and demanded to see the children. They made their way to the cellar but only encountered the swine. Searching the rest of the house they discovered the little girl lying under a bed; she was half-starved, bruised head to foot and had two black eyes. The children were taken into the care of the parish and the parents arrested.

When they appeared in court on 8 December 1809 at Hick's Hall in Middlesex, the court heard the harrowing story of the treatment meted out to Mary from her brother's testimony. He told the court that his stepmother often threw his younger sister into a tub of cold water and that she beat her with sticks, rods and a toasting fork and that the black eyes were as a result of a beating with the back of a spoon.

James Marlborough claimed that he had beaten Sarah for her ill-treatment of the children but was powerless to stop her when he was out of the house. As a result, he was sentenced to just 14 days in Newgate Prison and Sarah Marlborough was given a year in the Cold Bath Fields House of Correction.

* * * * *

Child-dropping was another common offence, often perpetrated by women who had been given the responsibility to look after a child on behalf of the parish. Having been given money to care for a child, a number of professional child-carers would then abandon the child in an adjoining parish and still collect funds for its upkeep. One such case was that of **Elizabeth Pugh** who had taken £300 to look after a child. She picked it up from a workhouse on 27 August 1809, but the same child was discovered at 9pm just four days later, abandoned in Castle Street, Holborn. Elizabeth Pugh and her father, Thomas, had not been very clever about abandoning the child. When they were tried on 20 January 1810 at the London Sessions, the prosecution was even able to produce the coachman that had dropped the Pughs and the child off. For abandoning the child and defrauding the parish of St Andrew, Holborn, the Pughs were given just six months each.

* * * * *

Another tragic case involved the death of 10-year-old Frances Colpitt, who had been apprenticed to **Esther Hibner** on 7 April 1829, one of many children that had been passed into the none-too-tender care of the Hibner family.

The children would be forced to sleep on the floor, covered only with an old rug. They were made to begin work at 3 or 4am and kept going until at least 11pm. At least three had already died but the Hibners were brought to court for the wilful murder of Frances and they appeared at the Old Bailey on 10 April 1829. When the little girl's body was examined she was covered in sores and the cause of death was probably an abscess on her lungs which had burst. The children in the household subsisted on a slice of bread and a cup of milk for breakfast and were rarely given any more food during the day. On Sundays they were locked up in the kitchen.

The three defendants, a mother and daughter both called Esther Hibner and their assistant Ann Robinson, had made Frances clean the stairs but she had collapsed due to exhaustion. The younger Esther took the little girl upstairs and flogged her and then sent her back down to finish off her work. The defendants claimed that the children had only been punished when they behaved badly and that they had always been treated with great kindness. It seemed that the majority of the cruelties had been carried out by the mother and, as a result, when the jury considered its verdicts, only she was sentenced to death, and her daughter and Robinson received 12 and four months imprisonment respectively in the House of Correction.

During the trial Esther Hibner's daughter smuggled a knife into the prison and her mother attempted to commit suicide. She was determined that she should not hang and the prison authorities were forced to put her in a straightjacket. Hibner was not to evade her punishment, however, and at 8am on Monday 13 April 1829 she was carried out to the gallows by two wardens. There was a huge crowd waiting to see her hang and many of the women that had come to see her die continued to shout abuse at her until life left her body.

* * * * *

The Kent family lived in a large three-storey house in a village near Trowbridge in Wiltshire. Samuel Savill Kent's first wife had produced 10 children, although only four of them were still alive when she died in 1852. Shortly after his wife's death Samuel married the children's governess, Miss Pratt, and by 1860 she had given birth to three children and was pregnant with the fourth. The two children who occupy the centre of this story are the 16-year-old **Constance Kent** and the three-year-old Francis.

Following the elevation of Miss Pratt to the new title of Mrs Kent, another governess and nurse had been employed in the shape of Elizabeth Gough. All of the family lived in the home, with Samuel and the new Mrs Kent sleeping on the second floor with their youngest daughter, and on the same floor were the rooms of Constance, William and a nursery which housed Francis and Elizabeth Gough. Servants occupied the top floor.

Elizabeth Gough woke up at 5am on 30 June 1860 and discovered to her horror that three-year-old Francis was not in his cot. Initially she believed that Mrs Kent had come into the nursery during the night and taken Francis to her own room. By 6am Elizabeth was dressed but her mistress had not yet arisen. When she did at 7am it became clear that she had not removed the child during the night. The house was searched and then the grounds and a window was found open in the drawing room. Initially it was believed that the child had been kidnapped and Samuel immediately went to the police to report the situation. Local villagers helped scour the local area and they discovered, to their horror, the little boy's body outside a privy in the grounds. There was a deep stab wound in the side of the child and his throat had been cut so deeply that the head was nearly severed.

By the time the body was discovered Samuel Kent had returned from Trowbridge with Inspector Foley. Their first discovery was a bloodstained nightdress that had been stuffed behind a boiler and a bloody handprint was found on a window.

Suspicion immediately fell on 16-year-old Constance, who for some time had felt that Mary Pratt's new children had superseded the surviving members of the original family. Mary Pratt had treated Constance badly ever since she had married her father and on more than one occasion Constance had been locked in a cellar.

After the inquest Foley arrested Constance and she spent a week in jail before the local magistrates decided that she had no case to answer. Foley then arrested Elizabeth Gough, but she, too, was quickly released. Samuel Kent then fell under suspicion and it was widely believed that he had committed the murder and that Elizabeth Gough had helped him. The police were getting nowhere and on 15 July Scotland Yard sent Inspector Whicher to Trowbridge to take over the investigations. He was convinced that Constance was guilty. All of the servants and family were re-interviewed and evidence began to emerge.

It seemed that the bloodstained nightgown had probably belonged to Constance, but that due to Foley's incompetence it had been washed and all traces of the blood had

Constance Kent.

vanished. Nevertheless Whicher arrested Constance again on 20 July, although the evidence against her was so circumstantial that she was released on bail.

Elizabeth Gough had, by this time, left the Kents employment and taken up a job as a seamstress. She was re-arrested and brought before the magistrates and again released due to lack of evidence.

The Kent family sold up and moved to Wales and in 1861 Constance was sent to a French convent under the name of Emily Kent. She returned to England in August 1863 and began training as a nurse in Brighton. Amazingly, on 25 April 1864, she appeared at the Bow Street offices of Sir Thomas Henry, the Chief Magistrate, in the company of

Reverend Wagner, the Director of St Mary's Home in Brighton, where she was training, and confessed to murdering Francis Kent.

She explained to Sir Thomas that 'Before the deed was done, no one knew of my intention, nor afterwards knew of my guilt. No one assisted me in the crime, nor in the evasion of discovery.' Constance was brought before the Assizes in Salisbury on 21 July 1865, pleading guilty to the murder of Francis Kent, and was sentenced to death. It was considered by the judge that because she had been so young when the murder had been committed, that her sentence should be reduced to life imprisonment.

In the event, she served 20 years at Millbank Prison and was released in 1885. On her release she changed her name to Ruth Emilie Kaye and emigrated to New South Wales. She died in hospital on 10 April 1944.

What is particularly significant about this case is the fact that Constance's description of the killing did not match what actually happened. She claimed that she had carried out the killing with a razor that she had stolen from her father's room. Medical examiners had established at the time that the wounds had been inflicted with a knife. Equally, the throat wound which was believed to have been the actual cause of death had not bled to the degree that would be expected if the child was still alive when the wound was inflicted. Constance claimed that this was how Francis had been killed, but medical opinion held that the cause of death was probably suffocation, with the wound inflicted after death. For some reason Constance had decided that at least in thought she was responsible for the death of Francis and although her case attracted considerable public attention and disquiet, it is very unlikely that she actually committed the crime.

* * * * *

1874 saw two child murders and three hangings as a result. **Mary Ann Barry** and Edwin Bailey, her common-law husband, were both found guilty of murdering their one-year-old child. It was revealed that they considered the child to be an awkward nuisance as it cramped their lifestyle as habitual thieves and alcoholics. More significantly, **Frances Stewart** gained the unenviable label of being the first grandmother in Britain to be convicted and hanged for the murder of a grandchild. She had been living with her daughter and son-in-law and had looked after one-year-old Henry Ernest Shrivener since he was born. Frances had been involved in a series of rows with the boy's parents and they had told her that they wanted her to leave their home. She abducted their child and threw him into the Thames at Poplar. Her execution was carried out at Newgate by the hangman William Marwood.

* * * * *

In the latter part of the 19th century, many women offered their services to the local parishes to take in illegitimate or unwanted babies. They would be paid anything from £10 or more for each child that they took into foster care or undertook to find a home for. Bearing in mind that there was virtually no law to protect children, and that there was a moral stigma attached to illegitimacy, these children passed into the care of women who would often dispose of them within days of the transaction being made.

Perhaps the most infamous was **Amelia Elizabeth Dyer**, whose sinister activities finally came to light in 1896 when she was tried at the Old Bailey on a specimen murder charge. The authorities and the general public were stunned at the scale of the murders that she had committed since beginning her revolting 'baby-farming' business.

Amelia Dyer, baby farmer.

Amelia Dyer was born in Bristol and married shortly before her daughter, Polly, was born. Dyer was a respected member of the Salvation Army and her husband worked in a vinegar factory. At the age of about 35 her marriage collapsed and she set up a baby farm in Long Ashton, but she was discovered by the authorities and sentenced to six weeks imprisonment. She remained in a workhouse until June 1895 when she moved to Reading.

She took a cottage in Piggott's Road in Caversham and advertised in the local paper 'Couple having no child would like the care of one or would adopt one. Terms £10.' Her first customers included a barmaid who handed over her 10-month-old daughter. She was followed by nine-year-old Willie Thornton and then another girl, aged four, and another baby. Significant, although Dyer did not know it, was the arrival of Doris Marmon, whose mother, Eleanor, gave Dyer £10 to look after her illegitimate child. Dyer also took in a little boy called Harry Simmons; a rich local woman brought this child in, claiming the boy was the son of a maid who had given birth to him and then absconded.

None of the children lasted very long, and on 30 March a bargeman pulled a brown paper parcel out of the Thames. When they unwrapped it they discovered the body of a baby girl. The child had been strangled with tape and a brick had been put into the parcel to weigh the little corpse down. On 2 April two more parcels were found stuffed into a carpet bag. It was to be proved later that these were the bodies of Harry Simmons and Doris Marmon.

Stupidly, although Dyer had adopted an assumed name of Mrs Thomas, she had wrapped one of the children in brown paper with her new name and address on it. It took the police only two days to find her.

In order to ensure that they had the right woman they sent a girl posing as an unmarried mother to enquire whether Dyer would be prepared to take her child for £100. The deal was agreed and when a police inspector arrived at the appointed time instead of the baby, Dyer was arrested.

It may be the case that Dyer was also masquerading as a Mrs Hardy and that in fact her now married daughter, Polly, and her son-in-law Arthur Palmer, also lived with her.

It became clear that many of the children lived barely 24 hours in Dyer's care. Even while in the workhouse she had operated under several different assumed names and had been carrying out her business for at least 20 years. No sooner had Dyer been taken to the police station than she attempted to commit suicide by stabbing herself with a pair of scissors. She then tried to strangle herself with a bootlace. More evidence was appearing daily, and 57-year-old Dyer became popularly known as the 'Reading Baby Farmer'. At least four other corpses were fished out of the Thames.

At some point before the trial Dyer made an admission to the police and said 'You'll know all mine by the tape around their necks'. According to Dyer neither her daughter nor her son-in-law had anything to do with the murders and disposal of the children. In fact Dyer wrote a letter to the Superintendent of Police and said 'I do most solemnly swear that neither of them had anything to do with it. They never knew I contemplated doing such a wicked thing until too late'. She had saved Polly but her daughter would become one of the major planks of the prosecution case.

Dyer was brought before Justice Hawkins on 21 May 1896. According to Polly's evidence, her mother had arrived at her home in Willesden with Doris Marmon in a carpet bag. Her mother had claimed that she was looking after the baby for a neighbour. Polly had left her mother and the child sitting by the fire in the kitchen and when she came back the baby had gone. Strangely, she recounted, her mother had chosen to sleep on the sofa in the kitchen with the carpet bag underneath her. Harold Simmons, the other baby, disappeared the following morning. When they took her to Paddington Station to catch the train to Reading, Arthur had carried the carpet bag and commented that it was very heavy. At some stage on her return journey Dyer had thrown the carpet bag into the Thames.

The defence counsel maintained that Dyer was insane and had suffered from depressions and delusions for a number of years. To counter this the prosecution presented evidence from Dr James Scott, the medical officer at Holloway Prison. He, above all, could pass professional judgement on Dyer's state of mind and concluded that Dyer was faking the symptoms of madness.

With the trial over the jury took just five minutes to pass a verdict of guilty on Dyer. They had rejected the defence counsel's pleas that she was insane. Before she was hanged on 10 June 1896 she reiterated her own guilt and wrote that she could not contemplate 'Drawing innocent people into trouble. What was done I did do myself'.

The extent of Dyer's crimes may never be known. Her notoriety survived her death and it was generally believed that her motive had been greed. In killing the children she could still draw fees from the parish or families and their absence would afford her with enough space to take in even more children.

* * * * *

Regrettably, whatever lessons were learned from the Dyer case, there was at least one other thriving baby farming business still to shock the nation. **Amelia Sach** and **Annie Walters**, who would become known as the 'Finchley Baby Farmers', ran a seemingly respectable nursing home in East Finchley. As a side-line they offered unmarried mothers the opportunity to leave their children with them. Sach and Walters claimed that for a variable fee, usually around £25, they would arrange for the children to be fostered. Mrs Sach would take the money and then the child would be passed on to Annie Walters. It was a neat setup as none of the murders actually took place at the nursing home.

Having split the proceeds the children would be conveyed to Walters's lodgings in

Islington. She had the outward appearance of being a very respectable woman in her fifties and she lodged with a policeman's family. She masqueraded as a short-term foster mother, often referring to the children as her 'little darlings'. They would stay with Walters for a short period of time and then be suffocated and dumped in the Thames or buried in a rubbish dump.

It seems that business was good and Walters usually had one child with her at any one time. However, due to the briskness of trade, Sach contacted her and told her that she had another child. Rather foolishly Walters asked her landlady to look after the little girl in her charge while she went to collect another baby. She was gone for some time and during this period the landlady changed the baby's nappy and discovered that it was not a girl but a boy. This aroused her suspicions, which she shared with her husband. They were both concerned that they had never seen any prospective foster parents at the lodgings and that the children appeared and disappeared very quickly. A few days after this event Walters told her landlady that the child had tragically died in its sleep.

On 15 November 1902 a Miss Galley paid Sach £25 to have her child adopted. This was the opportunity the police had been waiting for. The child remained with Walters for two days and then she was followed when seen to be carrying a bundle. The police followed her to the banks of the Thames and arrested her as she was about to throw it into the water. On searching her lodgings the police discovered chlorodyne, which Walters claimed was only used to help the children sleep.

To begin with she absolutely refused to divulge where she had got the children, but investigations eventually led to the Claymore House Nursing Home in East Finchley, run by Amelia Sach, then 29 years old. From the outset Sach claimed that she knew nothing of the fate of the children that she had entrusted to Walters's care. Clearly their stories were not believed in court and when they went on trial on 15 January 1903 at the Old Bailey before Justice Darling, they were both sentenced to death for murder. They have the dubious distinction of being the first women to be hanged at Holloway. Their execution took place on 3 February 1903.

* * * * *

Sach and Walters were not, however, the first women to be executed in the 20th century. That dubious honour goes to **Louise Josephine Masset**, who was hanged for the murder of her son on 9 January 1900.

Louise was a 33-year-old half French, half English woman, who had given birth to her illegitimate son, Manfred, in 1896. After the child's birth she had moved to Stoke Newington in London and placed the child in foster care with Helen Gentle from Tottenham. She paid Gentle 37 shillings a month and led her to believe that the money came from Manfred's father in France. This gave Louise the freedom to work as a governess and to offer piano lessons.

The situation changed in 1899 when Louise met and fell in love with Eudore Lucas. He was a Frenchman aged only 19 and it seems clear that due to their low income they considered marriage to be almost impossible. On 16 October Mrs Gentle received a letter from Louise. It explained, regrettably, that she needed to collect her son on 27 October and take him to France as his father had undertaken to care for him. In reality

Louise had very different plans for Manfred, and had, in fact, arranged to spend the weekend in Brighton with Eudore.

Before travelling to Helen Gentle's home in Stamford Hill, Louise took a brick from her back garden and put it in her bag. Louise arrived as planned and took Manfred and all of his clothes and boarded a bus for London Bridge railway station. The little boy was dressed in a blue frock and was wearing a sailor's hat. Louise and Manfred were seen in a waiting room at 1.45pm. A witness, Mrs Rees, later testified that Louise had told her at about 3pm that she was going to take the child to get something to eat. They were gone for three hours and when she returned Louise was alone and she caught the train to Brighton.

At 6.20pm a woman entered the ladies' lavatories at Dalston Junction Station and discovered the naked body of a young, male child. There were two pieces of brick lying next to the body. A doctor was immediately called and Dr Fennell discovered that the body was still warm and that the child had been beaten with the brick and then suffocated.

Strangely, Helen Gentle received another letter from Louise on Monday 30 October, informing her that Manfred missed her, and that although he had not been well on the Channel ferry, he was beginning to settle in with his father. Something must have aroused Gentle's suspicions and she presented herself to the police and asked to be shown the body of the child that had been found at the station. She was able to identify the body as that of Manfred and what was more damning was that the police had retrieved a parcel of children's clothes that had been abandoned at the left luggage office in Brighton. With it were Manfred's frock and sailor's hat.

The net was drawing in on Masset, compounded by the fact that a shop assistant identified Louise as having purchased a black shawl that had also been found at the murder scene. It seems that Masset was blissfully unaware of the police discoveries. However, when she later visited her sister her relative reported that she had seemed distressed.

After the police arrested her she was correctly identified by Mrs Rees, who had seen her with Manfred at London Bridge station. This was enough for the authorities to charge her with murder.

She came to trial in December 1899 and claimed that she had arranged for two baby farmers called Browning to look after Manfred for £18 per year. She even claimed to have given them £12 after having passed Manfred into their care. There was nothing to corroborate Louise's story; there was no receipt and, as far as the police were concerned, they could not trace two women called Mrs Browning. When the jury passed a guilty verdict Masset fainted and had to be revived with smelling salts so that she could hear the sentence. Petitions were sent to Queen Victoria by numerous French women who worked in London, but on 9 January 1900, at precisely 9am, Louise Masset was hanged by James Billington.

* * * * *

Ada Chard-Williams and her husband were also accused of being baby farmers and murderers. Although they were suspected of having killed several other children, the police could only positively link them to the death of one child.

In the summer of 1899 Florence Jones, an unmarried mother, had arranged with Chard-Williams to place her daughter, Selina, in the care of a Mrs Hewertson. When she later decided to check on the child's progress the address given to her by Chard-Williams did not exist. She had handed the baby over after answering an advertisement in a shop window. Whether Florence's search for her daughter had prompted it, or the murder had already been planned or executed is unknown, but a baby's body was found floating in the Thames in September. The child had been suffocated and it was a relatively easy task to match the distraught Florence with the body of her child.

The police eventually caught up with the couple and they were arrested and charged with the murder of Selina Jones. The Chard-Williamses denied that the body was that of Selina but could offer no explanation as to where the young child was if she was still alive. The police also had circumstantial evidence that several other children had disappeared after having been placed in the hands of these baby farmers, but nothing was clear enough for the police to press further charges. In the event this murder was sufficient to condemn Ada Chard-Williams to be hanged at Newgate on 6 March 1900. She was despatched by the hangman James Billington. Her husband was acquitted of all charges.

* * * * *

The murder of John Johnson in Glasgow in 1923 aroused passions for a number of notable reasons. Firstly the murderess, **Susan Newell**, was the first woman to be hanged in Scotland for 50 years. Equally, the horrific murder of the 13-year-old boy could never be adequately explained. He had been strangled and it was possible that Newell had either acted in rage or was insane. She had even tried to evade justice by blaming the murder on her husband. It left the public and officials perplexed and even when her last minutes were recounted, it only served to confuse even further.

Susan Newell was born in 1893 and by July 1923 was living in Coatbridge, a suburb of Glasgow, with her second husband John. With them was her eight-year-old daughter, Janet McLeod, a relic of her previous marriage. The family rowed continuously and after only three weeks of living in their rented flat in Newlands Road, their landlady, Mrs Young, told them that they would have to leave. It seems that Mrs Young had good cause, as on 19 June Susan had been reported to the police for assaulting her own husband. He had left and moved in with his sister.

Tragically, a 13-year-old newspaper boy called John Johnson knocked on the Newell's door at 6.45pm on 20 June. He was a busy lad who was well-known in the area for his industry and good humour. The door was answered by Susan, who asked him in and said she wanted a paper. John obviously knew something of the Newell family because he would not leave until Susan had paid him. For some reason Susan attacked John and strangled him and when her daughter, Janet, entered the flat she was told by her mother to help her wrap up the body in an old rug. As it turned out they decided on a bizarre and incredibly dangerous method of disposing of the body. They dumped John's corpse into an old pram and proceeded along the street, attracting confused stares from a number of witnesses.

They were heading towards Glasgow and a lorry driver even gave them a lift and put the pram and body onto the back of his truck. When he dropped them off at Duke Street he seemed to fail to notice that John's foot was sticking out of one end of the rug roll and that the top of his head was visible at the other end. He may not have noticed it, but a woman peeking out from behind net curtains certainly did; and she decided to follow them with her sister.

While they were trailing the mother and daughter they encountered a man whom they told to go and fetch the police. They watched as Susan and Janet left John's body near a tenement block.

By now the police were on the scene and they arrested Susan. During the walk she had obviously been considering how she could possibly explain the body in the pram. Immediately she told the police that her husband had murdered the little boy, and on fear of her own death she had been forced to take Janet with her to dispose of the body. The police charged round to John's sister's house and arrested him. Both partners were put on trial for the murder of John Johnson in September.

Until this point Janet had fully supported her mother's story, but in court before Lord Alness the story began to unravel. John Newell could prove that he had not been there when the boy was murdered and several witnesses could support his alibi. When Janet was called as a witness she carefully related to the court how she had come into the flat after playing outside and seen John Johnson's body lying on the sofa. She admitted helping her mother wrap the body up in the rug and accompanying her mother to dispose of the corpse. Tellingly, she also recounted that her mother had impressed upon her the importance of placing the blame for the murder on her stepfather.

The defence counsel tried to argue that Susan Newell must have been insane or at least temporarily deranged when she committed the murder. After all, there could have been no premeditation and there was no obvious motive. The prosecution used the testimony of Professor John Glaister, who had examined Susan while she was in prison on remand. He claimed that Susan Newell showed no signs of insanity or derangement and that this could not be a viable defence. In the event, the jury seemed to agree with the prosecution and after just 37 minutes returned a majority verdict of guilty. They added that under the circumstances the court should show Newell mercy and that she should not be sentenced to death.

Contrary to the jury's opinion, Alness did sentence Newell to hang, but he wanted first to establish beyond any doubt that she was sane. Psychiatrists at the Glasgow Prison in Duke Street supported Professor Glaister's opinion and the Secretary of State for Scotland duly set the execution date for 10 October 1923. When Newell was told that she was to be hanged she fainted, but by the fateful day she had recovered much of her composure. Newell refused to have a hood put over her head during the execution and thus became the last woman in Scotland to be hanged. She never admitted to her crime and was said to be the calmest and most courageous condemned prisoner that the executioner, John Ellis, had ever encountered.

* * * * *

Another major Scottish case hit the headlines in 1934. Despite the fact that there did not seem to be any motive and that most of the evidence was circumstantial, **Jeannie Ewan Donald** was found guilty of the murder of Helen Priestly.

Eight-year-old Helen lived in a tenement block in Aberdeen and went missing on 20 April 1934. She had been sent out by her 33-year-old mother, Agnes, at lunchtime to buy a loaf of bread from the local Co-Op. She was never seen alive again. Helen had not returned home before going back to school that afternoon but it was established that Helen had been seen at the bakery with a brown paper parcel under her arm, but after that had vanished into thin air.

The police thoroughly searched the local area but found nothing. One of Helen's school friends claimed to have seen Helen being dragged onto a bus by a strange man, but later the boy admitted that he had made it all up.

Shortly after 5am on 21 April Alexander Porter, a friend of Helen's father, John, arrived at the house to help him to continue to search the area for his daughter. To his horror he saw a sack, with a child's feet sticking out of it, partially hidden underneath the staircase. Within minutes the area was heaving with neighbours, crying and shouting, but the only people who ignored the hullabaloo were the Donald family. They lived directly below the Priestlys. They were not close friends and Jeannie Donald later said that when she had been woken up by all of the shouting her husband had simply put a pillow over his head and gone back to sleep.

When it was believed that the child had been raped, the hysteria reached fever pitch. The post-mortem was to prove this belief incorrect. The cause of death had been strangulation and the time of death no later than 2pm the previous day. Helen's body was still fully clothed and only her beret and panties were missing. Someone had attempted to make it look as if Helen had been raped. There were injuries that could have implied to the untrained eye that she had been sexually assaulted.

Suspicion immediately fell on the Donald family. They hated the Priestly family and the feeling was mutual.

When the police searched the Donald's house they found stains on the carpet which they believed to be blood and they promptly arrested Mr Donald. But after investigations not only were the stains not blood, but Mr Donald could prove that he had been at work at the time of the murder. The police then turned their attention to Jeannie Donald.

She elaborately explained all of her movements on 20 April, stating that she had left her flat at about 1pm to go and purchase eggs and oranges at the market. She had then visited a shop called Raggy Morrison to purchase some material for a dress for her daughter. She had not bought anything there as they did not have what she was looking for. She could accurately recount the time that she returned home as around 2.15pm, as she had bumped into a neighbour, Mary Topp. In the event, Mrs Topp thought it was closer to 2.30pm. After she had got home Jeannie said that she had then ironed a dress. As it turned out her detailed movements could be accurately checked by the police. Not only were the prices that she had given the police that she claimed to have paid for the eggs and oranges those that had been charged the previous week, but Morrisons had been closed that afternoon.

Catching Jeannie out in a series of lies was one thing, but linking her to the death of Helen was another. The police took away samples of hair from Jeannie's hairbrush, as well as household dust and carpet samples. These were compared to human hairs that had been found in the sack which had contained Helen's body; they matched. Even more

Jeannie Ewan Donald, murderer of Helen Priestly.

damning was the fact that there were cinders in Helen's hair and between two of her front teeth. These also matched ones found in the Donald's home.

Jeannie was charged and brought to trial in Edinburgh on 16 July 1934. Throughout the defence claimed that their client could not have had anything to do with the murder and that Helen had been raped by a man. The prosecution had radically different ideas

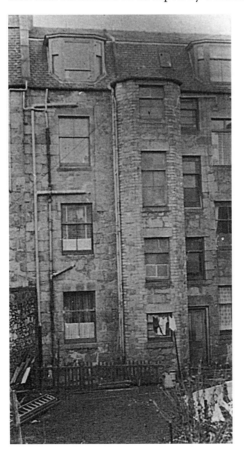

The home of Helen Priestly.

and could prove using elementary forensics that the fibres found in the sack matched those from the Donald household, that traces of vomit found on Helen's clothing had also been found on a flannel in the Donald's bathroom, and that the sack had an identical hole to those that had also been found in the Donald household. The sacks had been hung from a hook. The prosecution contended that Jeannie Donald had strangled Helen and then used a metal object to falsify evidence that the young girl had been raped. The prosecution believed that the cinders had found their way onto Helen's body because Jeannie Donald had put her body into the cinder box to hide it from the rest of the family, and that at some point in the early hours of the morning she had dumped the body in the sack under the stairs.

Even Jeannie's daughter, under cross-examination, admitted that on the day of the murder there had been a loaf from the Co-Op bakery in their kitchen.

In summing up after hearing all of the

evidence the judge told the jury 'You must dismiss from your mind any idea that evidence is unreliable merely because it is circumstantial, circumstantial evidence is just the evidence of proved facts.'

If the jury had had any qualms about finding Jeannie Donald guilty, the judge's words dispelled those fears. After just 16 minutes they returned a verdict of guilty. The judge sentenced Jeannie Donald to hang, but in the event her sentence was reduced to life imprisonment. Just 10 years later, with her husband dying of a terminal illness, Jeannie Donald was released on parole.

It is quite possible that Jeannie Donald had not meant to kill Helen Priestly. In fact it is perfectly possible that until the child was dead she had not laid a hand on her and had simply panicked. It was later proposed, after experts had examined the post-mortem evidence, that Helen had an enlarged thymus gland and that a shock may have caused her to faint and then choke on her own vomit. It is perfectly possible that Jeannie Donald had lain in wait for Helen Priestly in order to scare her, as the child was in the habit of ringing the Donald's doorbell and then running away. We will never know because Jeannie Donald declined to give evidence at her own trial.

* * * * *

Forensic evidence also spelled doom for **Nora Patricia Tierney** when she faced trial at the Old Bailey in October 1949 for the murder of three-year-old Marion Ward. Young Marion had been playing with Tierney's six-year-old daughter, Stephanie, at their home in Elsworthy Road, St John's Wood. When Marion's mother came to collect her daughter, Stephanie told her that Marion had gone off somewhere to play on her own. There was a huge police search involving hundreds of constables and local people. Three days elapsed before Marion's battered body was found in a derelict house close to her home. Her skull had been crushed with a hammer. All that the police had to go on was a woman's footprint close to the body.

Nora Tierney, then 29, was one of the first of the neighbours to be interviewed by the police. During the interview Tierney became extremely aggressive and once this was reported back to Chief Inspector Jamieson, he began to have suspicions. His first line of enquiry was to visit Tierney himself and request that she gave him her shoes so that she could be eliminated from the enquiries. Tierney was co-operative but when Jamieson asked her for samples of scrapings from under her fingernails, Tierney became hysterical. She blurted out that James, her husband, had killed the little girl and made her watch him do it. She was too terrified to come forward to the police and begged them to protect her.

The police arrested James Tierney and he could quickly prove that he had been nowhere near the house on the day the little girl had been murdered. Jamieson was certain that in Nora Tierney he had his killer.

At her trial in October one of her shoes exactly fitted the cast that had been taken at the scene of the crime. The police had also discovered fibres from Marion's jumper under her fingernails. The evidence was overwhelming but the motive was never really investigated. Regardless of this, after just 10 minutes, the jury found her guilty and the Old Bailey judge sentenced her to death. She did not hang for the offence as it became clear to prison psychiatrists that Nora Tierney's mind was deranged. Her sentence was commuted and she was sent to Broadmoor.

* * * * *

Another perplexing murder took place in 1953 when **Teresa Conroy** was charged with the murder of her 13-year-old son. The body was discovered by Michael Conroy, the boy's father. He had been labouring under the misapprehension that his wife and son were visiting relatives and was horrified to discover his son's body hidden under the mattress of a divan bed. When the police interviewed Teresa Conroy she initially claimed that she had no idea that her son was dead. Later she admitted that she had buried him under the mattress after the boy had suffered an epileptic fit and choked to death. The post-mortem proved otherwise; the cause of death was not choking. His blood had high levels of phenobarbitone and carbon monoxide. Teresa Conroy was found guilty of the murder of her son but was considered to be insane.

* * * * *

Another tragic case occurred in 1957 when 28-year-old **Joan Burns** was arrested and charged with the murder of her two daughters. Helen Lynne Burns was just four years old and her sister, Valerie Grace, only 10 weeks when they met their deaths. Their mother drowned them and then attempted to commit suicide. Joan had a long history of mental illness and had quite recently spent six months in a mental institution. When she was brought before the judge at Newcastle Crown Court on 8 October 1957 it was agreed that she was unfit to plead due to insanity and was therefore sentenced to be detained at Her Majesty's Pleasure.

* * * * *

Two years later another mother with a long history of mental illnesses murdered her two children. **Diana Bromley** was 39 in 1959 and despite having been into mental institutions at least three times, she had managed to bring up her two sons, Martin John, aged 13, and Stephen, aged 10. Diana had given the two children barbiturates and then had carried them into a garage where she had tried to finish them off with carbon monoxide fumes. This attempt failed so she strangled Martin and drowned his brother in the bath. After she had done this she cut both of their throats and then ran to a local pond and tried to drown herself.

When she appeared at the Surrey Assizes on 25 February 1959 she, too, was found unfit to plead due to insanity and was also detained at Her Majesty's Pleasure.

* * * * *

At the time of writing **Mary Bell**, at the age of just 11, is the youngest female killer to have ever stood trial in the United Kingdom. Mary Flora Bell was born in 1957 to a 17-year-old unmarried mother. When Mary was a year old her parents, William and Betty, married and moved to Newcastle-upon-Tyne. Mary's early childhood was a disaster, with her father rarely working and her mother in and out of psychiatric hospitals. At the age of three her mother had even tried to give her away to another woman at an adoption clinic.

Mary Bell and her accomplice, Norma Joyce Bell, who was no relation to her, probably started their murderous campaign long before the body of four-year-old Martin Brown was discovered. He was found in a derelict house on 25 May 1968. Initially the police thought that an empty pill bottle beside the body proved that the child had actually taken an overdose but the post-mortem revealed that Martin had been strangled.

The following day a local nursery school was broken into and vandalised. Notes and scribbles on the walls in children's handwriting were found, some of which referred to Martin Brown. The school installed an alarm system and when Mary and her 13-year-old friend Norma broke in a few days later, they were apprehended by the police, but no action was taken against them.

At some point Mary called at Martin Brown's house and asked his mother whether she could see him. His mother told her that he was dead, to which Mary was said to reply 'Yes I know he's dead. I wanted to see him in his coffin'. Martin's mother slammed the door in her face but both girls made frequent visits to ask strange questions of the distraught mother.

Two months passed and on 31 July a second body was found on some waste ground. This was the body of three-year-old Brian Howe; he too had been strangled and there were a number of cuts and puncture wounds on his stomach and legs. The police launched a massive enquiry, believing that they had an adult serial killer in the neighbourhood. Over 1,200 children were interviewed about strangers, where they played, who they had seen and what they had done on the day of the murders. Mary and Norma's answers appeared odd, suspicious and contradictory.

It was easy to prove that the two girls had written the notes left in the nursery school when their handwriting was compared to them. Some of their clothes were sent off for forensic examination and fibres from Mary's dress were linked to the murder scenes. Fibres from Norma's skirt linked her only to the murder of Brian Howe. Under interrogation they initially refused to talk until a solicitor was present but eventually they both accused one another of having carried out the murders. Norma claimed that Mary had attacked Brian and had squeezed his throat and had asked her to help her finish him off but she had run away. Later they had returned to the dead body and tried to carve their initials on his stomach with a razor.

Mary, meanwhile, put the blame on Norma. She said 'She squeezed it hard, you could tell it was hard because her fingers were going white. Brian was struggling and I was pulling her shoulders but she went mad.' She also claimed that Norma had gone to get the razor blade and scissors and it was her that had carved the marks on the little boy's body. When Mary was charged with the murder it was reported that she said 'That's alright with me'.

When Mary and Norma stood trial at Newcastle Assizes on 5 December 1968 they were both charged with the murders of Martin George Brown and Brian Edward Howe. From the outset it appeared that Mary was the ringleader and had led the more immature Norma into committing the murders. They had both blamed one another for killing Brian Howe and Norma claimed that Mary had continually talked about murdering him. One of their school friends, a 12-year-old boy, claimed to have heard Mary shouting 'I am a murderer' and that later she had shown him the house where Martin's body had been found. Norma's own mother testified that she had once had to jump in to stop Mary from strangling her 11-year-old daughter, Susan. In fact her husband had had to slap Mary to make her let go of Susan's throat.

The five women and seven men of the jury deliberated for four hours and acquitted Norma on both counts of murder. But Mary was found guilty of manslaughter on the grounds of diminished responsibility. There was little precedent for sentencing a girl of this age but Justice Cusack ordered that she should be detained for life.

No one seemed to want to take responsibility for Mary. Initially it was planned to send her to a remand centre in south-east London, but the local authority bowed to residents petitioning them that their children would be in danger should Mary escape. She was sent to a boy's approved school in Lancashire, but hit the headlines in 1977 when she escaped with another inmate and spent three days with two men. One of the men she slept with profited financially from his association with Mary Bell. He claimed that she had slept with him in order to get pregnant.

Throughout the seventies, on and off, her mother, who by now had become notorious in her own right for being a prostitute, sold a number of stories about her daughter and allowed letters and poems to be printed in the press. She also reported of Mary's life in various institutions, of Mary's self-mutilation, lesbian relationships, cross-dressing tendencies and demands to have a sex change.

Mary Bell was finally released on parole on 14 May 1980. She moved to Suffolk and started work in a children's nursery. Her probation officer convinced her that this was not an appropriate job and she moved back with her mother, met a man and became pregnant. It seemed that everywhere that Mary went someone leaked her true identity and there were a number of violent and ugly scenes when locals discovered who she really was. It was later revealed that Mary's mother had somehow made her daughter available to some of her clients and this may have been one of the catalysts that kindled her violent and aggressive tendencies. It has often been speculated whether Mary Bell would have become a long-term serial killer had she not been arrested at such a young age. She was certainly manipulative and very intelligent but it appears that now she has successfully controlled and understood herself in order to give her own daughter a normal life.

* * * * *

Beverley Allitt was born on 4 October 1973 and from an early age had always pinned her hopes on becoming a nurse. Unfortunately, given her rare psychological illness, Munchausen Syndrome by proxy, this was probably not her best career option. The disorder creates an uncontrollable urge to draw attention and in Allitt's case the attention was caused by causing injury to babies in her care.

Over a period of 58 days in the spring of 1991 there were 26 serious medical problems on the ward that looked after children at the Grantham and Kesteven Hospital. It resulted in the death of four children and a further nine were seriously hurt. By the middle of April a pattern had emerged and it was clear to the hospital authorities that there was a murderer at loose on the ward. The last death took place on 22 April when 15-month-old Claire Peck tragically died.

Dr Nelson Porter, one of the hospital's consultants, at first thought that one of the mothers on the ward could possibly have the syndrome. He sent blood samples and drip samples for analysis; there was a high reading of potassium present. The police were immediately called in and they began by looking at the staff rotas and comparing them to the incidents on the ward. A name came to the surface as being present at each tragedy; it was Beverley Allitt. The police were able to later prove that she had tampered with ventilators and pumps and introduced the potassium into intravenous drips.

On 26 July 1991 she was formally charged and arrested for murder. Further charges were to follow in November. It was a complex case to investigate and Allitt did not come to trial until 15 February 1993. She had been held at Rampton Psychiatric Hospital, which was a maximum security institution for the criminally insane. In addition to suffering from the syndrome, it was clear that Allitt also had anorexia. She had dropped down from a size 16 to a size 8 and had lost five stones in weight. She had also revisited a childhood habit of eating glass and scalding herself with hot water.

Allitt did not attend the whole of the trial, being too ill to be moved to the Nottingham Crown Court where the proceedings were being held. The jury found her guilty of murder and attempted murder on 11 May 1993 and after considerable deliberation Justice Latham sentenced Allitt to 13 life sentences on the four counts of murder and the nine counts of grievous bodily harm.

Government and public reaction to her crimes reached levels not seen for years. She was, after all, a nurse and, what was worse, her charges were small children who utterly relied on her professional integrity. She had exposed the dangers of under-funding in the National Health Service and the consequent lack of checks and balances.

Allitt was to hit the headlines again in August 1993 when she was admitted to Bassetlaw Hospital in Worksop after she mutilated herself with sharpened paper clips. Two months later she had confessed that she had carried out three of the murders and six of the other attacks. Although it was believed that the extent of the charges against Allitt was sufficient not only to prove that she had committed these crimes but also to take her permanently out of harm's way, it was always alleged that she had killed more patients. She had worked in various hospitals around Lincolnshire and Nottinghamshire and everywhere that had employed her began to look back at deaths and injuries on their wards and wonder whether Allitt was responsible.

* * * * *

Although many male killers, such as Shipman, Sutcliffe and Neilson, have engendered widespread condemnation and disgust, the majority of these women carried out their acts either alone or with other women and not with the help of a man. Mercifully cases where women kill children are rare and perhaps the only other contemporary cases were those of Rose West and Myra Hindley, but these were notable by the presence of a dominant male and both women claimed that they had been led to carry out their crimes by their partner.

BIBLIOGRAPHY

Alt, Betty and Sandra Wells *Wicked Women: Black Widows, Child Killers, and Other Women in Crime*, Paladin Press, 2000.

Askill, John and Martyn Sharpe *Angel of Death*, Michael O'Mara Books, 1993.

Bourke, Angela *Burning of Bridget Cleary: A True Story*, Viking Books, 2000.

Bridges, Yseult *How Charles Bravo Died*, Macmillan, 1972.

Clarkson, Wensley *Hell Hath No Fury*, Blake, 1991.

Gaute, J.H.H. and Robin Odell *The Murderers' Who's Who*, Harrap, 1979.

Goodman, Jonathan (Ed.) *Lady Killers*, ISIS Large Print Books, 1990.

Hamilton, Elizabeth *The Warwickshire Scandal*, Pan, 2000.

Hancock, Robert *Ruth Ellis The Last Woman To Be Hanged*, Weidenfeld and Nicolson, 1985.

Healey, Tim *Crimes of Passion*, Hamlyn, 1990.

Hodge, Harry and James(Eds) *Famous Trials*, Viking, 1984.

Hoff, Joan and Marian Yeates *The Cooper's Wife Is Missing: The Trials of Bridget Cleary*, Basic Books, 2000.

Honeycombe, Gordon *Murders of the Black Museum*, Hutchinson, 1982.

Honeycombe, Gordon *More Murders of the Black Museum*, Hutchinson, 1993.

Jones, Frank *Murderous Women*, Headline, 1991.

Kiely, David M. *Bloody Women*, Gill and Macmillan, 1999.

Lee, S. *Classic Murders of the North West*, Magazine Design and Publishing, 1999.

Linedecker, Clifford L. *Babyface Killers*, Saint Martin's Press, 2000.

Lustgarten, Edgar *The Woman In The Case*, Mayflower Books, 1965.

Martin *Chronicle of Crime*, Carlton Books, 1999.

Masters, Anthony *Rosa Lewis*, Weidenfeld and Nicolson, 1977.

Nicholas, Margaret *The World's Wickedest Women*, Octopus, 1984.

O'Connor, Niamh *The Black Widow*, The O'Brien Press, 2001.

Robins, Joyce *Lady Killers*, Bounty Books, 1993.

Roughead, William *Classic Crimes*, Pan, 1962.

Schurman-Kauflin, Deborah *The New Predator: Women Who Kill: Profiles of Female Serial Killers*, Algora Publishing, 2000.

Sereny, Gitta *The Case of Mary Bell*, Pimlico, 1995.

Sereny, Gitta *Cries Unheard: the Story of Mary Bell*, Macmillan, 1999.

Thompson, A. *Classic Murders of the North East*, Magazine Design and Publishing, 1998.

Walker, Gloria and Lynn Daly *Sexplicitly Yours*, Penguin, 1987.

Williams, Emlyn *Beyond Belief: the Moors Murderers*, Pan, 1992.

Wilson, Colin *The Mammoth Book of True Crime*, Robinson Publishing, 1988.

Wilson, Colin (Ed.) *Murder in the 1930s*, Robinson Publishing, 1992.

Wilson, Colin and Damon Wilson (Eds) *Murder in the 1940s*, Carroll and Graf, 1993.

Wilson, Colin *The Corpse Garden*, Magazine Design and Publishing, 1998.

INDEX

Adams, Agnes 186
Alden, Martha 14-15
Allen, Margaret 101
Allitt, Beverley 212-13
Andrews, Jane 71-2
Arden, Alice 8-9
Ashley, April 42
Barber, Elizabeth 13
Barber, Susan 160-1
Barney, Elvira 20-1
Barry, Mary Ann 200
Bartlett, Adelaide 148, 151-2, 163
Barton, Elizabeth 44
Bateman, Mary 138-9
Beddingfield, Ann 12
Bell, Mary 210-12, 214
Berghen, Catherine van 87
Bernhardt, Sarah 68
Berry, Charlotte de 75
Biggadyke, Priscilla 144
Blandy, Mary 132, 134
Blott, Elizabeth 186
Bonny, Ann 75
Branch, Elizabeth 190
Branch, Mary 190
Bravo, Florence 145, 151, 163
Bristol, Countess of 50-1, 53
Broadric, Anne 105-7
Bromley, Diana 210
Brooke, Daisy 66
Brown, Martha Elizabeth 107-8
Brownrigg, Elizabeth 189, 191-4
Brunswick, Caroline of 54-7
Bryant, Charlotte 157-8
Burns, Joan 210

Butler, Madam Mary 50
Byron, Emma 'Kitty' 15-16
Calvert, Louie 99
Cameron, Jean 78
Carew, Edith 153-4
Carleton, Mary 29-30
Catchpole, Margaret 79
Channel, Mary 130
Chantler, Wanda 122-3
Chard-Williams, Ada 204-5
Christofi, Styllou 7, 114-7
Chubb, Edith 102
Churchill, Deborah 87
Cleary, Bridget 33, 214
Conroy, Teresa 210
Cotton, Mary Ann 163-5
Cox, Jane 140, 146-7
Crouch, Eliza Emma 62
Cutpurse, Moll 176-7, 179-80
Dagoe, Hannah 184
Davies, Mandy Rice 40
Davis, Moll 49
Davison, Emily 36
Diblanc, Marguerite 96
Digby, Jane 59
Diver, Jenny 182
Dixon, Madge 79
Dixon, Margaret 189
Donald, Jeannie Ewan 206-9
Doyle, Mary 79
Duncan, Jilly 45
Dyer, Amelia Elizabeth 7, 189, 201
Edmondson, Mary 91
Edmunds, Christiana 108
Ellis, Ruth 7, 114, 118-21, 214
English, Christine 125-6

Fahmy, Marguerite 19-20
Fenning, Eliza 140
Fisher, Dorothy 112-13
Flanagan, Catherine 148
Frith, Mary 176-7
Fulham, Augusta 112
Garvie, Sheila 25-6
Godiva, Lady 28
Greeve, Elizabeth Harriet 184-5
Gwyn, Nell 47, 49-50
Hamilton, Lady Emma 31-2
Hamilton, Mary 30-1
Harris, Phoebe 182
Hawkins, Moll 181
Hayes, Catherine 9-10, 12
Hessel, Phoebe 76
Hibner, Esther 197
Higgins, Margaret 148
Hindley, Myra 7, 167-8, 175, 213
Housden, Jane 88, 182
Howard, Frances 45, 47
Howard, Rebecca 196
Hutchinson, Amy 131
Jeffries, Elizabeth 90
Jerome, Jennie 68
Jones, Betty 186, 188
Jones, Moll 179
Jordan, Jessie 38
Keeler, Christine 28, 40-1
Kent, Constance 198-9
Keppel, Alice 66
Keroualle, Louise de 49
King, Elizabeth 186
Lamb, Lady Caroline 57-8
Langtry, Lillie 66
Leach, Elizabeth 185
Lloyd, Sarah 185
London, Isabella 182

215

Lude, Lady 78
Lynch, Eliza Alicia 64
McCullough, Muriel 26-7
Macintosh, Lady Anne 78
M'Lachlan, Jessie 95-6
MacLean, Effie 45
Mainwaring, Mrs 108
Major, Ethel Lillie 155-6
Malcolm, Sarah 89
Manning, Maria 92-4
Marlborough, Sarah 196-7
Marrow, Ann 31
Mason, Elizabeth 131
Masset, Louise Josephine 203-4
Maw, Annette 123-4
Maw, Charlene 123-4
Maybrick, Florence 151-3
Meace, Jane 78
Megginson, Pamela 126
Merrifield, Louisa 160
Metyard, Sarah Morgan 194-5
Mills, Ann 78
Mitford, Unity Valkyrie 36
Moncreiffe, Harriet 68-9
Murphy, Christiane 182
Murray, Margaret 78
Nairn, Katharine 136
Napier, Barbara 45

Newell, Susan 205-6
Norcott, Mary 81-2
Norwood, Melita 39
O'Malley, Grace 73-5
O'Shea, Kitty 32
Pankhurst, Christabel 34
Pankhurst, Emmeline 34
Payne, Cynthia 28, 42-3
Pearcey, Mary 110
Pearl, Cora 62
Pcrry, Joan 83
Philpott, Gillian 126, 128
Phipoe, Maria Theresa 91
Pledge, Sarah 135
Pugh, Elizabeth 197
Raby, Moll 180
Ransom, Florence Iris Ouida 113
Rattenbury, Alma Victoria 22-4
Read, Mary 75-6
Richardson, Elizabeth 104-5
Rumbold, Freda 24
Sach, Amelia 202-3
Sampson, Agnes 45
Simpson, Wallis 70-1
Sleightholme, Yvonne 128
Smith, Madeleine 142, 151
Snell, Hannah 77
Spencer, Barbara 181

Stewart, Frances 200
Stopes, Marie 33-4
Swift, Sarah 86-7
Taylor, Louisa 147
Thompson, Edith Jessie 16
Tierney, Nora Patricia 209-10
Toole, Suzy 79
Tripp, Grace 88
Villiers, Barbara 49-50
Waddingham, Dorothea 156-7
Walter, Lucy 49
Walters, Annie 202
Walton, Philadelphia 186
Warner, Anne 182
Webster, Kate 97-9
West, Rosemary 7, 170, 173, 175, 213
Whale, Ann 135
White, Margaret 38
Whitney, Hannah 78
Williams, Ann 136
Wilson, Catherine 143-4, 148
Wilson, Mary Elizabeth 165
Young, Mary 182